The Truth (an ....guage

The Truth (and Untruth) of Language

Heidegger, Ricoeur, and Derrida on Disclosure and Displacement

Gert-Jan van der Heiden

DUQUESNE UNIVERSITY PRESS
PITTSBURGH, PENNSYLVANIA

Published in the United States of America by
DUQUESNE UNIVERSITY PRESS
600 Forbes Avenue
Pittsburgh, Pennsylvania 15282

Library of Congress Cataloging-in-Publication Data

Heiden, Gerrit Jan van der, 1976–
    The truth (and untruth) of language : Heidegger, Ricoeur, and Derrida on
disclosure and displacement / Gert-Jan van der Heiden.
        p. cm.
    Includes bibliographical references and index.
    ISBN 978-0-8207-0434-0 (pbk. : alk. paper)
    1. Hermeneutics. 2. Truth. 3. Language and languages—Philosophy.
4. Heidegger, Martin, 1889–1976. 5. Ricœur, Paul. 6. Derrida, Jacques.
I. Title. II. Title: Truth of language.
    BD241.H345 2010
    121'.680922—dc22
                                                                    2010000975

∞ Printed on acid-free paper.

Contents

Acknowledgments

The Faculty of Philosophy of the Radboud University Nijmegen proved to be a fruitful environment for working on this book. In particular, the Heidegger seminar was a very seminal place, and I would like to thank the people participating in it: (among others) Vincent Blok, Chris Bremmers, Nico Dieteren, Gerben Meynen, Andreea Parapuf, and Ben Vedder. In addition, I would like to thank the (other) people from the Department of Metaphysics, Michael Perrick, Gerrit Steunebrink, and Ad Vennix, who were always willing to read and discuss older versions of this study. In fall 2006, I spent four months at DePaul University in Chicago. During these months, the first contours of this study became visible, and I would like to thank Peter Gratton, Will McNeill, Michael Naas, and David Pellauer for giving me the opportunity to discuss the topics that engage me in this book. Finally, I would like to thank the Radboud Foundation for financially supporting my stay in Chicago.

Truth and Language

> A rhetorician of times past said that his trade was to make little
> things appear and be thought great....Those who mask and make up
> women do less harm, for it is a matter of small loss not to see them in
> their natural state; whereas the other men make a profession of
> deceiving not our eyes, but our judgment, and of adulterating and
> corrupting the essence of things.
>
> —Michel de Montaigne, *Of the Vanity of Words*

The above quote stems from the essay "Of the Vanity of Words." In
this essay, Michel de Montaigne warns his readers against the treacherous language of rhetoricians. Within the history of philosophy,
Montaigne's warnings are not isolated. The philosophical distrust of
language does not just concern the language of rhetoricians or soph-
ists, but often also includes the language of poets as Plato's *Republic* famously shows. Later and in a more general context, without
specifying a particular use of language, Edmund Husserl warns us
against the "seduction of language" (*Verführung der Sprache*).[1] Husserl, Montaigne, and, as I will argue, an entire philosophical tradition,
have worried that language may disguise the original meaning of an
expression because of the inherent ambiguity of words—a dimension
of language in which the rhetorician, the sophist, and the poet are in
their element. This ambiguity is said to threaten the philosophical
inquiry into the essence of things, and it is said to corrupt age-old
distinctions between truth and fiction, between the way beings are
and the way they appear to be. According to Montaigne, the trade of

1

a rhetorician is "to make little things appear and be thought great." In the hands of the rhetorician and the poet, language becomes an instrument that allows things to appear in a different, disguising, and secondary light, dissimulating the essence of things and leading us astray. This rhetorical play would thus deceive our judgment and would endanger the sober inquiry into the essence of beings that is said to mark genuine philosophy.

By calling his essay "Of the *Vanity* of Words" (my italics), Montaigne suggests that this rhetorical danger is caused by the super-fluousness and the redundancy of words. In the first place, this superfluousness concerns the ambiguous language of the rhetorician, the sophist, and the poet. In the second place, it hints at the funda-mental seduction of language as such, to which Husserl is attentive: language allows beings to appear, but it also veils them. Montaigne's comments, however, combine danger and ornament to characterize rhetorical language: the danger is caused by an ornament. In this way, these comments provide a perfect example of what Derrida has analyzed as the "dangerous supplement."[2] Montaigne's words encap-sulate the danger that rhetoric and poetics pose to philosophy by arguing that this danger is caused by a supplement, by an addition, by a redundancy that, essentially, can be avoided. In the wake of the hope that this danger can be avoided, projects arise in which one dreams the ultimate philosophical dream of the construction of a per-fect language and a *mathesis universalis,* a language in which every ambiguity is dissolved and pure univocality has taken its place.

Contemporary hermeneutic philosophy — and here I use the term in the broad sense of including the projects of Martin Heidegger, Hans-Georg Gadamer, Paul Ricoeur, as well as Jacques Derrida — proceeds from a fundamentally different perspective on the relation between thought and language. What hermeneutics challenges first and fore-most is Montaigne's claim of the "vanity of words." In Ricoeur's description, hermeneutics is a philosophy that begins with language.[3] Thus, for hermeneutics, language and its fundamental ambiguity are inevitable in every effort to address the philosophical question of the essence and the truth of being(s). In fact, contemporary hermeneutics proceeds from the idea that language is the most fundamental *opening* of the world. Language lets beings appear, but not as something they are not—as opposed to their true essence—but it lets things appear *in the first place* and thus grants our access to them. Without language nothing appears and no understanding is possible. In fact, as Heidegger argues in his reading of Plato's allegory of the cave as well as his allegory of the river *Lēthē,* without appearances and without unconcealment, the human being would be impossible.[4] Gadamer argues that language is the medium in which human understanding occurs.[5] One of the basic questions of these hermeneutic and deconstructive currents of thought is the question of what this indispensability of language means for metaphysics, for our understanding of being, and for our understanding of truth.

Even though hermeneutics centers itself on this basic, pivotal relation between language and being, this relation is understood in different ways by Heidegger, Ricoeur, and Derrida. In this study, I argue that we can discern at least two important lines of thought that are developed to deal with this relation. The first consideration is captured by the term *disclosure*. This first line of thought develops the above mentioned idea that nothing appears without language. This line of thought is developed very clearly in Heidegger's later work. The disclosure of language characterizes language's relation to being and truth. Being is the element thanks to which and in which beings are (present). Truth is reinterpreted by Heidegger as the unconcealment of beings. Within this perspective on being and truth, language plays a fundamental role: Heidegger understands the essence of language as the ability of language to bring beings forth out of concealment into unconcealment. The highest calling of language, and especially poetic language, is therefore to be the occurrence of truth. The second consideration is captured by the term *displacement*. This term concerns every linguistic phenomena that involves a displacement of a word or a group of words from one (con)text to another, or from one language to another, or from one generation to another. Thus, it involves a whole range of linguistic phenomena such as metaphor, quoting, translation, transmission, poetic mimesis, and so on. Displacement goes to the heart of what Montaigne found to be the danger of language. In hermeneutic thought, this danger of displacement is no longer conceived as an avoidable supplement, but often as a positive and productive dimension of phenomena of language. Taken in this sense, displacement is an important element in the thought of Derrida and Ricoeur, although in different ways. Under the heading of the displacement of language, multiple issues will be addressed in this study, as the untruth, the repeatability, and the ideality of language. The goal of this study is to articulate the different hermeneutic positions concerning the pair disclosure and displacement as well as to show the consequences of these differences for an understanding of the relation between truth and language in contemporary hermeneutic thought.

THE EXPRESSIVE VIEW OF LANGUAGE

Even though an entire philosophical tradition discusses the problematic nature of language for thinking, this does not mean that a more favorable account of language simply lacks. In the *Rhetoric,* Aristotle notes that poetic language, such as metaphor, is capable of showing lifeless things as alive and as active.[6] In his reading of Aristotle, Ricoeur suggests that poetic language shows reality as a budding and an opening flower, that is, poetics has the capacity to awaken the slumbering possibilities of reality and to depict them as if they were actualized.[7] Aristotle's understanding of poetic language has been a source of inspiration for contemporary hermeneutics to rethink the importance of language. Aristotle's conception of poetic language elaborates a more favorable conception of language in which the *articulation* of a being allows us to become aware of this being and its possibilities *in the first place* and in an elevated way. Such a poetic articulation is not something added to reality, but it is the medium in which reality is opened up and given to us. Here, we see the first contours of what we could call an *expressive* dimension of language.

In a very general sense, this expressive view of language (*logos*) is as old as philosophy itself. In Platonic and Neo-Platonic thought reality is seen as the expression of a divine and cosmic *Logos*. In Augustine's thought the *Verbum* of God lies at the heart of creation.[8] In this account, the expressive dimension of the Word is creative in an eminent sense; the expressiveness of (God's) language creates the world. However, this outstanding form of creation is not attributed to human language. Plato's view of the creative aspect of language in book 10 of the *Republic* is typical. Unlike Aristotle, who seems to possess a definite awareness of the expressivity of poetics, Plato has Socrates argue that poetics is marked by a distance to truth. This distance is called *mimesis*.[9] Due to this distance between truth and poetics, the poet must be watched over and regulated by the philosopher.[10] In Aristotle's account of poetics the same word, mimesis, is conceived as a form of presentation: it concerns the poetic depiction of something lifeless as alive. In Plato's account, however, the poet is nothing but an imitator of the genuine maker (*demiurge*); the poet is further away from truth than the divine craftsman and even than the ordinary craftsman, who, unlike the poet, still deserves to be called a maker.[11]

During the eighteenth century in the work of the Romantics, the importance of the expressive dimension of language for human experience is brought to the fore with much verve. The works of Hamann, Herder, and especially Humboldt argued in favor of the expressive and presentational dimension of language for the human experience of the world.[12] Humboldt "makes of language the defining pivot of man and the determinant of his place in reality." In Humboldt's understanding, human language and human articulation are thoroughly creative. As Steiner says, "Speech is *poiesis* and human linguistic articulation is centrally creative."[13] For the Romantics, the creativity of language is not limited to the Word of God, but human language itself is creative and has the capacity to create poetic worlds.

Moreover, the Romantics show a particular awareness of another problem as well. Emphasizing the creativity of *human* language introduces another problem. There is not just one, unique human language. Human beings speak in multiple tongues. The creativity of human language is always the creativity found in a particular tongue.

Consequently, the attention to the disclosive power of human language also opens up the problematic of the multiplicity of languages. The question arises of how these different disclosures are related. The early Romantics (*Frühromantik*), such as Ludwig Tieck and August Wilhelm von Schlegel, have worked on this problem of multiplicity and the connected problem of the relations between languages as realms of disclosure by their unique translations. Therefore, the affirmation of the creative and disclosive power of human language is accompanied by the problem of the apparent differences and displacements *between* languages. From Romantic thought on, the problem of disclosure is accompanied by the problem of displacement, by the problem of translation, transition, and tradition, by the problem of the in-between of language*s* as well as the problem of the repetition of (the meaning of) what has been said from one language to another.[14]

Without a doubt, hermeneutic philosophy is highly indebted to these developments in Romantic thought. Although Heidegger is always very cautious not to interpret language as the expression of an inward self or subjectivity—modern subjectivity is one of his main adversaries—his attention to language develops exactly the disclosive dimension of language that the Romantics still found in the expressiveness of language. Heidegger concentrates on the disclosive dimension of language, developing its ontological implications through his work on truth as *alētheia* or unconcealment (*Unverborgenheit*). He determines the essence of language as the capacity of language to show (*zeigen*) beings. In particular, he shares with the Romantics a deep affinity for poetry. In his quest for the essence of language, he turns to poetics (*Dichtung*) as a guide for approaching this question. For Heidegger, thinking and poeticizing are not drifted apart by the wedge of a platonic mimesis. Rather, the poetic experience of language that is manifest in a poem guides the thinker on his or her way to the essence of language. In the *Metaphysics*, Aristotle briefly notes that a *philomuthos*, a lover of myth, is in a certain respect like a *philosophos*, a lover of wisdom.[15] Heidegger's thinking on the relation between *Denken* (thinking) and *Dichten* (poeticizing) reinforces and deepens this resemblance between the thinker and the lover of myths. In fact, since poetry guides the thinker on the way to language, he or she cannot be but a lover of myths, a *philomuthos*. Thus, it will come as no surprise that it is exactly the German translation of the Greek word *muthos*—*die Sage*—that grants the *philomuthos* Heidegger the appropriate word for the essence of language.

Purposes of this Study

Within contemporary hermeneutics Heidegger's work on the relation between poetic language, being, and truth deserves a prominent place. His major influence on the development of contemporary hermeneutics is obvious: hermeneutic thinkers after him have all felt an obligation to respond to him and to comment on his work. Due to this particular role of Heidegger's thought for contemporary hermeneutics, I will devote chapter 1 to Heidegger's discussion of truth, untruth, understanding, and language in order to capture the interpretation of disclosure and displacement that follows from it. This chapter prepares the following chapters that will often refer back to the results of the first one. These three subsequent chapters will be thematic in nature: they discuss the themes of writing, metaphor, and mimesis, respectively, in the thought of Heidegger, Ricoeur, and Derrida, and to lesser degree also Gadamer. The goal of these case studies is to achieve a better understanding of the notions of disclosure and displacement and their relation in the work of each of these thinkers. We shall see that Ricoeur and Derrida take up other inheritances of the Romantic thought on language: the importance of displacement, transition, and tradition as well as a reflection on the meaning of the multiplicity of human language will be addressed by means of a study of writing, metaphor, and mimesis.

Hermeneutics after Heidegger can be divided into two main schools. On the one hand, one distinguishes hermeneutics in the more strict sense of the word. Hermeneutics, being derived from the name of the Greek messenger god Hermes, concerns the interpretation of meaning sent in language. This type of hermeneutic thought concentrates on theories of interpretation and understanding, and it approaches these questions from the perspective of the *primacy of meaning*. Interpretation and understanding is thus understood as the articulation and the appropriation of meaning. Within this strand of thought poetics is thought as the innovation or the invention of meaning. This *invention* of meaning precedes and inspires the philosophical elaboration of concepts. Poetics provides a richer language than the conceptual language of philosophy or even the language in normal, everyday conversation, since it creates meaning and brings beings to the fore in a completely new, unheard-of way. This invention of meaning expands our experience of the world. The two main representatives of this line of thought are Gadamer and Ricoeur. On the other hand, one finds the school of thought known as deconstruction represented by Derrida. Derrida's attention to language differs from the first school's attention to language, especially as it regards the question of the primacy of meaning. For Derrida, meaning is neither the origin nor the goal of language. Rather, meaning is an effect of a more fundamental aspect of language, which Derrida calls *différance*, and which is closely connected to the supplementary nature of language, as well as to displacement. According to Derrida, this displacement is at the heart of the transformative dimension of (poetic) language. Yet, this displacement is itself not of the order of what is uncovered or brought to presence. Displacement, supplementarity, and *différance* do not concern the primacy of unconcealment; they concern the original contamination of concealment and unconcealment that enables the appearance of meaning and beings in language.

These two approaches of what is primary in language are clearly distinct. In terms of the relation between truth and language, the first school tends to emphasize the disclosure of meaning in language; the second school emphasizes the importance of untruth in relation to and as a condition of truth as disclosure. The flash of wit of the second approach is to argue that this untruth is primary, whereas it is usually approached as a secondary phenomenon, as we shall see later on. To put Heidegger's influence on contemporary hermeneutic thought into perspective and to demonstrate the richness of his thought on truth and language, it is important to discuss both of these two approaches because they emphasize, elaborate, and criticize different aspects in Heidegger's work on truth and language.

Finally, let me briefly indicate why I have chosen writing, metaphor, and mimesis as the case studies. In relation to Heidegger's emphasis on the disclosure of language, the theme of displacement becomes important thanks to the reflection on writing and textuality in the hermeneutic thought of Gadamer, Ricoeur, and Derrida. Therefore, the second chapter will demonstrate how the element of displacement is brought into play after Heidegger and his tendency to approach displacement as a form of *pseudos* or *Verstellen*. In particular, chapter 2 will deal with the question of how hermeneutic thought deals with the ancient depiction of writing as a decay of speech in the light of the more favorable quality of writing as that which enables the repetition of what has been said or written in another context than the context in which it originated.

The topics of metaphor and mimesis both bring up the problem of truth and *poetic* language. Poetic language does not mean poetry *stricto sensu*, but I use it here as an elliptical expression for the poetic aspects of language. My inquiry into metaphor and mimesis is therefore, in the first place, an inquiry into the metaphoric and mimetic dimensions of language. Within the realm of this study, metaphor and mimesis are particularly interesting since they both involve disclosure as well as displacement. Both deal with the *disclosive* and *creative* aspect of language. Moreover, they both have an intrinsic relation to displacement as well. As its Greek origin shows — *metapherein* — metaphor has classically been determined as a transference. In metaphor, a word is displaced and transferred to another domain. Similarly, mimesis is never simply presentation or disclosure, but always also *re*presentation or displacement. Human action is both presented (disclosed) and represented in a tragedy. Because metaphor and mimesis are intrinsically related to disclosure and to displacement, a discussion of these topics immediately touches the heart of the matter of this study: how is the relation between disclosure and displacement understood in Heidegger's, Ricoeur's, and Derrida's discussion of (poetic) language and truth?

These latter two topics are also motivated by the questions that engage all three: How to bring to language those dimensions of reality that have not yet been said or thought? And what does the occurrence of such a bringing to language mean for us and for "reality"? A reflection on the meaning of the pair of concepts disclosure and displacement in the work of Heidegger, Ricoeur, and Derrida on truth and language is first and foremost an effort to understand how these three writers try to approach this unthought-of dimension of and in language.

ONE

Heidegger on Disclosure and Language

For now I had begun to believe, despite all the talk of science around me, that there was a magic in spoken words.
— Ralph Ellison, *The Invisible Man*

Heidegger's concern with the notion of truth and his reinterpretation of the Greek notion *alētheia* is an abiding theme in his thought. In fact, as one of the *Feldweg-Gespräche* suggests, his entire work consists in bringing the word *alētheia* back to language and in thinking that which the Greeks experienced in it.[1] Against the background of the history of metaphysics, the claim that the word *alētheia* is obfuscated may seem odd: this history provides us with a whole range of different and often very subtle concepts of truth. Nevertheless, Heidegger is convinced that these concepts have forgotten something essential about truth and the corresponding account of being. To introduce this chapter on Heidegger's account of truth and language, and in particular to introduce the notions of disclosure and displacement that will play a crucial role throughout this book to understand the relation between Heidegger's, Ricoeur's and Derrida's thought, let us briefly consider Heidegger's critique of the metaphysical conceptions of truth and the alternative he proposes.

To capture his critique, Heidegger's analysis of the scholastic concept of truth is illuminating and exemplary. In this concept, truth is

defined as an agreement between subject and object (*veritas est adaequatio rei et intellectus*).[2] This correspondence between object (*res*)
and the subject's idea of this object is grounded in the divine intellect.
Objects *are* because they are created, and in scholastic understanding
being created means that a being (*ens creatum*) exists if and only if it
corresponds to the divine idea. Thus, the divine ideas are true because
created beings *as* created beings correspond to the divine intellect. As
a consequence, in order to be true, the ideas in the human intellect
should correspond to the eternal, divine ideas.[3] Hence, truth consists
in the correspondence of every created being—object and human
intellect—to a highest being, the divine intellect or creator, which is
the measure of all existence and beingness (*Seiendheit*).

Although other concepts of truth are developed in the history of
metaphysics, Heidegger argues that each of these is structurally the
same as the scholastic one: each of these concepts presupposes the
identification of a highest being as the measure of beingness of all
beings; truth consists in the correspondence to this highest being.
Basically, this is also what Heidegger means by the onto-theo-logical constitution of metaphysics: the primary *ontological* question of
"What do all beings have in common?" is always caught up in the
theological quest for the highest being. This onto-theo-logical constitution has important consequences for how metaphysics deals with a
number of fundamental issues.

Let me mention two of these onto-theo-logical issues that are
important to our survey: the problem of totality and the problem
of actuality and presence. Since the highest being is the measure of
all beingness, a being *is more* to the extent that it *corresponds better* to this highest being.[4] As a consequence, this highest being does
not only become the measure of the truth of other beings, but also
becomes the ordering principle: it orders the other beings in accordance to their degree of being. In this sense, beings are part of a totality ordered by the highest being.[5] This relation between the order
and its highest being is problematic. On the one hand, as its ordering
principle, the highest being is different from this order and, as such,
cannot belong to it as one of its elements. On the other hand, if this

order is to capture and hierarchize all beings in accordance with their degrees of being, then the highest being should be part of it, namely as its completion. Since the highest being is perfect, it is considered to be fully actual and without any potentialities: it is devoid of any absence or privation. Since the highest being is the measure of all beingness, this actuality and this presence is transferred to the concept of being itself. Being is interpreted as presence (*Anwesenheit*) and more in particular as the completely present highest being.

As opposed to these conceptions of truth and their related conceptions of being, Heidegger argues that a more basic dimension of truth is forgotten:

> In whatever manner beings are interpreted—whether as spirit, after the fashion of spiritualism; or as matter and force, after the fashion of materialism; or as becoming and life; or as representation, will, substance, subject, or *energeia;* or as eternal recurrence of the same—every time beings as beings appear in the light of Being. Wherever metaphysics represents beings, Being has been cleared. Being has arrived in a state of unconcealedness (*alētheia*). But whether and how Being brings such unconcealedness with it, whether and how It brings itself with in, and as, metaphysics, remains veiled.[6]

In this quote, Heidegger does not only criticize the metaphysics of Plato, Aristotle, or Aquinas, but his critique stretches out to the thought of Leibniz, Spinoza, Kant, Schopenhauer, and Nietzsche as well. Each of these metaphysical enterprises conceives being from the viewpoint of a particular being, whether it is will, substance, spirit, Aristotle's god as the highest and final goal of all beings or Plato's Idea of the Good. Heidegger argues that the metaphysical project itself as the effort to think being as a being depends on a more original gift, namely the gift by which beings are given to us as present in the first place. Differently put, by insisting on the highest being as the anchor point for being, metaphysics forgets to address the question of how this highest being—and every other being for that matter—can appear in the first place. It forgets to pose the question: What is it that grants every being, including the highest being its presence? What movement of presencing (*Anwesen*) is at stake here?

These questions indicate that the metaphysical project presupposes a realm of the open that grants us accessibility to beings.

This realm of openness guides Heidegger's understanding of truth. In fact, the truth of being concerns the very *disclosure* or unconcealment (*alētheia*) of this open: being brings unconcealment with it and brings beings into unconcealment. If one follows Heidegger in this regard and considers being as a name for the accessibility of beings, it is clear that any conception of being that interprets being as a particular being is problematic: the presence of this particular being, say God, depends on this open to appear and to be. Consequently, to think being in light of this being conceals being as this realm of the open and distorts it. In fact, as Heidegger argues already in *Sein und Zeit*, and as we shall see further on in this chapter, metaphysics puts the relation between being and beings upside down. Instead of noting that we interpret beings always in the light of a primordial understanding of being (*Seinsverständnis*), it suggests that we reverse this relation and interpret being as a particular, highest being. This reversal or *displacement* is the typical movement of metaphysics by which it conceals being and forgets the question of being.

This relation between metaphysics and the question of being is typical for Heidegger's work. On the one hand, the project of metaphysics presupposes the truth of being; in this sense, metaphysics is a derivative and belongs to the realm of truth as disclosure. On the other hand, this project distorts and displaces this primordial disclosure. To overcome this distortion, the dismantling (*Abbau, Destruktion*) of the history of metaphysics is necessary. Numerous interpretations of being form the many layers that cover up the question of being in the history of metaphysics. The destruction of philosophy aims to tear these layers down in order to lay bare the primordial realm of the open to which each and every interpretation of being belongs.[7] This project of dismantling allows Heidegger to propose alternatives to both of the two characteristics of the highest being I mentioned above: totality and absolute presence.

In the first place, by arguing that the unconcealment of being is more primordial than any highest being, he proposes an alternative conception of being in general or as a whole.[8] Rather than insisting on a primordial multiplicity of beings or of being, Heidegger thinks being as that which is common to all beings, and more specifically which grants all beings their being. However, by distinguishing being from beings, Heidegger proposes a way of thinking this "in common" beyond the idea of a totality ordered by a highest being. He proposes a way of thinking the co-belonging of beings without reducing either of them to each other or to another being.[9] In the rest of this chapter, I shall show how he develops an alternative to totality in his conceptions of co-belonging, the whole, and gathering. These aspects are crucial for his conception of language, and they will guide parts of Derrida's reading of Heidegger's work on language.

In the second place, the destruction of metaphysics aims to overcome the distortion of the question of being. The concealment of being is a feature of Heidegger's thought on being from the outset. For instance, in *Sein und Zeit* he writes, "Yet what remains *hidden* in an egregious sense, or which relapses and gets *covered up* again, or which shows itself only '*in disguise*,' is not just this [being] or that, but rather the *Being* of [beings]."[10] The disguise that is described here characterizes a type of concealment attached to any kind of horizon. An entity can only appear thanks to its horizon. By withdrawing itself in the background, the horizon allows the entity to appear in the foreground. This implies that our understanding of being remains implicit when we are dealing with particular beings in the world, although it is always presupposed. In relation to the metaphysical distortion and the everyday disguise, truth gives itself to think as a struggle with concealment. This struggle itself is primary. If a full and absolute presence were possible, as metaphysics claims, then any concealment is a privation of presence due to the feebleness of the human or to unfortunate (everyday) situations. Plato's allegory of the cave in the seventh book of the *Republic* might be read as an example of this. The concealment in the cave is not essential, but it is merely a mishap of the human, which can be overcome thanks to rationality. According to Heidegger, however, concealment is unavoidable with respect to the question of being. Truth as disclosure is a struggle with concealment without being attracted by a complete presence. This upsets the account of a highest being. For instance in Aristotle's account of God, the highest being is both pure actuality and presence, and for that reason it is the ultimate *telos* attracting every movement.

The Heideggerian struggle, however, is a struggle drawn toward that which withdraws itself. This implies that this struggle is creative in the sense that it needs to bring forth a world (*hervorbringen*) into unconcealment out of concealment, as Heidegger puts it in "*Der Ursprung des Kunstwerkes.*" This creativity of truth is the creativity of finitude. We belong to a whole that we cannot encompass; this marks our finitude. The whole of being fundamentally *withdraws* itself, but it attracts us *not as the absolutely present and actual* being, but exactly as that which withdraws itself. Only when the whole is intrinsically concealed as the as-yet unthought, is the creative task to uncover it and to disclose it, the most fundamental task of thinking. In the following, we shall see that language and in particular poetic language is the human means to disclose. As Heidegger already writes in *Sein und Zeit* in his explanation of phenomenology, "The 'Being-true' of the *logos* as *alētheuein* [wresting of truth] means that in *legein* as *apophainesthai* [to let beings be seen from themselves] the [beings] *of which* one is talking must be taken out of their hiddenness; one must let them be seen as something unhidden (*alēthes*); that is, they must be *discovered*."[11] At the same time this means that in the above description a certain transition has taken place with respect to the notion of concealment. The withdrawal of being is not simply due to the disguise and the distortion of metaphysics or of everyday interpretations of being—the latter two refer back to a primary form of openness to which they belong. The destruction of these latter two disguises aims at the truth or the meaning of being, but there it does not find simple unconcealment. In fact, being itself, although it gives itself to think in the beginning of Western thought as presencing is always marked by concealment as well. When we are drawn to being, we are *drawn to what withdraws itself.* This concealment is no longer of the order of a displacement referring back to a primary disclosure.

To fully understand what truth as unconcealment means in Heidegger's work, it is necessary to understand concealment as well, both in its displacing and in its more primordial form. This will be done in the third section of this chapter. As a hypothesis, to be examined more closely in this section, we could say that the distortion and displacement of metaphysics is secondary to disclosure since it takes place within the realm of disclosure, whereas the withdrawal of being concerns the provenance of disclosure and is therefore primary to disclosure.

Disclosure and Being-In in *Sein und Zeit*

In order to develop the themes mentioned in the above introduction and to prepare my discussion of the relation between Heidegger, Ricoeur, and Derrida, which will guide us through the next chapters, it is necessary to turn to Heidegger's conception of truth and language in *Sein und Zeit* first. To some extent, the themes and the sections from *Sein und Zeit* that will be discussed are well-known, but rather than simply repeating the well-known facts, I will approach them in light of the pair disclosure and displacement: What do these sections and themes tell us about the meaning of disclosure and displacement in Heidegger's thought? Perhaps the best place to begin is in section 44c of *Sein und Zeit* because it is here that Heidegger nicely labels and distinguishes the different forms of disclosedness (*Erschlossenheit*) of Dasein and immediately relates them to closedness.

Thrownness, Project, and Falling

In the first sections of *Sein und Zeit*, Heidegger makes it immediately clear that the problem of his book is the meaning of being and the understanding of being that characterizes the being called Dasein. Rather than accounting for the beingness of Dasein or of any other being by relating it to some highest and transcendent being as its measure, Heidegger develops the being of Dasein as a being-in-the-world (*In-der-Welt-sein*). The "meta" position of the highest being in metaphysics is left behind, and instead Dasein is approached from

the perspective of its "in": the world is the element in which Dasein always is, and in particular it is the element that lets beings be
encountered by Dasein. Consequently, beings do not appear as isolated entities, but as innerwordly beings that belong with Dasein to
a world.[12] This turn toward being-in alters Heidegger's conception
of truth accordingly. The truth of our understanding of a being is
no longer determined by the degree to which our understanding is
in correspondence to the actual essence of the being outside a given
situation. Instead, the question of truth becomes the question of our
openness to beings as beings in the world. How are beings accessible
in the first place? In *Sein und Zeit*, it is the disclosedness of Dasein
which accounts for this accessibility and thus guides the fundamental
notion of truth.[13] What does Heidegger mean by disclosedness and
how is it intrinsically related to forms of concealment or closedness?

Thrownness and *Befindlichkeit*

The first kind of disclosedness is called *thrownness* and is discussed in
Heidegger's analysis of *Befindlichkeit*.[14] Thrownness means that we
are always already thrown into a world with others and with other
beings. *Befindlichkeit* refers to the way in which Dasein finds itself
within a world in which certain beings have already been disclosed
in a particular way. Therefore, they are familiar and accessible, always
already meaningful and significant.[15] To describe this openness to
beings, Heidegger introduces the notion of mood (*Stimmung*). A
mood attunes us to a particular being as a being in the whole of
the world. That is to say, each mood has always already disclosed
being-in as a whole, and thus it provides a particular accessibility of
beings.[16] In this way, he thematizes our openness to the whole of the
world without thinking it from the viewpoint of a totality ordered by
a highest being.

To understand how these notions of thrownness and *Befindlichkeit*
are related to the notions of understanding and interpretation in
Heidegger's thought, consider the following example. While we are
enjoying a movie, the music playing during a particular scene can
help us to interpret this scene. The music attunes us to what happens

in the movie. It situates us in the movie and therewith gives us expectations of what will happen next. For instance, if we are looking at a scene in which a man silently approaches a woman from behind and an ominous sound accompanies the scene, then we will fear the worst of what will happen next: will she be stabbed, murdered, raped? However, if the same scene is accompanied by some sweet, romantic tune, then we will expect that the couple will be caught in a fond embrace in the next moments of the film. By attuning us to the scene, the music allows us to anticipate what will happen next, or better, it allows us to anticipate the plot in which the scene stands. The anticipation is not a "free-floating potentiality-for-being," but it is rather motivated and oriented by this attunement.[17] Because the music allows us to anticipate the plot—the whole of the movie—it allows us to interpret the meaning of the scene within this plot. The attunement of the music to the scene orients us and therefore allows us to understand and to interpret the scene. Without an anticipation of the plot we cannot understand anything: the scene cannot be understood as an isolated, separate scene, but only as part of the whole. If we are not attuned to a scene—either by music or in another way—then our expectations concerning the next scene would not be embedded in and motivated by the coherence in which we are thrown. These expectations would be complete arbitrary and unmotivated. In fact, we would be completely *disoriented* in the movie. This shows that attunement and anticipation allow us to be *orientated* within the whole, without having to encompass it. As such, Dasein is open to what happens in the movie or is encountered in a world without having to grasp the whole order. Moreover, this openness is not derived from a more original representation of the world as a totality to which Dasein tries to accord its own perspective. In fact, every effort to represent the world is always already secondary to and derived from this original orientation by attunement and anticipation.

Project and Understanding

The example of the movie has already brought us to the second form of disclosedness, namely, understanding conceived as project or projection (*Entwurf*). The music, I claimed, attunes us to a scene and allows us to anticipate the plot of the movie. Heidegger calls this kind of motivated anticipation *project*. The world in which Dasein is thrown contains particular possibilities; it is the task of understanding to project these possibilities out before us. In projecting, Dasein throws possibilities out of its particular situation ahead of itself. But Dasein is ahead of itself in its project *in order to come back* to its own situation and interpret particular beings (or a scene) in light of the possibilities that it has thrown ahead of itself.

Again, the movie example is helpful to understand this "being ahead of itself." The anticipation of the whole of the movie is a form of being ahead of yourself. The film has not ended yet, but in order to understand its scenes we anticipate its ending as its genuine possibility. We become most strikingly aware of this "being ahead of ourselves" if the next scene turns out to be quite different than our expectations of it. However, let me emphasize that Heidegger is not interested in the question of whether we are right or wrong concerning any *actual* plot. What matters to him is that we are always, as beings in the world, already anticipating that which comes next. It is this anticipation and not the adequacy of our anticipation that allows us to interpret the scene while we are watching it. Because this anticipation does not need to coincide with what actually will happen, Heidegger does not say that we anticipate the *actual*, real plot. Instead he speaks about projecting *possibilities* and about being ahead of ourselves. In anticipating its project, understanding gathers the scene into a *possible* coherence. In fact, Heidegger has an intrinsic reason to focus on possibilities here. In the case of a movie, it makes sense to try to capture the real plot since there (often) is one. Yet, in the case of Dasein's being-in-the-world, an actual plot is never attained since such an actual plot requires that Dasein attains its end. However, in the case of Dasein, this end is its death. Death, as Heidegger explains, is for Dasein never an actuality: as long as Dasein is, its death is possible, and as soon as its death arrives, Dasein is no longer. Hence, Dasein can only relate to its death as to its possibility. Consequently, the end of being-in-the-world can never be related to as an actuality but only as a possibility; in fact, it is Dasein's ultimate possibility. Therefore, our being-in-the-world does not allow for a totalizing grasp. Since no totality is given, disclosedness is primordially composed of the attuning orientation, the motivated anticipation and the explicating return to the beings we encounter.

His particular understanding of the end as possibility means that Heidegger's analysis of understanding as anticipation should not be mistaken for a teleology.[18] In a teleological account of interpretation, the process of interpretation is looking for and attracted by a present and actual *telos*, or, as Derrida calls it, a transcendental signified—for instance, the actual plot of a movie, or the actual meaning of a text. At this point, a possible difference with Gadamer and Ricoeur announces itself, as we shall see in the next chapter. Although the *telos* may be concealed *for the interpreter* in a teleological account, the possible complete presence of this *telos* is presupposed in this account of interpretation. In this conception, interpretation is a way of dealing with and an effort to overcome the concealment of this *telos*. Consequently, the end of interpretation, in the double sense of the word, is the actual presence of the goal. Heidegger, however, tries to show that the anticipation of possibilities projects a coherence, and this projected coherence of possibilities makes interpretation possible. Hence, no transcendental signified is presupposed by interpretation, only the project of understanding. Consequently, Heidegger's conception of understanding is an inventive one: it creates and discovers the whole thanks to which interpretation is possible.[19]

Falling and Untruth

The counterpart of Dasein understanding its ownmost possibility (*eigenste Sein-können*) and its authentic disclosedness (*eigentliche Erschlossenheit*), is *falling*.[20] Falling is a form of closedness, that is, a closing of Dasein's possibilities. Instead of trying to understand a being itself, Dasein has the tendency to repeat what "they"[21] say, and it has the tendency to lose itself in the everyday world and to hold to what has already been discovered and to what is familiar.[22] Let me elaborate two different aspects of Dasein's fallenness.

First, one could wonder to what extent the closure of falling is different from the disclosure of thrownness. Like the closure of falling, the disclosure of thrownness means that beings have always already been discovered and that beings are to a certain extent familiar to us. So why does Heidegger describe thrownness as a form of disclosedness and falling as a form of closedness? A brief example may clarify this. Suppose that we are reading a philosophical text that is impenetrable for us. It just does not become meaningful when we try to read it. In this case, insightful secondary literature or inspiring courses can provide us with interpretations of this text that help us to read it. Thanks to these interpretations this text is no longer mute to us, but becomes significant. Thanks to these interpretations we are attuned to the text in a particular way. This enables us to read the text ourselves and to interpret it in light of different reading possibilities. In this way, our understanding is motivated by these interpretations, but our understanding need not coincide with the interpretations that open up the text. However, if we would treat these interpretations as normative and as the fixed interpretation of the meaning of the text, then the same interpretations no longer let us encounter the text as *that which can be understood*. In this case, we simply parrot the interpretation instead of trying to understand the text. What happens here is that the interpretation, which in the first place disclosed the text to us, closes the text off as something that can be understood. These two functions of the same interpretation are clearly distinct. This does mean, though, that what once helped us to understand something may later obstruct genuine understanding. Similarly, thrownness, which *motivates* the anticipation of our understanding, is different from falling, which *disguises* our ownmost possibility of understanding.

Second, the closure of falling has a specific character. Although it is a form of concealment, it is not a *lack* of appearance or presence. Heidegger uses the word *Verstellen* to describe this closedness. *Verstellen* means "to disguise" or "to distort," but a better translation would be "to displace," since the "dis" captures the meaning of *Ver* in German and *stellen* can be translated as to posit or to place. This word describes a concealment that takes place within the realm of what is unconcealed. Falling displaces beings and this does not mean that it completely hides a being, but rather that *it shows a being as something it is not*. Heidegger's analysis of idle talk provides a perfect example of what this means. In his analysis of idle talk, Heidegger points to the problem of repetition. The repetition of what has been said in "gossiping" and "passing the word along," leads to an understanding of things that is not guided by one's own, proper understanding, but "what is said-in-the-talk as such...takes on an authoritative character. Things are so because one says so."[23] Clearly, this appearance of a thing in what *they* say about it is not without a relation to what a being is. As what has already been discovered, the appearance refers back to an original discovery. Yet, at the same time, as that which has already been discovered, it conceals this discovery as well as the potential for a renewed discovery. In fact, what has been discovered may obstruct discovery, as Heidegger reminds us: "Only in so far as entities within-the-world [*innerweltliches Seiendes*] have been uncovered along with Dasein, have such entities, as possibly encounterable within-the-world, been covered up (hidden) or disguised. It is therefore essential that Dasein should explicitly appropriate what has already been uncovered, defend it *against* semblance and disguise, and assure itself of its uncoveredness again and again."[24] The danger of semblance and disguise, the danger of the closure of falling happens to those beings that have already been disclosed. Heidegger's account of displacement consists precisely of this: it is this mixture of concealment and unconcealment as well as of disclosure and closure that marks the disguise of falling.

To deepen our understanding of these dimensions of falling, I propose to use the word *trace*. What has been said, and that which is passed on in idle talk, is a trace of saying because it refers back to an original saying, and it does not bring this saying itself to presence. These two aspects are characteristic of a trace: a footstep in the snow refers back to a person, but it does not present this person. Moreover, because a trace is also something in itself, it may lead us astray and focus us on itself instead of on its origin. If this happens, a trace conceals its origin. This also applies to what has already been discovered: this may conceal the possibility of discovery. It is particularly interesting that Heidegger suggests in the section of *Sein und Zeit* on idle talk that the difference between "gossip [*Nachreden*]" and "what has been drawn from primordial sources" is still discernable in saying and in hearsay [*Hörensagen*], but is no longer discernable by the reader once it has been written down.[25] In this sense, the text is a culmination point of the trace's concealment and of the concealment of falling in the passing on of what has been said! Clearly, this has important consequences for Heidegger's conception of writing and the text, as I shall discuss in the next chapter. To anticipate this discussion, let me note that Derrida uses the term *trace* in a slightly different way. As I noted, the trace is a secondary notion for Heidegger: it refers back to a primordial possibility of discovery. In Derrida's and Levinas's account of the trace, it is no longer considered to be secondary. In their conception, a trace refers back to something that has never been present and that will never be present. In this way, the trace, though referring, is primary. Or rather, the trace is all there is in terms of signification and presence. By linking the Heideggerian notion of *Verstellen* to the trace, I aim to show that these notions are all related to a particular concept of untruth, namely, an untruth that belongs to the domain of appearing. As we shall see further on in this chapter, Heidegger consistently uses the Greek word *pseudos* to describe this form of "untruth." As opposed to this untruth, Heidegger also pays attention to untruth as *lēthē*. In fact, as he claims the Greek privative *a-lētheia* refers to the primacy of this notion. This twofold concealment is discussed in relation to Heidegger's discussion of Plato's parable of the cave.

Interpretation and Assertion

The task of interpretation, in distinction to the project of understanding, is to provide an *explicit* understanding of a being. In Heidegger's analysis of interpretation, in section 32 of *Sein und Zeit*, we can trace both the importance of *orientation* and of the *primacy of the whole* in his account of the *hermeneutic "as"* of interpretation: "that which is explicitly understood has the structure of *something as something.*"[26] To understand the difference between the hermeneutic "as" and the apophantic "as," that is, between interpretation and assertion (*Aussage*), the notions of orientation and whole are crucial.

Understanding, as I noted, is the gathering of beings into a possible coherence that precedes the discernment of any particular being. This coherence orients interpretation. Heidegger calls this orientation the *fore-structure* of understanding.[27] This fore-structure implies that interpretation does not address a being in its isolation; instead it is motivated and oriented by the whole of understanding. The primacy of the whole returns in Heidegger's explanation of the as-structure of interpretation. In order to conceive of something *as* something or to interpret X *as* Y means already interpreting X in its togetherness (*Beisammen*) with Y.[28] Interpretation does not address either X or Y as isolated beings, but it interprets X from the point of view of its belonging together with Y. The combination of the fore- and as-structures leads to Heidegger's description of meaning: "*Meaning is the 'upon which' of a projection in terms of which something becomes intelligible as something; it gets its structure from a fore-having, a fore-sight, and a fore-conception.*"[29]

Heidegger's description of the hermeneutic as-structure and his explanation of the disclosure of meaning as the "upon which" of understanding and interpretation has been an important influence for Ricoeur's theory of metaphor. In line with Gadamer's understanding of the fundamental metaphoricity of language, Ricoeur describes a metaphor such as "X is Y" or "X is as Y" ("man is a wolf" or "man is as a wolf") from the perspective of the co-belonging of X and Y. In the theory of metaphor, this togetherness of X and Y is called resemblance. The primacy of this co-belonging of beings over their isolability allows Ricoeur to describe metaphor as the capacity to disclose new meanings. At the same time, as we shall see in the third chapter, there is an important difference between Heidegger's description of the hermeneutic as, his description of the apophantic as, and Ricoeur's description of what I propose to call the metaphoric as. To understand this, we first need to deal with Heidegger's account of the apophantic *as*, which can be found in section 33 where he discusses the *assertion*.

Heidegger's analysis of assertions serves a twofold goal — the first of which is to describe *logos* as showing. Throughout his discussion of *logos* as assertion, as discourse (*Rede*), and as language in general, Heidegger points out that in *On Interpretation* Aristotle uses the notion of *logos* in the sense of *apophansis*. In this way, Aristotle connects the essence of language with showing and pointing out since the Greek *apophansis* means just these things, according to Heidegger.[30] An assertion lets a being be seen without mediation and as it is. Language does not place itself between us and the beings we are talking about by presenting an image, picture, or representation of these beings, but it effaces itself in order to let the beings show themselves as they are.[31]

This showing quality of language is equiprimordial to *Befindlichkeit* and understanding.[32] Discourse (*Rede*) articulates the understanding. This opens up a new dimension of Dasein's disclosedness. Besides understanding and interpretation, *articulation* allows Dasein to *show* beings in their uncoveredness. Heidegger relates this showing quality of articulation to the classical determination of the essence of the human — *zōon logon echon*. He argues, "Man shows himself as the entity which talks. This does not signify that the possibility of vocal utterance is peculiar to him, but rather that he is the [being] which is such as to discover the world and Dasein itself."[33] In this section, Heidegger interprets the classical definition of human beings in line with his own conception of truth. That human beings speak means that they discover the world and discover themselves through language. Disclosure takes place in articulation. Thus, the apophantic dimension of language relates language to truth as disclosure. Of course, this also means that Heidegger relates assertions to the disclosedness of Dasein in understanding. He takes great care to show that the relation between words and things is not a connection between two given beings. A word is not in the first place a representation of a being. Instead, an assertion shows a being as it has been disclosed by the understanding. By founding the assertion in the understanding, Heidegger tries to show that the assertion is not *another* place of access to the world different from the understanding, but that the assertion itself is founded in Dasein's fundamental disclosedness. It is only through Dasein's understanding that assertion and beings belong together—and neither the assertion nor the being that is asserted can exist outside of this primordial understanding. On this point, Heidegger will change his mind as can be seen in *Unterwegs zur Sprache*.

The second goal of Heidegger's analysis of assertions is to develop the idea of *logos* as disguise. An assertion speaks about something, and it is the place where the being it speaks about is shown. However, an assertion is more than that—and here a shift takes place from the disclosive showing of an assertion to its displacing and concealing dimension in Heidegger's analysis. Instead of being simply the place where beings are shown, an assertion may become a ready-to-hand being itself, available for everyone who can speak. Thus, as something ready-to-hand, it may be repeated and passed on. This readiness-to-hand of the assertion introduces the problem of falling as disguise as well as the problem of the representational character of language: the togetherness in understanding of the assertion and the being it asserts is dissolved; the assertion and the being it asserts become two separate ready-to-hand (and even present-at-hand) beings. Once they are separate, one has to account for their correspondence. Hence, this process leads to the determination of truth as correspondence, as Heidegger claims. Hence, the nature of the assertion inaugurates the derivative concept of truth as correspondence. How does this come about?

The assertion is a *derivative* mode of interpretation.[34] "Derivative" points to the *resemblance* of interpretation and assertion as well as to the *decay* of assertion. Assertion resembles interpretation since it has a similar as-structure that is founded in the togetherness of beings projected by the understanding; it points something out "on the basis of what has already been disclosed in understanding."[35] Yet, an assertion is also a form of decay. Unlike interpretation, the assertion tends to conceal the whole out of which beings are interpreted. It does so by bringing being to the fore *as present-at-hand*. Whereas interpretation carries the visible traces of the coherence of understanding in its as-structure, the apophantic as of assertion "no longer reaches out into a totality of involvements."[36] Thus, the decay of assertion introduces a closure similar to that of falling: it closes off the authentic disclosedness as the primordial phenomenon of truth.

Moreover, this decay of the assertion coincides with its becoming *repeatable*. This repeatability always concerns what has been said. What has been said is secondary and refers back to the original saying out of the understanding, but by its decay it can appear to be something independent—thus concealing its foundation in the understanding. This detachment of "what has been said" from an original saying plays an important part in Ricoeur's analysis of *distanciation*, as we shall see in next chapter. Unlike Heidegger, Ricoeur will not describe this distanciation as a decay. In fact, he shows us that Heidegger's account of the decay of assertion lacks a more favorable and positive interpretation of the repeatability of what has been expressed. Heidegger seems to forget the positive dimension of repeatability. He only argues that the assertion may disguise authentic disclosedness, leading to a metaphysical conception of truth as agreement. This suggests once more that Heidegger tends to understand repetition, representation, transference, and displacement as mere secondary phenomena that tend to conceal a more primary disclosure.

TWOFOLD CONCEALMENT

To deepen our understanding of Heidegger's conception of truth and untruth, this section is devoted to his twofold determination of concealment as *pseudos* and *lēthē*. However, to see how this problematic arises out of his analysis of the problem of truth, I will first turn to Heidegger's reading of Plato's allegory of the cave. This reading presents us with some basic aspects of Heidegger's conception of truth and, in addition, allows me to discuss briefly the problem of a change of the essence of truth that according to Heidegger occurred in Western thought.

Heidegger's Reading of the Allegory of the Cave

In the winter term of 1933/34, Heidegger lectured on Plato's allegory of the cave.[37] This allegory is the famous place of a final battle (*Kampf*), Heidegger argues, between two concepts of truth in Greek thought: truth as *alētheia* or unconcealment and truth as *orthotes* or correctness.[38] Here a change in the essence of truth has taken place in Western thought. One of the main objections directed against Heidegger's analysis of the concept of truth in Greek thought concerns exactly his claim that the Greeks once had an explicit understanding of truth as unconcealment and that the essence of truth has changed from this understanding to an understanding of correctness in the history of philosophy. After the Presocratics, truth simply means correctness. To come to terms with these objections, I will first describe this transition in Plato's parable and secondly show how the phenomena of concealment is indispensable to understand Heidegger's final position with respect to this problem of the change of the essence of truth in the history of Western metaphysics.

A Twofold Truth in Plato's Allegory of the Cave

The prisoners in Plato's cave, as is well-known, have been living in this cave all their lives. They are fettered in such a way that they can only see the wall in front of them. In the cave, a fire burns behind their backs. In front of this fire, but behind the prisoners' backs, people carry around all kinds of artifacts. The light of the fire projects the shadows of these artifacts on the wall. Because the prisoners have never seen these artifacts, they do not recognize that they only see shadows, and they take the shadows to be the true things. They need to be liberated from this situation in order to see things as they truly are. The allegory describes the difficulties of being liberated from the cave as well as the somewhat unexpected return of a liberated prisoner to the cave. In his lectures, Heidegger divides the allegory into four stages: (1) the situation of the human beings in the cave; (2) the first attempt to liberate a human being; (3) the actual liberation of one human being; (4) the return of that human being into the cave.[39]

In his analysis of the first stage, Heidegger explains that the allegory is, strictly speaking, not about freeing prisoners from darkness. The prisoners are always already in a certain light; they always already perceive certain appearances, namely, the shadows on the wall. This means that beings are always already *uncovered* to some extent. Like human beings in their everyday situation, the prisoners are always already related to beings in their unconcealedness, and they stand always already amid appearances.[40] Therefore, the allegory is an allegory on truth as unconcealment from the outset: how does Dasein relate to what appears? As a parable on truth as unconcealment, it is also a parable on the concealment of this unconcealment as such. Although the prisoners stand amid appearances, these appearances are not given to them *as unconcealed*.[41] This means that if the shadows were given to them *as* shadows, then they would know of the difference between the shadows and their origin. However, the whole in which these appearances and the prisoners are related is concealed to the prisoners.

In the second stage, a prisoner is liberated from his chains. Therefore, the prisoner can turn toward the objects and toward the light of the fire burning in the cave. The appearance of the light of the fire is determined by Plato as *more uncovered*. This appearance is not merely an appearance like the shadows, but it has an increased uncoveredness.[42] Hence, Plato introduces a *comparison* in which he discusses the idea of *orthotes*, correctness. In this second stage, the second dimension of truth comes into play in the allegory: the appearance of the fire in the cave is more correct, is more uncovered, and therefore *is* more than the shadows. Yet, the prisoner does not recognize this appearance of the fire *as* more correct. The prisoner merely sees another appearance. The only comparison the prisoner can make is the comparison between the *bearable* appearance of the shadow on the wall and the *painful* flickering of the fire. The prisoner prefers the bearable shadow to the painful fire and thus returns to the illusion.[43]

Heidegger makes two important remarks. In the first place, he notices that the fire in the cave needs to appear first before the prisoner can be confronted with the question about which appearance is better and is more right. In this sense, truth as comparison and truth as correctness always presupposes truth as unconcealment. For instance, at this stage, it would not make sense to compare the shadow on the wall with the sun burning outside the cave, because the sun has not yet appeared. The sun is still simply concealed. Truth as correctness or comparison, and consequently also the idea of a reality ordered in agreement with degrees of being, can only take place within the realm of unconcealment.[44] In the second place, he notes that despite the appearance of the fire in the cave, the prisoner does not recognize the fire as more uncovered than the shadows. Although the fire of the cave is no longer denied to him, but shown to him thanks to his liberation, the fire does not appear to him as a fire, that is, as the light that allows the shadows to appear: the liberated prisoner does not know of the relation between the fire and the shadows. Although this relation is known to us, the readers, it remains in the dark for the prisoner and *therefore* he wants to return to his old situation.[45]

The battle between the two concepts of truth reaches its culmination point in the third stage. At this point, a prisoner is freed from the cave and brought into the light of the sun. In his discussion, Heidegger does not refer to the allegory but to Plato's own explanation of it. The light of the sun represents the Idea. In Plato's description of the Idea, this battle between the two concepts of truth can still be traced. Yet, the depiction of the Idea as the *most unconcealed* and the *most being* being also relates the Platonic Idea to the fully present and actual being in which no concealment remains. That is, it refers us to the onto-theo-logy of Plato's metaphysics: the Idea is the measure of the beingness of all other beings. It also refers us to the concept of truth as agreement: the Idea is the measure of truth of every being. In the next to last section of his lectures on the allegory—for good reason titled, "The disappearing of the ground experience [*Grunderfahrung*] of *alētheia*"—Heidegger describes how Plato's particular discussion of the Idea no longer questions the realm of unconcealment, but restricts itself to unconcealed beings.[46] This movement in the allegory marks the shift from a discussion of the realm of the open as such, that is, of the ontological, to a discussion of the highest beings, that is, of the ontic. Because of this shift, truth as unconcealment is obfuscated and truth as the agreement between beings is the only truth that matters to Plato at the end of the allegory.[47]

This brief examination of Heidegger's reading of the first three stages of Plato's allegory of the cave shows how in Plato's allegory, the realm of unconcealment is prior to the realm of truth as correctness. As a reading of the allegory, it makes sense. However, to come back to the objection I raised in the beginning of this section, can Heidegger maintain that this reading traces a change of the essence of truth in Greek thought itself?[48]

During the time of his 1933 lectures, Heidegger indeed claims that the Greeks have experienced and conceptually grasped the concept of truth as unconcealment and the concept of truth as correctness.[49] Yet, at the same time, he argues that the "battle" that takes place in Plato's allegory is neither consciously known nor explicitly wanted by Plato.[50] It seems somewhat strange, to say the least, that if the Greeks had indeed conceptually grasped both concepts of truth, that this battle would have gone unnoticed by Plato. Apparently, the Greeks experienced this truth in such a way that it remains implicit and not thematized. In *Zur Sache des Denkens,* Heidegger goes one step further and withdraws the claim that the Greeks had already grasped or experienced truth as unconcealment. He writes that the Greeks *named* truth *alētheia* and that they *spoke out of* truth as unconcealment, but that they did not actually *think* or *experience* it as such: "In scope of this question, we must acknowledge the fact that *alētheia,* unconcealment in the sense of the opening of presence, was originally only experienced as *orthotes,* as the correctness of representations and statements. But then the assertion about the essential transformation of truth, that is, from unconcealment to correctness, is also untenable."[51] Although Heidegger acknowledges that the claim of the essential transformation of truth is untenable, he still claims that *alētheia* provides more to be thought about than the Greeks have thought in it.[52] He insists on his interpretation of *alētheia* as presencing—

not because the Greeks experienced this, but because it is the *con-cealed wealth* of the Greek language that Heidegger brings to pres-ence in his thought. Hence, even though the Greeks have never thought *alētheia* as unconcealment, this particular meaning belongs to the *unthought* of the Greek notion of *a-lētheia*. This unthought-of meaning is the Greek legacy to us. Therefore, Heidegger's reading of Plato's allegory of the cave is still relevant after his withdrawal of the claim that the Greeks experienced *a-lētheia* as unconcealment since it shows how this unconcealment is present in Plato's thought. It is the subject matter that counts, as Heidegger puts it, and not the etymology.[53]

His remarks in *Zur Sache des Denkens* are important because they reflect a fundamental aspect of Heidegger's thought: for him, the unthought of a thought and the unsaid of what has been said or writ-ten is the greatest gift a thought and a book bestows upon us — greater than what is actually and explicitly thought and said.[54] This concealed wealth of a text or of a language contains the essence of this text or this language. What is explicitly said or thought thus conceals the whole out of which it speaks and thinks. Concealment preserves this essence, withholding it from presence but at the same time holding it ready to be brought to presence. Heidegger's thought on conceal-ment moves within this state of expectancy: language and thought is pregnant with meaning to be brought to presence. Therefore, think-ing does not refuse itself what has not yet been unconcealed since only this concealment can be the source and the provenance from which truth can come to presence. In a situation comparable to that of the prisoner, the philosopher should not blind him or herself to this concealment, but should try to bring it into the open.

The Question of Untruth

Let us return to Plato's allegory. The fourth and final stage of the parable tells us how the liberated prisoner, who has dwelt in the light of the sun for some time, goes back down into the cave to free the other prisoners. By looking back on his or her life in the cave and by returning to it, the liberated prisoner learns to understand fully the

situation of the cave. Now the prisoner knows that a certain unconcealment exists in the cave, but also that this unconcealment *hides* and
disguises: the shadows do not appear as the things themselves, but as
shadows, that is, as mere appearances.[55]

In just a few remarks, Heidegger shows that his conception of
truth as unconcealment also implies a revision of the traditional concept of untruth. Untruth is not simply that which is false. More is at
stake than simple falsity. Heidegger distinguishes two forms of concealment. He distinguishes between *the concealment of what has not
yet been uncovered* and *the concealment of the mere appearance that disguises.* Looking back at his freedom, the prisoner comprehends that
his liberation involves a *setting apart* (*Auseinandersetzung*) between
what is and that which is *mere appearance.* A mere appearance does
not show a being as it is, but disguises, distorts, and displaces this
being.[56] In the first stage, the shadow is a good example of displacement. The shadow shines, but not *as* shadow; it appears as the real
thing instead of as a shadow of an artifact. This form of concealment
is deceptive and deceitful; it leads us astray and covers up the whole of
unconcealment that enables it. Plato calls this disguising appearance
pseudos, and Heidegger uses the term *Verstellen* or displacement.

Moreover, this setting apart involves the uncovering of what *has
not yet been* uncovered: the light of the fire, the true objects, the
(light of the) sun, and the whole of unconcealment in which these
beings belong together. For the prisoner in chains, these elements
are all concealed: in the first stage, they do not even appear to him.
The privative *a-lētheia* refers to the Greek word *lēthē,* concealment
or forgetting, which according to Heidegger is the Greek word for
this simple concealment. He also calls it *Versagen* or refusal. This
aspect of concealment implies that unconcealment must be torn out
and wrested from concealment.[57] Truth only happens in a battle with
this twofold untruth; it occurs by setting itself apart from what disguises and displaces, and by wresting from that which withdraws.
Both aspects of untruth show that truth only occurs as a battle with
concealment. Therefore, "the truth as such does not exist," "truth is
not a possession," and "no pure unconcealment exists."[58] This also

implies that Heidegger does not understand untruth as a lack of presence or actuality, but as a part of the essence of truth as disclosure.

The Distinction between *Pseudos* and *Lēthē*

In the final section of his lecture course, Heidegger returns to the distinction between two forms of concealment and introduces their Greek names: *pseudos* and *lēthē*. *Lēthē* is a form of concealment referring to what has *not yet* been unconcealed. Heidegger describes *pseudos* as a form of concealment that covers up something after it has been unconcealed before.[59] To illustrate what *pseudos* means, Heidegger discusses the word "pseudonym."[60] The word "pseudonym" does not simply mean a false name. Instead, it is a cover (*Deckname*) behind which the writer conceals himself. In his *Parmenides* lectures, Heidegger even argues that pseudonym is not simply a name to cover up (*Deckname*), but in reference to Kierkegaard's use of pseudonyms, he argues that certain pseudonyms show something essential about the works written under those pseudonyms, although they disguise the name of the author at the same time.[61] The example of Kierkegaard's pseudonyms show that a pseudonym is neither a false name nor a name that simply covers up the identity of the author. It rather lets something appear, although in a twisted and distorted way and by keeping something secret.

In the same manner, the Greek meaning of the word *pseudos* is not simply falsity, but involves both concealment and letting something appear. Concealment is brought about by the fact that *pseudos* shows a being *as it is not*; it twists and distorts (*verdrehen, verkehren*).[62] The fundamental meaning (*Grundbedeutung*) of *pseudos* is *Verstellen*, that is, displacement or disguise.[63] As Gadamer puts it, *pseudos* is not simply errancy, but it indicates the uncanniness typical of appearances.[64] What we see here is that Heidegger retrieves the notion of *pseudos* under the aspect of truth as unconcealment. The translation of *pseudos* as *falsum* is in this respect as concealing as the translation of *alētheia* as *veritas,* which is a translation that distorts the Greek experience of truth as unconcealment into the Roman concept of truth as correspondence (*veritas est adaequatio intellectus ad rem*). This translation conceals how *pseudos* itself is a key word in the Greek understanding of truth and untruth as a relation of unconcealment and concealment.

Heidegger stresses that the displacement of *pseudos* takes place in the realm of unconcealment. It is one appearance or one being that displaces another or that displaces the realm of the open that allows this appearance to take place. He gives the example of a door that is displaced (*ver-stellen*) by a cupboard put in front of it. The presence of the cupboard imposes itself on us, but it may impose itself to such a degree that it appears as if there is no door behind it.[65] We could add to this example the shadow as it appears to a chained prisoner in Plato's cave. The shadows appear to be the real artifacts themselves and thus they displace and disguise the actual artifacts: it seems to the prisoners that there are no artifacts behind the shadows.

These two examples imply that *pseudos* is not more original than disclosure, but it is the other way around: *pseudos* belongs to a realm of unconcealment. *Pseudos* concerns a displacement within a realm of unconcealment due to which we lose track of the whole in which those distorting appearances are given to us. *Pseudos* displaces the whole. This implies that there is a close connection between *pseudos* and the notion of the trace I introduced above. The appearance implied in *pseudos* is a trace of the realm of unconcealment to which it belongs, but this trace cannot disclose this realm. Instead, it tends to conceal it. Two linguistic examples of *pseudos* impose themselves on us: (1) Heidegger argued that the assertion tends to conceal the disclosure from which it stems. As an assertion, it still points out a being, but as ready-to-hand it conceals the belonging together of itself and this being, grounded in understanding. (2) Another example might be found in translation. Translated words always refer back to an original language, but they cannot disclose this original whole from which they stem. Obviously, a translated word means something in the language in which it is translated—for instance, *veritas* and *falsum* definitely mean something in Latin—but it is exactly this appearance of meaning which conceals the original meaning of the word and implies an unmistakable loss that can only be made undone by going back to the original realm in which the words appeared for the first time.[66]

These examples show that *pseudos* is a highly complicated form of concealment on the basis of appearances. It involves at the same time appearing and hiding; it depends on the realm of the open, but it also distorts this realm and closes it down. According to Heidegger, this also implies that *pseudos* is secondary to the whole of unconcealment in which beings appear because it needs the unconcealment that it nevertheless distorts. Although *pseudos* deprives us of seeing the whole by distorting it, it takes place within a whole or refers back to it. This is exactly the problem of the onto-theo-logy of metaphysics: one being displaces and disguises the whole of being. This implies that *pseudos* cannot be simply opposed to *alētheia*, and this can be seen in the Greek language, according to Heidegger, where it is not the proper antonym of *alētheia*.

The true antonym of *alētheia* is *lēthē*, simple concealment. The realm of *lēthē*, primary concealment, is the realm in which truth rests. Heidegger writes in his essay "Logos": "The *A-lētheia* rests in *Lēthē*, drawing from it and laying before us whatever remains deposited in *Lēthē*. . . . Unconcealment needs concealment, *Lēthē*, as a reservoir upon which disclosure can, as it were, draw."[67] As such, truth as disclosure draws from a realm that retains what has not yet been uncovered. The contrast with *pseudos* is striking. *Pseudos* closes off what was once disclosed to us. *Lēthē* precedes any appearance; unlike *pseudos*, it is simple concealment. Though *lēthē* withholds disclosure, it is also the realm from which disclosure draws. Therefore, *lēthē* not only withholds truth, but also holds it at the ready. It is the condition of possibility of the occurrence of truth.

In "*Vom Wesen der Wahrheit*," Heidegger confirms this when he writes, "Concealment deprives [*versagt*] *alētheia* of disclosure yet does not render it *sterēsis* (privation); rather, concealment preserves what is most proper to *alētheia* as its own."[68] By refusing disclosure, this concealment retains and preserves what is proper to *alētheia*. *Lēthē* as concealment is the realm of a concealed wealth that lies ready and awaits disclosure; it is a well from which *alētheia* draws.

The difference between *pseudos* and *lēthē* is marked by the lack of any appearance or disclosure in *lēthē*. This is an important difference because *pseudos* leads us astray on the basis of concealing *appearances*. It is the appearance that distorts, disguises, and displaces. The withholding that marks *lēthē* is of a different kind. It does not lead astray; it simply refuses disclosure. As this refusal and as this withdrawal, it also draws *alētheia* as that which withdraws the essence of *alētheia*. Therefore, *lēthē* can be called the genuine *beginning* or provenance of truth.

Obviously, *lēthē* as forgetting is not to be confused with ordinary forgetting. The forgetting addressed in *lēthē* has nothing to do with the feebleness of human memory. It is an aspect of being itself. Forgetting is not merely a psychological circumstance, but has an ontological meaning and is related to the question of truth and being. Therefore, Heidegger does not translate *lanthanō* as "I conceal," but as "I am concealed."[69] By this translation, he shows that for Greek thought, concealment and forgetfulness are not effects brought about by a fault of human memory, but that they reign in the open as the provenance of the open. In this sense, *lēthē* does not depend on human forgetting, but concerns a primordial forgetting in the being of human beings.[70] In sum, *pseudos* is a sign or a trace that displaces the being to which it refers. Heidegger describes *lēthē* as a forgetfulness without any sign. No appearance refers to it. It is simply withdrawn.[71] Therefore, the forgetfulness of *lēthē* is a forgetting of forgetting.[72]

Remembering Lēthē

Heidegger introduces *lēthē* as the counter essence (*Gegenwesen*) to *alētheia*. This notion brings to mind a number of questions. Why is this primary, simple concealment so important for him if his thought centers around disclosure? Moreover, how can we think this forgetfulness even as it leads to a forgetting of this forgetfulness? Finally, how can we speak about it given that it is said to have withdrawn into oblivion? *Lēthē* is a crucial phenomenon since it is involved in the essence of truth and in the Greek understanding of the essence of human beings. In §7 of *Parmenides,* Heidegger turns to the myth of Er at the end of Plato's *Republic,* the myth involving the river *Lēthē.*[73] This myth, he argues, preserves the remembrance of concealment and oblivion that mark human essence: "Yet the *essence* of man…is saved only when man, as the being he is, harkens to the legend [*Sage*] of concealment. Only in that way can he follow what unconcealedness itself and disclosure of the unconcealed demand in their essence."[74] To explain the importance of this myth of concealment, we have to introduce two aspects of Heidegger's thought that are brought into play in this section of the *Parmenides.*

In the first place, when Heidegger speaks about the essence of human beings, he speaks very classically about human *logos.* But he interprets *logos* or language as the letting appear of beings. Thus, when he speaks about the "essence of human beings [*das Wesen des Menschen*]," he speaks about language in relation to truth as disclosure. And when he writes that the essence of human beings is saved only when humans harken to the myth of concealment, this implies that disclosure always takes place against the background of a primary concealment. The task of disclosure consists in bringing to presence what is utterly and simply concealed. A fixed, purely present *telos* is not what attracts thinking. Rather thinking's task is to disclose what conceals itself and to save what is unconcealed from a hiding withdrawal (*verhehlenden Entzugs*). In this task, thinking is a response to the appeal of being (*Anspruch des Seins*).[75] The possibility of this task of thinking implies that although *lēthē* or forgetfulness reigns over humanity, it does not reign completely; otherwise humanity could not be as it is. In terms of Plato's myth, Heidegger writes that the one who constantly drinks from the water of the river of oblivion could not be on earth as a human being.[76] If *lēthē* were to reign fully, concealment would be all-enclosing and human being as *zōon echon logon,* as the being that speaks, would be impossible because the truth of language consists in bringing what is concealed into unconcealment.[77] Only because disclosure as the bringing forth from concealment into unconcealment is a possibility of being, human being as a speaking being is possible. This disclosedness is even presupposed by

human being's everyday existence, as Heidegger showed in his reading of Plato's allegory of the cave: even the chained prisoner always
already stands amid discovered beings and is therefore concerned with
unconcealment. These two implications—disclosure taking place
against a background of concealment and the fact that forgetfulness
does not reign completely—also imply that the disclosure attained by
human beings in language is nothing but a continual struggle with a
fundamental oblivion.

In the second place, Heidegger argues that the Greeks experienced
logos and *muthos* as *Sage* or saying, with the latter being the fundamental realm of unconcealment. The myth of *lēthē* is therefore an
almost paradoxical form of a saying that allows the essence of concealment to come to presence. "For the Greeks," Heidegger writes,
"the withdrawing and self-withdrawing concealment is the simplest
of the simple, preserved for them in their experience of the unconcealed and therein allowed to come into presence."[78] Let us recall
Heidegger's description of the task of philosophical thinking in "*Vom
Wesen der Wahrheit*": "Philosophical thinking is the gentle releasement that does not renounce the concealment of being as a whole.
Philosophical thinking is especially the stern and resolute openness
that does not disrupt the concealing but entreats its unbroken essence
into the open region of understanding and thus into its own truth."[79]
Here we see that the philosophical task is completed by a myth that
indeed brings the unbroken essence of concealment into the open. In
this sense, thinking is not opposed to myth but is guided by myths
that keep in memory what needs to be thought. Therefore, the thinker
is and can only be a *philomuthos*, a lover of myths. Plato's work shows
this more than the work of any other philosopher, despite his denigration of the poets in the same *Republic*.[80]

The myth on *lēthē* is important to Heidegger because it is an original saying (*muthos*) that speaks of and shows the beginning of truth
and of saying. The myth on the river *Lēthē* preserves and remembers
the essence of concealment in relation to the essence of man and shows
the importance of concealment as the essence of truth. Heidegger
writes, "This remembering utterance [*Sagen*] of the *muthos* preserves

the primordial unveiling of the essence of *lēthē* and at the same time helps us to think more attentively the domain in which Homer already mentions the counter-word to *lēthē, alētheia.*"[81] For Heidegger, this gives rise to a *chiasmatic relation* between concealment and unconcealment. We have already seen how he argues that the essence of concealment is preserved in a myth, the realm of unconcealment, but he also argues that the essence of truth is both retained and kept ready in *lēthē.* Concealment is not just the realm that withholds truth, but it is also a concealment that keeps the essence of discovery ready.[82] Heidegger's description of *lēthē* as that which has not yet been unconcealed implies the same thing. *Lēthē* concerns a concealment that awaits the arrival of truth as disclosure. In his *Parmenides* lectures, Heidegger articulates this by his play on the word *vorenthalten,* which he writes with a hyphen as *vor-enthalten.* By doing this, he stresses that *lēthē* withholds, but also that it retains (*enthalten*) the essence of unconcealment in advance (*im voraus*).[83] In this way, concealment is ahead of unconcealment and contains the possibility of disclosure. As such, *lēthē* is also different from *pseudos.* The distortion of everyday life proceeds from the conviction "that something is preserved the soonest and is preservable the easiest when it is constantly at hand and graspable."[84] In our examination of *Sein und Zeit,* we have seen that Heidegger discusses the latter "thoughtless opinion" in his analysis of what has been expressed and thus has already become ready-to-hand. This Heideggerian example leads us immediately to the problem of the materiality of writing and its contribution to transference, which we will discuss in the next chapter. Opposed to this preservation of the saying in the written form, Heidegger writes, "But in truth, and that now means for us truth in the sense of the essence of uncncealedness, it is self-withdrawing concealment that in the highest way disposes human beings to preserving and to faithfulness."[85]

Applied to the example of the text, this means that the readiness-to-hand of the text does not preserve meaning. In its immediate availability, the text presents an indifference between what is mere gossip and what has been drawn from primordial sources.[86] As such, for thoughtless opinion, the text effaces the difference between a response to the appeal of being and the unthoughtful repetition of particular interpretations of being. At the same time, Heidegger draws our attention to the myth on *lēthē*, which tells us about a preservation of something that is not immediately available, at hand, or graspable, but that is characterized as unthought and unsaid, and that is kept ready to be brought to presence in a disclosing interpretation as a thinking response to the appeal of being. Opposed to the indifferent preservation of the text, Heidegger draws our attention to what the myth says on *lēthē* as a genuine preservation, and on the possibility to listen to this and be true to this myth. It is in myth, the outstanding form of unconcealment, that this essence of concealment as *lēthē* is preserved, and concealment in turn retains the essence of truth and keeps it ready in advance.

Let me conclude this section on the preservation of *lēthē* with a remark preparing the problematic of textuality and writing that will be discussed in the next chapter. If Plato's myth of Er is indeed the place where we can still hear the preservation of *lēthē*, what does it mean that this myth is transmitted to us *in writing*? Should we not conclude that the text's preservation, marked by the indifference between gossip and what has been drawn from a genuine appeal of being sources, affects the myth's preservation? In the next chapter, I will show how Heidegger's attention to writing in *Was heißt Denken* as well as Derrida's and Ricoeur's attention to the materiality of writing in the process of transmission arise in the wake of these questions.

A Twofold Concealment in "Der Ursprung des Kunstwerkes"

In "*Der Ursprung des Kunstwerkes*" a distinction similar to the one between *pseudos* and *lēthē* can be found.[87] In this text, Heidegger articulates these two forms of concealment as *einfaches Versagen*, and *Verstellen*, respectively. We have already come across his use of *Verstellen* in *Sein und Zeit* in relation to closedness and falling. In *Sein und Zeit*, *Verstellen* expresses how what has been discovered can disguise the possibility of a proper disclosedness (in understanding). *Verstellen* preserves the uncanniness of the displacement brought about by a mere appearance. The uncanniness of this displacement concerns the experience that Heidegger has, for instance, elaborated in his analysis of anxiety (*Angst*).[88] In anxiety, the always already meaningful beings, with which we feel at home in our world, become utterly insignificant. This no-longer-being-at-home— *Unheimlichkeit*—or uncanniness resides (potentially) in the appearance of every being: the familiarity and meaningfulness of beings may be disrupted. However, this uncanniness is not a negative phenomenon. In Heidegger's analysis of anxiety, the uncanniness means positively the disclosure of Dasein's being-in-the-world as such. In a more general sense, it is in this uncanniness through which an appeal of being may be heard. *Pseudos* as *Verstellen* is therefore never simply a false or incorrect representation of the world in an assertion, but it concerns the concealment of being and the concealment of the realm of the open in which (displacing) appearances are always already given.

In *"Der Ursprung des Kunstwerkes," Verstellen* is described similarly as a form of concealment that obstructs, displaces, and veils beings and the realm of the open. Heidegger writes, "One being places itself in front of another being, the one helps to hide [*verschleiern*] the other, the former obscures the latter, a few obstruct many, one denies all. Here concealment is not simple refusal. Rather, a being appears, but it presents itself other than it is. This concealment is dissembling [*das Verstellen*]." This kind of concealment takes place within the lighting that it displaces. The above quote also discusses another form of concealment, which Heidegger calls *einfaches Versagen*, simple refusal. This name should remind us of *lēthē*, which, as we saw in the previous section, is "the most simple of simples" to the Greeks. Unlike displacement, this simple refusal does not put us on the wrong track by way of appearances. Instead, Heidegger writes, "concealment as refusal is not simply and only the limit of knowledge in any given circumstance, but the beginning of the lighting that is lighted."[89] Concealment as simple refusal is the beginning or the provenance (*Herkunft*) of lighting (*Lichtung*). This type of concealment does not concern an appearance that may lead us astray. It is a simple concealment, a simple refusal of any appearance and openness.

Yet, this simple concealment is the provenance of disclosure, which means that disclosure does not occur because we are attracted by a purely actual and present final goal. Disclosure is not in the service of such a pure and present being. Instead, disclosure concerns the very bringing to presence of being itself. Therefore, disclosure is essentially a struggle with untruth. It proceeds from a wresting and robbing from the simple refusal of disclosure, and it sets itself apart from concealment as displacement.

Heidegger describes lighting as the open place occurring in the midst of being as a whole. This open place "grants and guarantees to us humans a passage to these beings." As such, beings can only appear to us if they stand within this lighting. Truth takes place as this lighting in a "battle" with concealment as *Verstellen* and as *einfaches Versagen,* both as displacement and as simple refusal.[90] Therefore, he can claim that the essence of truth is untruth, that is to say that truth only occurs in a struggle with appearances that displace the whole of the lighting in which we are. And truth is also a struggle with the concealment that simply refuses us any appearance at all and that stands at the origin of the open place in which beings appear in the first place.

Despite the conceptual distinction between concealment as simple refusal and concealment as displacement, Heidegger writes in "*Der Ursprung des Kunstwerkes,*" "We are never fully certain, whether it is the one or the other." Apparently it is difficult to say with what concealment we are dealing; they are always given together. Taking them together under one name "concealment," Heidegger writes, "Concealment conceals and dissembles [*verstellt*] itself."[91] The reason that these two forms of concealment are always entangled is of course due to the fact that the human being is always already in a realm of unconcealment. The human being is always already amid appearances that displace the whole in which it stands. This is the meaning of Heidegger's conception of everydayness, which he argues is involved in the first stage of Plato's allegory of the cave. Therefore, the human being never confronts *lēthē* alone; it is always already struggling against distorting appearances as well.

This entanglement is an important aspect of Heidegger's thought on concealment for this study because it prepares the way for the analysis of the relation between Heidegger and Derrida. One could articulate this relation by saying that Derrida radicalizes this entanglement. I proposed above to relate Heidegger's understanding of *pseudos* and *Verstellen* to the notion of the trace. A trace is an entity that refers to but does not present its origin. In line with Levinas, Derrida radicalizes the concept of the trace.[92] According to Derrida, a trace refers, but it refers to something which has never been present and which will never be present. By adding this aspect, Derrida's conception of the trace does not simply place the trace on the level of *pseudos* or Heidegger's notion of displacement, but rather provides an entrance to thinking the entanglement of displacement and simple refusal. The Derridean trace does not displace the realm of disclosure in which we are, but displaces something that is simply refused to us. The phenomenon of translation provides an example of this somewhat abstract description of the Derridean trace (this example will be elaborated more conceptually in chapter 4). A translation of a foreign text is a trace of this text: since no translation can fully capture the origin in all its dimensions, it lets the foreign text appear in our own language by displacing (and perhaps even distorting) it. Yet, this trace does not refer to a realm of disclosure in which we are: it does not refer to our own language, but rather refers to a realm of disclosure to which we do not belong, namely the foreign language or the idiom of the foreign writer to which the original text belongs. This linguistic example shows that the notion of the trace and of displacement might very well transcend the Heideggerian realm of *pseudos*. In fact, this example shows that the entanglement of displacement and simple refusal should not be thought in relation to disclosure as such, but in relation to the *repetition* of disclosure and to the *transference* of one realm of disclosure to another, and perhaps even to transference as a conditions of possibility of disclosure(s) as such. These questions will be taken up in the next three chapters which will provide examples of linguistic phenomena that all include transference: writing, metaphor, mimesis, and translation.

LANGUAGE AND TRUTH

In the analysis of *Sein und Zeit,* we have seen how Heidegger argues
that language is apophantic. This means that language does not give
a representation of the world, but points beings out and shows beings
out of themselves. This apophantic dimension of language is grounded
in the fundamental phenomenon of truth, namely the disclosedness
of Dasein. In his later work, the showing character of language is no
longer understood as a derivative of Dasein's disclosedness.[93] Instead,
language and especially poetic language are the original realm of disclosure themselves: *Sage* and *muthos* guide him in his effort to think
the essence of language.

Experiencing Language

Let us first discuss what is involved in Heidegger's interest in language in his later work. In the introduction to "*Das Wesen der
Sprache,*" Heidegger writes that he intends to bring his audience face
to face with the possibility of experiencing language in such a way
that our relation (*Verhältnis*) with language is brought to language.[94]
He wants to do so while describing both the how and the essence of
language.

Heidegger sharply distinguishes his efforts to experience language from the so-called sciences of language. According to him,
the knowledge of language in linguistics, philology, and philosophy
of language ultimately produces a metalanguage (*Metasprache*). This
metalanguage belongs to metaphysics.[95] Although he does not say
much about this metalanguage, it is not difficult to understand why
he relates the production of metalanguages to metaphysics. Like
metaphysics, this metalanguage forgets that a mother tongue is in
the first place a realm of unconcealment that allows us to experience
the world: it is in the expressions of language that the world comes
to be. The effort to produce a metalanguage is an effort to produce
an unambiguous, computable language. The representation of the
world in such a computable language allows us to approach the world
as something computable and manipulable.[96] The effort to produce a

computable language forgets to ask what this endeavor says about the essence of being and of language. Paraphrasing Heidegger's examinations in "*Der Satz vom Grund*," we could say that this effort obeys (*ist gehörig*) a particular understanding of being, but does not listen to (*hören*) the appeal of being that precedes it. In this sense, the production of a metalanguage forgets to raise the question of being *and* forgets to inquire into the essence of language as the realm of unconcealment. In their efforts to *produce* language, the linguistic sciences forget to *experience* language as the realm to which they belong and that precedes their efforts. The project of a metalanguage refuses itself from the outset the possibility to find truth as disclosure in the heart of language.

Heidegger's rejection of a metalanguage is to be contrasted with his affirmation of our primordial belonging to language as the realm of the open. Before being able to produce a language, we belong to language, and to inquire into this belonging, we need to comply with (*sich fügen*) this language in order to experience how language discloses the world.[97] To have an experience of language is to become *experienced in* language; it is to listen to language and to find the appropriate words to articulate what language is. This essence of language is not a present essence to which our understanding would be attracted. Its presence depends on language itself and its articulations; this essence may be wrested from concealment only by means of articulation. In this sense, truth as disclosure and language are coexistent in humans. To become acquainted with the concealed depth and the power of expression of language is the goal of an experience with language. This is the reason why Heidegger does not turn toward a technical metalanguage. However, he does not turn toward our everyday use of language either. Although many things are brought to language in everyday speaking, language *itself* and the way language opens up the world is not brought to language in everyday speaking. To undergo an experience with language (*eine Erfahrung mit der Sprache machen*) means to bring language itself to language. According to Heidegger, one may find this kind of experience with language in the work and the words of the poets. Poets are acquainted with the depth and the power of expression of language. Poets aim at bringing language itself to language and thus undergo an experience with language. In this way, they articulate the opening quality of language in their poetic language. Therefore, Heidegger's effort to undergo a *thinking* experience with language is guided by poetry and the *poeticizing* experience with language. This surmised kinship between poetry and thought, which needs to be experienced itself, guides Heidegger's reflection on the essence of language and of thought in *Unterwegs zur Sprache.*[98]

The depths of language conceal the essence of language. As Heidegger points out, in our everyday use of language, much is brought to language, but language itself is seldom brought to language. In fact, to be on the way to this essence is to be on the way to something that has never yet been said before, that is, brought out in language. We cannot be certain whether language *gives* or *refuses* the appropriate word to say this essence. As Heidegger writes, "But when the issue is to put into language something which has never yet been spoken, then everything depends on whether language gives or withholds [*versagen*] the appropriate word."[99]

The gift of this appropriate word, which is nothing but the appropriation of the essence of language, is called *Ereignis*. This difficult word in Heidegger's thought is related to *eigen,* which means "proper," and to *eignen,* which we could translate as "to propriate" in order to show the relation to words such as "appropriation" (*zueignung*) or expressions such as "the appropriate word" (*Das geeignete Wort*).[100] In German, the word *Ereignis* means also "event." The combination of these meanings gives us a hint of what Heidegger means by *Ereignis:* it is the "event of appropriation," as it has been translated. In the context of our discussion of language, *Ereignis* concerns a gift of language in which the essence of language is disclosed to us. Heidegger writes that *Ereignis* can be experienced as that which gives or grants.[101] What it gives and what it grants is that which is most proper to us, namely the realm of the open to which we belong. Considering the central role of the notions of proper (*eigentlich*), appropriation (*Aneignung*), and the event of appropriation (*Ereignis*), we see how important the chain of words related to the German *eigen* and *eignen* is to Heidegger's thought. Yet, unlike a more common sense meaning of a word such as "appropriation," this chain of words never concerns that which we grasp, master, or control. Rather, it is related to the essence of language, which is beyond our control. Thus, although Heidegger speaks about appropriation here, *Ereignis* does not indicate the event of capturing or of mastery. The essence of language cannot be encompassed by us because we belong to language.[102]

This latter aspect is true in general for Heidegger's use of the word *Ereignis*. Every appropriation also implies expropriation (*Enteignis*) because the event of giving itself withdraws behind the gift it presents. This gift, reaching, or advent withdraws itself in the gift of presencing (*Anwesen*). This expropriation is, as before, the provenance and the beginning of lighting. Therefore, Heidegger relates this expropriation to the withdrawal of *lēthē*.[103] This intricate relationship between appropriation and concealment is essential to his thought: he never understands what is most proper to us as that which can be thought as pure presence. Quite the contrary, he tries to reassess the notion of the proper outside of the realm of a metaphysics of presence. This means that Heidegger thinks the important hermeneutic concept of appropriation in a particular way. He does not think it as taking possession of and taking control over something by representing it to consciousness, but appropriation as well as interpretation are thought by him as responses to an appeal that precedes these responses. This appeal can never be recovered by the response. It can be understood as a complying with the realm to which we always already belong. If one understands "proper" and "one's own" in this sense, it becomes clear why Heidegger can argue that responding to the appeal of being brings human beings into that which is most proper to them. This is justly called "appropriation" or "propriation," but in this explanation of appropriation the appeal and the event that gives precede, elicit, and escape the appropriation. Therefore, concealment plays an essential part in Heidegger's thought of the *Ereignis,* the event of appropriation. Concealment is not only that which leads us astray

(*Verstellen*), but concealment (*lēthē, einfaches Versagen*) is also the unheard-of realm of potentiality and wealth that any disclosing articulation draws from. This also applies to language. If language could ever be exhausted by us, then disclosive language as the essence of human beings disappears. In fact, if language could be exhausted, it would be nothing more than a perfectible and computable instrument of human beings.

Language as Showing

Heidegger's writings on language are guided by the experience poets have had with language.[104] In one notable section of *Unterwegs zur Sprache,* Heidegger turns to the poem *Das Wort* by Stefan George, and it is the last phrase of this poem that draws his special attention: "*Kein Ding sei wo das Wort gebricht.*" Its translation reads as follows: "Where words break off no thing may be." According to Heidegger, this means that the appearance of beings requires words. Beings are brought into the open thanks to their articulation in language: "The word alone gives being to the thing."[105]

To some extent, this creative dimension of language is an experience of everyday life. Beings, events, people, natural or political phenomena—they all appear in a different light as soon as we articulate them differently. People who possess the capacity to bring beings to light and to let them shine in all their splendor or desecration are called eloquent. Heidegger, we could say, is not interested in eloquence as a capacity of human beings, but as the essence of language. The eloquence of language shows beings and lets them shine forth.[106] Ricoeur proposes to call this aspect of language "*invention.*"[107] This word, in the French, is paradoxical because it refers to both creation and discovery. Ricoeur finds the creative and discovering aspects of language most clearly in poetic language. Poetry is creative; it opens the world and brings beings to presence, but by this creative opening it finds and discovers beings as they are.

This also means that the eloquence of (poetic) language should not be confused with something merely ornamental. Eloquence does not embellish a being. In common sense, eloquence is at best helpful but never sufficient to discuss the essence of a being. To discuss an essence, philosophy needs to get away from any embellishment. If we call Heidegger's attention to the showing of language "eloquence," then this eloquence is not external to the way a being is. The eloquence that makes a being shine allows this very being its presence and being. This is what Heidegger claims in his explanation of the phrase from *das Wort*.

The poem *Das Wort* shows us something about the relation between words and things.[108] This relation (*Verhältnis*) is not a connection (*Beziehung*) between two separate beings, between a word on one side and a thing on the other. As we have already seen, such a connection is an indication of the displacement and the disguise of the co-belonging of word and thing. In *Sein und Zeit*, Heidegger grounds this co-belonging in the disclosedness of Dasein's understanding. In *Unterwegs zur Sprache*, however, this relation is found in language itself. Heidegger writes, "What is it that the poet reaches? Not mere knowledge. He obtains entrance into the relation of word and thing. The relation is not, however, a connection between the thing that is on one side and the word that is on the other. The word itself is the relation which in each instance retains the thing within itself in such a manner that it 'is' a thing."[109] In poetry, truth and reality occurs, and being is brought into the open. The poetic phrase *Kein Ding sei wo das Wort gebricht* also implies that language is a quest for an appropriate word, as Heidegger writes, "Everything depends on whether language gives or withholds [*versagen*] the appropriate word."[110] This means that common, everyday language does not have the power to let a being shine in its presence. The novel, inventive speech of poetry is required to let truth occur and to bring it out of concealment into unconcealment.[111] *Ereignis* as the event in which the appropriate word is said is the event of truth and the occurrence of reality; the appropriate, novel word is said so that there may be a being, and so that this being is unconcealed and appears to us in its presence.

This event of disclosure is the essence of language, according to Heidegger. He calls this essence of language "saying" (*Sage*). As in

Sein und Zeit, where he discusses the apophantic character of language, he emphasizes that language as saying is showing. *Sagen* comes from the old German word *sagan,* which means to show and to let appear.[112] As such, saying is in the first place a showing. From the above quote it follows that the showing of language is not external to the essence of a being; instead, the showing of language retains (*einbehalten*) how a being is. Poetic language as creative is therefore immediately related to disclosure and to discovery. Its creativity concerns bringing to light what has not yet been said, and it concerns saying the appropriate word where words are still lacking. What lacks an articulation does not only lack an announcement (*Verlautbarung*) but has not yet been shown and has not yet arrived in appearance.[113]

From a metaphysical point of view, this is incomprehensible. Of course, no one denies that a good articulation helps us to understand a being better. Yet, for traditional metaphysics, this articulation can only be helpful. Language is but a tool. It may help one to get to learn the essence of a being. However, from a metaphysical point of view, an articulation has nothing to do with the essence of a being as such because the essence of a being is already given and actual. Heidegger contests exactly this aspect of metaphysics. The task of language is not to represent a being, but to present a being, to let a being be present. Articulation as bringing to presence releases the presence of a being in the first place. Of course, this does not mean that every time we talk and utter something, truth occurs. In my reading of *Sein und Zeit,* I discussed the intrinsic possibility of disguise found in parroting and repetition. In *Unterwegs zur Sprache,* Heidegger follows up on these remarks. He points out that saying (as showing) is not the same as speaking. One can speak endlessly without saying anything, that is, without showing anything.[114] In his analysis of language, Heidegger does not promote a new kind of sophistry in which every uttered opinion would contribute to understanding the being of beings. Instead, he pays tribute to language as the realm that gives a being the freedom to be and releases a being to appear.

It is only in the wake of this conception of language and its relation to being and truth that we can understand why themes such as poetry, language, literature, rhetoric, metaphor, and so on, have become so important for philosophers inspired by Heidegger. Without the intrinsic relation of language as saying to disclosure and being, these themes would not have the same urgency for a philosopher.

Language as Gathering

In "*Logos (Heraklit, Fragment 50)*," Heidegger furthers his examination of the relation between truth, being, and language through a reading of Heraclitus' fragment B 50. He argues that the Greeks experienced *Logos* as the name of the being of beings. Although *Logos* is explained in the history of philosophy as *ratio, verbum,* or logic, Heidegger argues that *Logos* meant for the Greeks in the first place both speech (*Sprache*) and bringing to language (*zur Sprache bringen*). Heidegger writes, "'To bring to language' means to secure [*bergen*] Being in the essence of language." Being is preserved in language because language lets beings appear from themselves. As in *Sein und Zeit*, Heidegger invokes once more Aristotle's interpretation of *legein* as *apophainesthai* to prove this point in "*Logos.*"[115]

One of the features of this essay is that Heidegger interprets *Logos* as *legende Lese,* that is, as a gathering that lets present beings lie together. He has three aspects in mind when he explicates *legein* as such a gathering: language brings beings to presence; it brings present beings together in their presence; and it preserves them in their presence. These three aspects—disclosing, collecting, and preserving—demonstrate that language lets beings be at our disposal (*vorliegen lassen*) because language discloses and preserves the being-present of beings, but language does so always by bringing them together (*Beisammen-vorliegen-lassen*).

To understand why gathering is always involved in the appearance of beings, we could think of the unity of a story or a lecture. A story provides a narration of a series of events, and a story tells us how certain people act in certain ways for certain motives in certain circumstances. This suggests at first glance that a story is discordant: it is composed of a series of distinct events, and it is composed of a multiplicity of ingredients such as agents, motives, goals, circumstances, actions, and so on. However, if we listen to a story and try to understand it, we do not let ourselves be thrown off by this apparent discordance, but instead we are focused on the whole of story—its plot or intrigue. The intrigue renders the story intelligible. Each element of the story has its place in the story and is only meaningful to a listener as element of the whole of this story.

In a similar way, beings belong together in being. Being is like an intrigue, the whole that withdraws itself behind each of the beings, but that lets every being be present. In "*Logos*," Heidegger translates *ho Logos* as *legende Lese,* which means that *Logos* lets all beings appear together in their presence (*Anwesen*). The whole of *Logos* itself is not present. It withdraws itself. Nevertheless, it attracts us as that which withdraws itself. The reader of a story tries to attune him or herself to the plot of the story. Likewise, a human being tries to listen (*hören*) to *Logos*. Heidegger explains this listening as the speech of a mortal human: *homologein.* This speech does not speak out of itself, but is grounded in listening to and complying with *ho Logos.* At this point, there is obviously an important difference with the example of a story and its intrigue. A reader can anticipate a plot because an author has configured it. In the case of *legein*, however, a human being may listen (*hören*) properly to *Logos* because he or she has already heard *Logos.* Humanity has already heard *Logos* because it belongs (*gehören*) to *Logos.*[116] This belonging to *Logos* precedes a human being's own listening and speaking. A human being always already belongs to the unconcealed-concealed whole of *Logos,* and therefore he or she can comply with this whole.

Heidegger takes great care to distinguish *Logos* as the whole from a metaphysical point of view that identifies the whole under the aspect of a highest, most actual, and present being. He takes on this point in his reflection on Heraclitus's discussion of *hen panta.* Heidegger points out that *hen,* the whole of what is present,[117] does not coincide with Zeus, the highest and most present being among beings. Heidegger argues that only if *hen* is not understood as *Logos* but as *panta,* then the whole of present beings shows itself under the rule of a highest being, Zeus.[118] Heidegger thus does not interpret *Logos* as a specific being. Instead he interprets it as being itself. To consider the whole of beings under the aspect of one particular being is the same as considering the intrigue of a story under the aspect of one event. But this misses how the whole withdraws itself and grants each of its parts its particular place thanks to this withdrawing.[119]

Aristotle has argued that a good plot contains a turning point. How can a plot have a turning point, which requires at least two parts, if the plot would be conceived only under the aspect of one of its parts? A plot with a turning point shows the tension between the parts in the whole. Similarly, Heidegger understands the gathering of saying in a Heraclitean way as the gathering of day and night, winter and summer, peace and war, the present and the absent — in sum as the gathering of opposites.[120] The whole is not ruled over by a supreme presence or a supreme light such as the sun, and the night is not the privation of light. Rather, the whole lets night and day be together and lets them show their own particular appearance as well as their mutual difference. After all, the night has its own mode of unconcealment in which the sky is disclosed to us in a way the day never can.

I want to conclude this section by pointing to a particular difficulty in Heidegger's understanding of the relation between *Logos* and *legein*. On the one hand, as the authentic listening of mortals, *legein* is the same (*das Selbe*) as *Logos*. *Logos* only occurs (*ereignet*) as *legein*. Thus, the *Ereignis* of *Logos* takes place as the authentic listening of mortals.[121] On the other hand, *legein* as *homologein* is not at all the same as *Logos*. Despite this difference between *Logos* and *homologein,* Heidegger rejects the idea that *Logos* is the exaggeration of *homologein* or that *homologein* is the imitation of *Logos*. It is clear why he rejects this solution: it would lead to a Platonic dichotomy between a godly word and an imitative human word. Instead, he suggests that the *legein* of *Logos* and the *legein* of *homologein* find their provenance in the simple middle between them.[122] He does not discuss this middle in this essay. Nevertheless, the remarks leading up to this simple middle are interesting. They show that Heidegger presents us with the alternative of *either* a dichotomy due to which mortal language

becomes an imitation of a godly language, *or* a primordial co-belonging, which implies a more encompassing *legein*. What is missing in this
either/or approach is a third possibility, namely a mimesis between
different mortal languages. In this essay, Heidegger approaches the
problem of the multiplicity of language, by addressing two forms of
legein—*Logos* and *homologein*—but these two forms are not equal;
they stand in a particular hierarchical relation to each other. As a
consequence, he can only opt for the second option because the first
option leads to a Platonic solution, that is, to a conception of *homologein* that lacks *Logos*. The particular hierarchical relation between
the two forms of *legein* from which Heidegger's analysis proceeds
obstructs a third possibility: to think a more primordial multiplicity
between languages without describing either of the languages as a
decay of the other.

One could argue that Heidegger is led to this hierarchy by
Heraclitus. This may be true, but his reading here is not an isolated
case. In Heidegger's reflections on the problem of translation we have
seen that he tends to describe translation either as a form of decay or
as a form of interpretation that takes place in one language. The multiplicity of languages leads to particular linguistic phenomena, such as
transference, mimesis, translation, displacement, metaphor, and so on.
From the example of translation and from this reading of Heraclitus,
we know what either/or approach to expect in Heidegger's discussion of these phenomena: either decaying displacement or an original (co-)belonging without displacement at all. This shows that he
ultimately does not abandon some of the basic elements of his view
of language demonstrated in *Sein und Zeit*. In his view, language is
either a decaying of the original, or an original co-belonging without
the problems of displacement found in language.

Despite Heidegger's care to keep a metaphysical account of totality away from his understanding of the whole and of the gathering of
the *Logos*, Derrida is troubled by a number of aspects of Heidegger's
account of language. In fact, Heidegger's attention to propriation
and appropriation, his account of language as *Sage* and showing, and
his account of *legein* as gathering are all three highly problematic

in Derrida's perspective. Derrida insists on the trace that does not belong and on the multiplicity of languages that upsets any gathering and co-belonging. The question of the essence of language becomes highly problematic if multiple languages exist. Moreover, what does gathering mean if not unifying different and irreducible languages? These problems are at the heart of Derrida's reading of Heidegger. He will not repeat Heidegger's point of view, in which language is approached from the perspective of disclosure. He rather focuses first and foremost on the problem of displacement: when multiple languages exist, what does the displacement and transference from one language to the other has to tell us about language? Does this not always upset both the primacy of showing and of gathering?

The elements of Heidegger's thought which we discussed in this chapter, provide us with a background for both Heidegger's understanding of writing, metaphor, and mimesis in the next chapters as well as a background for Ricoeur's and Derrida's reading of Heidegger. The relation between disclosure, displacement, and language will be the guideline for the next chapters. In them, we discuss the productive value of displacement and distanciation, which seems to go unnoticed in Heidegger's work, but is crucial to Derrida's and Ricoeur's thought on the creative dimension of (poetic) language. In this way, they also further Heidegger's conception of poetic language as the realm of disclosure *par excellence,* as we shall see in their account of metaphor, poetry, mimesis, and literature.

TWO

The Transference of Writing

In the beginning, that is the fiction, there was writing. That is to say, a fable, some writing.

—Jacques Derrida, *Psyche*

Socrates: It is a discourse that is written down, with knowledge, in the soul of the listener; it can defend itself, and it knows for whom it should speak and for whom it should remain silent.
Phaedrus: You mean the living, breathing discourse of the man who knows, of which the written one can be fairly called an image?

—Plato, *Phaedrus*

In the previous chapter I discussed how Heidegger's thought emphasizes the primacy of disclosure in relation to displacement. The latter is first and foremost understood as concealment as *pseudos*. This primacy of disclosure was traced clearly in his account of the essence of language as saying. However, there is more to language than the mere event of disclosure in saying. There is also writing. Especially for the hermeneutic strands of thought developed in the wake of Heidegger's work, such as Gadamer's or Ricoeur's, writing gives language the quality of a "persistent existence," as Husserl calls it. Thanks to this dimension of writing, texts can be handed down to us and a text can be read in other contexts than the one in which it was written. Thus, a tradition becomes possible as the *re*reading and *re*interpretation of the text. Writing, in sum, is a condition of possibility of the transferability and repeatability of language and is as such the condition of possibility for hermeneutic consciousness.

Needless to say, the transference of writing is a form of displacement. Therefore, in view of our discussion in the previous chapter, it need not surprise us that Heidegger often relates writing to the problem of *pseudos,* that is, to the problem of a distorting displacement that corrupts and obstructs the ownmost possibility of language and thinking: disclosure. In the previous chapter, we have already seen the first contours of this tendency in Heidegger's thought. For him, the repetition and permanence of language is not only secondary to disclosure, but also conceals this essence of language. Therefore, it comes as no surprise that he dismisses writing in *Was heißt Denken?* as a flight from thinking.[1] Apparently, the turn to thinking can only be a turn to language as saying, that is, disclosure.[2] This chapter deals mainly with other accounts of the transference of writing. In particular, it is discussed how Ricoeur and Derrida (and to a lesser degree also Gadamer) provide a more favorable account of the displacing quality of writing and how they relate it to disclosure. Thus, it will be shown how the framework of disclosure and displacement offers us a clear perspective on the relation between Heidegger, Ricoeur, and Derrida on truth, untruth, and language.

ON THE WAY TO WRITING

Writing is dangerous, treacherous, and seductive. Although any kind of language poses a threat to philosophy, writing is much more threatening than speech. At least, this is Plato's opinion as we can find it in the *Second Letter,* the *Seventh Letter,* and the *Phaedrus.* Plato's "attack against writing is not an isolated example in the history of our culture," as Ricoeur writes, and as Derrida demonstrates in, for instance, *La dissémination* and *De la grammatologie.*[3] The same hierarchy between speech and writing can still be traced in Heidegger's thought. Therefore, as a point of departure, let me briefly describe Plato's objections against writing.

Plato considers the danger of misunderstanding in writing so devastating that he argues that one should avoid writing down any serious philosophical thought. Living speech is but a tool to turn the soul of a philosopher toward the truth. As Plato argues in book 7 of the *Republic,* "Education is not what some people declare it to be, namely, putting knowledge into souls that lack it."[4] Instead, education, which involves the living conversation between teacher and pupil, aims at turning the "whole soul" of the pupil "until it is able to study that which is and the brightest thing that is, namely, the one we call the good."[5] This means that living speech does not contain truth itself. It is one step away from truth, so to speak. As Plato writes on the knowledge his own teachings contain: "For this knowledge is not something that can be put into words like other sciences; but after long-continued intercourse between teacher and pupil, in joint pursuit of the subject, suddenly, like light flashing forth when a fire is kindled, it is born in the soul and straight way nourishes itself."[6] Only in a dialogue in which the teacher is present and in which teacher and pupil both strive for truth in good will and without envy, "only then, when reason and knowledge are at the very extremity of human effort, can they illuminate the nature of any object."[7] Writing, in turn, is two steps away from truth since it is merely an image of this living speech. As an image it lacks the possibility to enter into a dialogue with someone. Consequently, writing lacks the very movement of dialectic, which in living speech is the movement toward truth. Especially in relation to Plato's own teachings this is highly problematic. Since writing speaks to everyone without distinction, even to those who are not qualified to understand the philosophical teachings of Plato, it is imperative that these teachings are not written down. In the *Second Letter,* Plato notes that to the masses probably no teachings are so laughable as his philosophical doctrines. Even some of his students, who unlike the masses are capable of understanding their truth, did not see the evident truth of his teachings immediately, but only learned to see it after 30 years of careful examination.[8] These difficulties of the spoken communication of philosophical truth are aggravated in writing: the danger of writing is that once truth has been written down, it may fall into the hands of someone who is not qualified for it and who will thus mock the truths it contains.[9]

Therefore, Plato has not written down his teachings, as he notes in the *Second Letter*. In writing, we would expose this priceless wisdom to the envy and the criticism of those unqualified. The Platonic "rage" against writing culminates in the following phrases from the *Seventh Letter:* "Whenever we see a book…we can be sure that if the author is really serious, this book does not contain his best thoughts; they are stored away with the fairest of his possessions. And if he has committed these serious thoughts to writing, it is because men, not the gods, 'have taken his wits away.'"[10] To give a brief overview of the concerns I mentioned above, let me discuss three problems of writing that Plato raises in the *Phaedrus.*

The first problem is that writing conceals. In the last part of the *Phaedrus,* Socrates tells the Egyptian myth of the origin of writing.[11] In this myth, writing is introduced by Theuth, its inventor, as a helpful means and a remedy (*pharmakon*). It would make the Egyptians wiser by improving their memories. However, king Thamus, to whom Theuth offers the gift of writing, objects that instead of improving their memories, writing will make the Egyptians forgetful. King Thamus's objection might remind us of Heidegger's remarks on the repeatability of "what has been expressed" (*das Ausgesprochene*). What has been written down can be repeated, but this repetition can easily obstruct genuine appropriation and understanding. If many things are written down, King Thamus says, then people become the hearers of many things, but they will know nothing. He continues, "You provide your students with the *appearance* of wisdom, not with its reality."[12] Writing appears and shows itself as wisdom and as understanding, but it turns out that this appearance is mere appearance and a concealment of true understanding.

With Heidegger's analysis of *pseudos* in the back of our minds, it is difficult not to see how this Egyptian myth implies a relation between writing and *pseudos.* Writing refers back to a genuine understanding and a genuine memory; in this sense it is a trace. At the same time, however, it lacks this understanding and memory. But this is not all. If writing were to present itself as such a lack, Plato would probably have been much more gentle on writing. However, writing presents itself *as* understanding and *as* memory. Hence, writing shows itself *as something it is not*. Thus, the untruth of writing is for Plato the untruth of the uncanny concealment of *pseudos*, which Heidegger rediscovered in his interpretation of this Greek notion.

Another problem of writing concerns the absence of truth. For Plato, the main difference between speech and writing is the difference between the presence and the absence of truth, that is, writing is marked by the absence of the speaking subject whose soul is turned toward the truth. Although, strictly speaking, not every speech implies the presence of truth, speech does allow for such a presence. In writing, however, the one who speaks is absent.[13] This has important implications. In a conversation, we can ask the one who speaks to clarify him or herself. If the speaker's soul is indeed turned toward the truth, he or she can give another articulation that helps us to understand his or her words. Writing, however, is not accompanied by any understanding. As soon as "anyone asks them anything, they remain most solemnly silent," Plato argues.[14] Written words only repeat themselves identically, without any clarification. Due to the absence of the original thinking from which the words stem, *they cannot explicate themselves*, because explication is saying the same thing in different words for clarification. Due to this utter lack of self-explication, writing is a bastard form of language. Since it lacks the movement of dialogue and dialectic, it lacks the movement toward truth contained in living speech.

In the myth, King Thamus clarifies this by saying that writing is composed of "signs that belong to others."[15] This can be interpreted in line with Heidegger's comments on assertions that are ready-to-hand. In writing, we take up words that are not our own and that do not stem from our own understanding. They are external to our understanding. Of course, one could wonder whether this is not a problem for speaking as well. In fact, it is. That is to say, it is a problem for certain forms of speech. As we have seen in the previous chapter, Heidegger notes that if we speak in truisms and clichés, we speak while saying nothing. Of course, Plato would agree with this. However, in the Platonic dialogues, the speaker can be questioned to go beyond such accepted clichés. This dialectic movement often ends in *aporia,* but this means that speaking provides the opportunity for this dialectic. Writing does not. Consequently, writing, which also borrows words from elsewhere, cannot be questioned when it lapses into *doxa* or opinion.

The final problem is the weakness and danger of writing. As a consequence of the absence of the speaker, writing is weak and feeble. Plato compares writing to an orphan who lacks the protection of its father. Due to the absence of understanding, written words do not know to whom to turn and to whom not to turn. *They address everyone without distinction,* even though the words are not meant for everyone because not everyone is capable of understanding their meaning. This makes writing liable to misunderstanding and abuse.

This particular feebleness of writing is also its danger. Writing can roam about everywhere. Because it addresses everyone without distinction and because it does not provide its own interpretation, its meaning can be disseminated. This seems to contradict what we discussed as the second problem, namely that writing remains solemnly silent. Inspired by Derrida's reading of the *Phaedrus,* we could say that writing remains silent *about its original meaning.* At the same time, it speaks rapidly and gives every interpreter something to understand. This multiplicity of interpretations is writing's feebleness: it is not capable of defending and presenting its original meaning. At the same time, this multiplicity is its danger because it confronts us once more with the typical concealment of writing. It conceals its original meaning by letting another appear. Therefore, Plato not only compares writing to a deplorable orphan, but also to an illegitimate son, to a bastard of truth: it appears to present the thing itself, but in truth presents a mere appearance.[16]

Along these three lines, we see how Plato depicts writing as a secondary form of language. On the one hand, this means that writing does not live up to the potential of language, namely to be a dialectic tool that helps the soul to turn to the good. Writing is a secondary form of language that has lost the guidance of reality and truth. On the other hand, this loss takes the form of a concealment. Writing does not show itself as the loss it is. Writing appears as a depiction of the truth. Thus writing brings into play the uncanniness of concealment. This problem can also be found in Husserl's description of the seduction of language in "*Der Ursprung der Geometrie.*" Language seduces us to follow the associations it evokes, thereby leading us away from the truth that has been expressed in it and that can and should be reactivated by the philosopher.[17]

Against the background of this understanding of writing, it should come as no surprise that many thinkers in hermeneutics have felt compelled to respond to Plato's denigration of writing. Since hermeneutics proceeds from the primacy of the text that has been handed down to us, it needs to explain how it deals with the loss of understanding as well as with the uncanny concealment of writing. How can the transference of writing be understood differently? More precisely, hermeneutics needs to show how the *loss of an original* understanding can be conceived as the *condition of possibility of a repetition* of understanding. To see how it deals with this, let me first turn to Gadamer.

Gadamer on Language

According to Gadamer, "In writing, language gains its true ideality [*Geistigkeit*], for in encountering a written tradition understanding consciousness acquires its full sovereignty."[18] Can one think of a greater contrast to Plato's objections than the one expressed in this quote? The quote does not say anything about a loss of understanding that would be caused by writing. In fact, it claims the exact opposite. It claims that hermeneutic understanding "acquires its full sovereignty" and its true spirituality (*Geistigkeit*) in writing.[19] Yet, this should not be taken to mean that writing no longer conceals for Gadamer. A few lines before this quote, it reads, "Thus written texts presents the real hermeneutical task. Writing is self-alienation. Overcoming it, reading the text, is thus the highest task of understanding."[20] This latter quote is rather striking given the first. On the one hand, it is only in writing that language reaches a pure intelligibility to which hermeneutic understanding responds. On the other hand, writing is an alienated speech that needs to be changed *back* into speech. In the first quote, writing is said to have the ability to reach the fullness of intelligibility; in the second quote, writing is said to be a loss of speech that needs to be overcome to become intelligible. Where does this leave us?

Before answering this question, let me first note that the second quote does not refer writing back to an understanding in which it is grounded, but rather to an original speech. To some extent, this does not come as a surprise. Writing grounded in speech repeats the Aristotelian idea that writing is a representation of speech. Yet, this idea is usually accompanied by the idea that speech itself is also a representation, namely of affections in the soul in Aristotle's case, which would make writing a representation of a representation.[21] In Gadamer's conception of the relation between understanding and language, this is not the case. Thus, he provides us with an important alternative account of the relation between language and truth to Plato's and Aristotle's conception of this relation. What does this imply for the relation between speech, writing, and (hermeneutic) understanding?

Language as the Medium of Understanding

According to Plato, the intimate relation between truth and language is grounded in a specific hierarchy between the two. Simply put, either language is derived from an understanding of that which is most real (depicted in the *Phaedrus* as speech accompanied by such an understanding), or language does not comply with this understanding (depicted in the *Phaedrus* as writing roaming about everywhere and addressing everybody). Language is at its best a vehicle that enables the communication of wisdom. Gadamer proposes a different conception of the relation between understanding and language. Language is not merely a vehicle of communication, but language is the *medium* of understanding.[22] Understanding cannot be separated from language because understanding takes place in language as articulation and interpretation. At the beginning of the third part of *Wahrheit und Methode,* Gadamer makes the following important remark concerning the relation between language and (hermeneutic) understanding: "*Rather, language is the universal medium in which understanding occurs. Understanding occurs in interpreting*....All understanding is interpretation, and all interpretation takes place in the medium of a language that allows the object to come into words and yet is at the same time the interpreter's own language."[23] Understanding does not precede language, Gadamer argues, but occurs in and through the articulation of language. This idea is central to hermeneutics in the most broad sense of the word. In his critique of Husserl in *La voix et le phénomène*, Derrida makes a similar claim. Derrida argues that as long as we try to separate understanding from language, then every articulation is, strictly speaking, external to understanding. Yet, every understanding, even our self-understanding, takes a detour through articulation and language. We understand ourselves in the light of the articulation that a language can provide. Therefore, as long as we insist on a pure understanding *without* words, which depicts language as a mere tool, then we will miss the point that this pure understanding is contaminated again and again because we articulate and come to understanding by means of this articulation and because there is no understanding preceding this articulation.[24] Therefore, a pure intuition, the aim of Husserlian phenomenology, is impossible; all intuitions are mediated through discourse.

Although Derrida's "detour" is not the same as Gadamer's "medium" and "occurring," one similarity is clear: understanding takes place within the realm opened up by language. According to Gadamer, our understanding (of a text) always operates within "the whole of possible meanings in which we linguistically [*sprechend und aussprachebereit*] move."[25] It is language *as speech* to which we belong as speaking beings. For Gadamer, language as speech is a realm of possible articulations. Our understanding moves within this realm: what cannot be articulated in language cannot be understood. Gadamer's conception of language as the medium of understanding repeats Heidegger's elaboration of language in a threefold way.

In the first place, the preceding analysis shows how Gadamer comprehends *language as showing*. Articulation brings the subject matter

(*Sache*) of a dialogue or a text to speech. This implies that a subject matter appears only in and by articulation. Hence, it is articulation that allows the subject matter to be presented for hermeneutic consciousness. In the second place, Gadamer's analysis of dialogue (*Gespräch*) could be read as repeating Heidegger's conception of *language as gathering*. The idea of gathering can be traced in Gadamer's conception of the fusion of horizons (*Horizontverschmelzung*) that occurs in dialogues. "Dialogue," Gadamer writes, "is a process of coming to an understanding."[26] This, of course, is not a description of every actual dialogue, but a definition of what Gadamer proposes to call a dialogue. In a dialogue (in Gadamer's use of the word), the participants try to come to a better understanding of the subject matter that concerns them both. Both participants bring their own horizon into play in this conversation. This means that they both articulate their own opinions on the subject matter. However, in a true dialogue (as opposed to a debate), they do not intend to maintain these opinions or enforce them upon the other participant, but rather they risk these opinions in order to come to a better understanding of the subject matter.[27] Each person in the dialogue listens to the opinions of the other not with regard to the other as an individual, but with regard to the "substantive rightness" (*sachliche Recht*) of these opinions.[28]

The ultimate goal of a dialogue is a fusion of horizons. Gadamer takes great care to distinguish this fusion of horizons from the reflective dialectics of Hegel. The fusion of horizons is not the synthesis found in Hegel's dialectics, that is, it does not propose a new totality encompassing two different horizons and is not guided by the teleological ideal of complete self-presence. Gadamer's fusion does not withdraw us from our belonging to a horizon or from our belonging to language. In fact, fusion is the work of language. Gadamer emphasizes, "*the fusion of horizons that takes place in understanding is actually the achievement of language.*"[29] To understand what he means by this, it is essential to keep the model of a dialogue in mind. In a dialogue, both participants speak, and they speak in their own language.[30] Their voices are different and remain different; they do not merge. Yet, at the same time, their voices articulate the same subject matter. This subject matter unifies the partners in a dialogue, and this unity is in accord with the unity of the instance of speech to which they both belong: the dialogue. Not consciousness but speech as dialogue *gathers* the articulations of the participants into a whole. The idea that the participants belong to the dialogue should be taken as radically as possible. Their articulations are not simply *their* articulations; in a dialogue they are articulations *of the dialogue*. The subject matter is not brought to speech in a dispersed multiplicity of articulations that are subsequently connected in a dialogue. Rather, the dialogue is the whole of an occurrence of speech in which the multiplicity of articulations take place. In this way, the gathering of the dialogue corresponds to the unity of the subject matter that can be brought to language in multiple ways and in multiple contexts.

Finally, we can point to a third resemblance with Heidegger's work. According to Heidegger, the essence of language withdraws itself behind the beings it shows; language itself hardly ever comes to language.[31] Gadamer also affirms that the medium of language itself is itself not understood in a dialogue. It is a subject matter that is understood. The medium, on the other hand, in which this understanding occurs, withdraws itself and remains unthematized in dialogue such that it can be the horizon in which the subject matter is presented.

Nevertheless, with respect to the notion of the text, a genuine difference between Heidegger's and Gadamer's conception of language can be found. To be precise, Gadamer's conception of writing as alienation is in line with Heidegger's concerns about writing. However, his main concerns with respect to writing concern the ideality of writing, which forms an important difference with Heidegger's account of language as disclosure and with Plato's de-privileging of writing. It introduces us to a positive account of transference. Let me briefly discuss these two aspects of Gadamer's conception of writing.

Writing and the Ideality of Language

The texts in a tradition are the genuine objects (*Gegenstand*) of hermeneutic understanding. These texts have a particular function. In three ways, they introduce a more purified situation for hermeneutic consciousness. In the first place, the text purifies the presentation of the subject matter from all accidental aspects of a dialogue that distract our attention from this subject matter and tend to disguise it. As Gadamer writes, "In writing, the meaning of what is spoken exists purely for itself, completely detached from all emotional elements of expression and conversation [*Kundgabe*]." Moreover, the text confronts the interpreter with an horizon that stems from another time. In a dialogue we always speak with people from our time, but in the interpreter's "dialogue" with a text his or her horizon is deepened.[32] Finally, the text shows that meaning is not confined to the horizon of the author or the world of its intended addressees. Thus, Gadamer claims the exact opposite of Plato. The text is not a loss of an original understanding, but it shows that the meaning of a text transgresses the original understanding of the author. Therefore, Gadamer can claim that the meaning of the text is given freely to anyone who can read.[33] Plato's description of the danger of concealment is changed into the democratic principle of an equal opening of the text for everyone.

These aspects together form the *ideality of language*. This ideality is the principle of the repeatability of the subject matter of a text in every context. As Gadamer writes, "What is identical in the repetition is only what was actually deposited in the written record." The identity does not depend on the author's understanding. What is repeatable is what is identical behind each writing. Yet, the identity of the subject matter is an abstract identity. It needs a concretion of meaning, as Gadamer calls it.[34] The subject matter is never present as such. It only accounts for the possibility of repeating the same subject matter in different contexts. The actual presentation of the subject matter requires interpretation. Such an interpretation depends on the language and the horizon, or pre-understanding of the interpreter. Therefore, interpretations differ. They all *present* the same subject matter *in different ways*.

To understand Gadamer's relation to Heidegger, Ricoeur, and Derrida, it is important to stress that the ideality of language leads to a particular tension with Gadamer's emphasis on speech as the realm of presentation. The subject matter of the text could be seen as a *transcendental signified* in Derrida's sense of the word.[35] The concept of a transcendental signified is developed by Derrida to characterize a particular understanding of interpretation. A transcendental signified is a signified of a text that is beyond the actual process of interpretation, but which is at the same time the condition of possibility of interpretation because it attracts and orients the interpretation. In this sense, the process of interpretation is teleologically motivated by this transcendental signified. The transcendental signified accounts for the unity of the process of interpretation. In this sense, Gadamer's concept of the subject matter of a text can be interpreted as a transcendental signified since the subject matter is indeed the condition of possibility of the interpretation of a text: it attracts and orients every interpretation, and it lends unity to the different interpretations of the same text—every interpretation brings to language the same subject matter. Moreover, the subject matter of the text is strictly speaking beyond and outside of the process of interpretation. The presentation of the subject matter occurs only in and by means of different and multiple articulations. Therefore, the subject matter is only present in multiple and different ways. Thus, one is led to wonder where the unity of the subject matter is actually given.

As we have seen before, Gadamer tries to account for this unity by invoking his notion of dialogue. He compares the interpretation of a text with a dialogue between the text and its interpreter. The dialogue is an instance of speech in which multiple horizons are gathered. For Gadamer, the model of the dialogue is the model to understand interpretation: interpretation of a text is like a dialogue with a text. This is clearly a logocentric model, but let us take this model and its logocentrism for granted for now and concentrate on Gadamer's idealism. This model accounts for the unity of the horizons of the text and the interpreter in a specific interpretation that takes place here and now, *in actu*. Yet, Gadamer's conception of the ideality does not only assert something about this interpretation, here and now, but it also asserts that it is the same subject matter of a particular text that is interpreted again and again in different interpretations of the same text. Thus, despite the differences of contexts in which a text may give itself to read, it is the same subject matter of this particular text that is brought to presence in interpretation. This presupposition, however, moves beyond speech and beyond the unity that the model of the dialogue can account for. The ideality of language *presupposes a unity of the subject matter of a text beyond the realms of dialogues in act.*

Writing as Alienation

The latter conclusion on the ideality of language is in contrast with Gadamer's analysis of writing as the *alienation of speech.* Writing as alienation means in Gadamer's thought that writing needs to be *"changed back into speech and meaning."* Apparently, writing does conceal meaning and replaces the meaningful speech of dialogue with mere written signs.[36] A text itself cannot *say or present* its meaning. It needs the help of the interpreter who articulates this meaning.

This turn in Gadamer's description of writing is problematic. If writing needs to be changed *back*, then writing *refers back* to a previous articulation. Any articulation occurs in a particular language and a particular situation. Yet, he also asserts that the repetition of interpretation does not refer back to such a previous situation, but instead opens up the ideality of language. I propose to interpret this tension in Gadamer's thought on hermeneutics as a tension between two conceptions of language: language as disclosure and language as transference. The first belongs to speech and the latter to writing. In the conception of language as *disclosure,* the essence of language is its capacity to bring meaning to speech and to show beings as they are. In this conception, meaning is presented and belongs to the realm of disclosure as that which is understood, and the text is an alienation from this realm of disclosure. In the conception of language as *transference,* on the other hand, language is marked by its capacity of transmission. For Gadamer (as well as for Ricoeur as we shall see below), this transference of language concerns the repeatability of meaning, that is, the ideality of meaning.

This brief explication shows how, even though Gadamer tends to privilege a particular conception of language as speech, namely dialogue, over the text, he also emphasizes that the text is the out-standing condition for hermeneutics. In this way, he wards off Plato's attacks on writing. Especially, his elaboration of language as a medium is important here. It shows how understanding presupposes language since it can only take place in and as language. This is a general con-viction in hermeneutics. Yet, the question of what this exactly means and what this tells us about transference divides different philoso-phers in the hermeneutic tradition. Gadamer underlines the disclosive character of articulation and interpretation as well as the ideality of meaning. In the next sections we shall see how Ricoeur proposes a different account of this transference, and how Derrida even contests the primacy of the disclosure of language as such.

RICOEUR ON TEXT AND DISTANCIATION

In Ricoeur's thought, the notion of the text plays a crucial role. He discusses it in the light of one central concept, as can be seen from the following quote: "In my view, the text is much more than a particular case of intersubjective communication: *it is the paradigm of distancia-tion* in communication. As such, it displays a fundamental character-istic of the very historicity of human experience, namely, that it is communication in and through distance."[37] Like Gadamer, Ricoeur stresses the importance of language as a medium for our understand-ing and our experience of the world, but more than Gadamer, he stresses the importance of distance and the many aspects of this dis-tance. In each of these aspects, distance in human communication is *productive*. This productive nature of distance can only be found par-tially in Gadamer's work. He acknowledges that texts coming from another historical period may deepen our experience of the world. In this sense, the distancing at work in the transference of writing is productive for our experience. However, he describes other dimen-sions of this particular distancing as alienation: in the previous section we came across the alienation of speech and meaning in writing, but also the methodical distance a science adopts is for him a form of alienation. At these points and in immediate opposition to Gadamer,

Ricoeur proposes another perspective on the distance and the transference at work in written language. In fact, this is one of his main
contributions to hermeneutics and marks the difference between his
and Gadamer's work: the rigorous conceptualization of the produc-
tivity of distance in his account of distanciation.[38]

Let me point out that a discussion on the role of disclosure and displacement could also begin with other aspects of Ricoeur's thought on
language. In fact, if we are searching for similarities with Heidegger's
account of saying and showing as the most original dimension of
language, it would not be difficult to find some striking quotes. For
instance, in the 1960s when his work is devoted to a thorough analysis of the relation between interpretation and symbolic language,
Ricoeur writes that a symbol "marks the breakthrough of language
toward something other than itself." He calls this breakthrough the
symbol's "*opening*," and he continues, "This breakthrough is *saying;*
and saying is showing."[39] Hence, at the heart of symbolic language,
we find the same aspects that characterize Heidegger's conception of
the disclosure of language: saying and showing. Yet, if we would take
this point of departure and insist on this similarity, we would miss
how the notion of distanciation developed in the 1970s and 1980s
leads to a more specific account of the relation between disclosure
and displacement that can be traced in Ricoeur's hermeneutics of this
period. Therefore, a thorough discussion of the disclosive dimension
of (poetic) language will have to wait until the next two chapters.
First, Ricoeur's conception of distanciation needs to be understood
as a particular interpretation of displacement.

Fourfold Distanciation

To understand how the question of distanciation imposes itself on
Ricoeur, it is important to note that his account of hermeneutics
changes from the 1960s to the 1970s. In *Interpretation Theory*, he
notes that from the 1970s onward, the field of hermeneutics is no
longer restricted to the problem of double meaning alone—as it was
in his account of the symbol in the 1960s—but concerns "the whole

problem of discourse, including writing and literary composition."
Once he has extended the field of hermeneutics in such a way that
it includes the problem of discourse, the "hermeneutic function of
distanciation" becomes visible and can be addressed.[40] What are the
different aspects and levels of distanciation he distinguishes and how
do they position Ricoeur in relation to Heidegger, Gadamer, and
Derrida?

Distanciation in Discourse

In my discussion of Plato and Gadamer, the difference between speech
and writing was my point of departure. To understand distanciation,
we need to take our starting point elsewhere: not in the difference
between speech and writing, but in the dialectic of discourse itself.
The notion of discourse was first developed to conceive of language
first and foremost at a semantic level. As Émile Benveniste already
explained, discourse does not concern the structure of language
(*langue*) as a closed system of signs examined in structuralism and
semiotics, but rather concerns the occurrence of language in speech.[41]
For Benveniste, this occurrence of language is the most primordial
aspect of language: before a language can be studied scientifically or
sentences can be decomposed in signs, it must be spoken first. Following these ideas of Benveniste, Ricoeur argues that an account of
language should start with an account of what happens in this event
of language.[42] The question of what happens in this event brings us to
semantics: The occurrence of language is the opening up of signification and meaning. Effectuated in speech, discourse unfolds itself in
semantic entities that cannot be reduced to their underlying structure
of signs.[43] In more down to earth language, when we speak, we do not
speak signs but we speak meaningful sentences or whole stories that
can be understood. Of course, these semantic and intelligible unities
can be broken down or decomposed, but then we lose the meaningfulness of the utterance and only find signs and the underlying
structure of language. In sum, in contrast to structuralism and semiotics, which claim that only the sign-structure of language (*langue*)
is intelligible as opposed to the occurrence of language (*parole*), the

account of this occurrence as discourse demonstrates that this occurrence has its own unity and intelligibility: "discourse is understood as meaning," as Ricoeur puts it.[44]

Apart from the discussion with structuralism, it is clear that Ricoeur recognizes in Benveniste's notion of discourse a particular hermeneutic experience of language that can also be found in Heidegger's work. Language happens as speech, that is, it happens as a saying that opens up the space of meaning. This implies that every interpretation is indebted to this primacy of the event of language: interpretation presupposes that a space of meaning is opened up so that the interpretation can explicate and appropriate it. In this sense, Jean-Luc Nancy's discussion of Ricoeur's hermeneutics in *Le partage des voix* is both right and wrong. He is right to insist on the fact that interpretation as the explication of meaning presupposes a primordial opening up of meaning. Meaning can only be understood and interpreted if it is somehow disclosed. However, he is wrong to think that Ricoeur's account of hermeneutics would not discuss this opening up of meaning: Ricoeur's account of discourse provides a discussion.[45] At the same time, it is clear that Ricoeur is not on a par with Nancy's account, but to understand this difference it is not enough to discuss the difference between the disclosure of the horizon of meaning in the event of language and the explication of the disclosed meaning within the boundaries of this horizon. We need to turn to the relation between event and signification. For Nancy, sense and event coincide; discourse is always occurring as sense. On the other hand, though he acknowledges that signification always occurs as event, Ricoeur argues that signification is not bound up in this event: it transgresses this event. A simple example can clarify this: Even when I am absent at a certain conversation, one of the participants can tell me later what was discussed. The event of this conversation is unique and unrepeatable, but the meaning that was disclosed during this conversation is repeatable and can be retold at a later moment and in a different conversation. Clearly, this retelling occurs again as event, but as another one. This dialectic between event and signification is typical for discourse.[46] Discourse is event and signification, but as signification it is not merely event since meaning can distance itself from the event of its occurrence. This displacement of meaning with respect to the original locus of its disclosure is the first form of distanciation in discourse.

Displacement as the distanciation of the event of discourse has particular implications: It implies that the event of saying is to be distinguished from the meaning of what is said.[47] For instance, as the event of a conversation, discourse refers to a particular world—the world shared by the conversation partners—and has a particular addressee. In these examples, distanciation implies that what is said distances itself from the particular world and the particular addressee referred to in saying. This difference between the event of saying and the repeatability of what is said runs parallel to Heidegger's distinction between expressing (*aussprechen*) and that "what is expressed" (*das Ausgesprochene*) that we can find in *Sein und Zeit*.[48] What is expressed can detach itself from understanding and for that very reason can be repeated. However, since expressing originally speaks out of understanding, this detachment means also that it uproots that what is expressed from its original understanding. As such, this repeatability is a sign of decay. Although an assertion remains apophantic in nature, this pointing out may be repeated without genuine understanding, that is, without a genuine disclosedness of the being that is spoken about. As such, this repetition more than likely leads to a false appearance, a *pseudos* of understanding. The repeatable statement turns out to be a mere effect of an original disclosure that tends to conceal this original event of disclosure. In contrast to Heidegger, Ricoeur insists that it is exactly this effect that can be understood. In this sense, the phenomenon of understanding cannot be accounted for fully out of its occurrence as speech or understanding in the Heideggerian sense of the word. If signification and meaning give themselves to be understood, the phenomenon of displacement as distanciation is not simply a decay or a loss of understanding but it is rather the phenomenon that accounts for the possibility of the gift of hermeneutic understanding itself. In this sense, distanciation is productive.

In order to turn to writing and the text, let me briefly note how Ricoeur also tries to deal with Derrida's work by means of this dialectic between event and signification. He writes, "To hold, as Jacques Derrida does, that writing has a root distinct from speech and that this foundation has been misunderstood due to our having paid excessive attention to speech, its voice, and its *logos,* is to overlook the grounding of both modes of the actualization of discourse in the dialectical constitution of discourse."[49] This comment avoids a debate with Derrida since it does not go into the real issues. In the first place, it misses a certain similarity between his and Derrida's project. On a very superficial level we can say that both Ricoeur and Derrida approach the difference between speech and writing as the difference between disclosure and displacement, and both aim to show, in opposition to Heidegger, the importance of this displacement in any account of language. However, in Ricoeur's account of this latter difference, displacement is understood as the distanciation of meaning. The problem of displacement is understood under the aspect of meaning. This particular aspect allows him to interpret distanciation as a productive displacement. Is this correct? Can the repeatability of writing be understood as the repeatability of meaning? Derrida introduces the notion of iterability (*itérabilité*) to describe the repeatability of writing, but this repeatability is not the repeatability of meaning. These similarities and differences between Ricoeur's conception of distanciation and Derrida's conception of iterability are studied in a very profound and clear way in the studies of Lawlor.[50] Here, of course, I do not want to repeat these themes, but reinterpret them in the light of the relation between disclosure and displacement: By adding Heidegger into the equation, it becomes possible to demonstrate how the similarities and differences between Ricoeur's and Derrida's conception of writing go back to a different account of disclosure and displacement, and thus to a different relation to Heidegger's work.

From the perspective of disclosure, which is first and foremost the disclosive event of discourse, a particular question arises with respect to Ricoeur's account of the first level of distanciation: How does he reconcile the singularity of discourse as event with the repeatability of discourse as signification and meaning? On the one hand, he follows Gadamer and claims that it is the same meaning that is repeated.[51] Meaning is marked by a certain ideality. On the other hand, also in line with Gadamer, Ricoeur argues that the appropriation and understanding of meaning only occurs in an event of interpretation—a hermeneutic dialogue, as Gadamer puts it. This means that every appearance and appropriation of meaning is marked by the event's singularity. How can he reconcile this sameness and ideality of meaning with the irreducible multiplicity of its appearance in different events of interpretations? With regard to this fundamental question, Derrida's account of the repeatability of writing as iterability (*itérabilité*) rather than as the repeatability of meaning proposes a remarkable answer. In Derrida's etymology, the Latin *iter,* which means "anew" or "again," would stem from the Sanskrit *itara,* which means "other."[52] The name "iterability" stresses that the repetition of writing involves otherness. Is this not exactly what happens in the process of interpretation, namely that writing allows meaning to appear again, but never as the same, but as different, marked as it is by the new, singular context in which it reappears? This would dissolve the idea of ideality. Or rather, it shows that ideality tries to relativize the differentiation at work in the transference of writing: to aim at the same, ideal meaning or the same, ideal subject matter, Derrida suggests, presupposes the exclusion of the reappearance of the text in unthought-of and unheard-of contexts of discussion in which the boundaries of this ideality might be transgressed.[53]

Distanciation as Writing

With these questions, we are already at the heart of the question of writing and the text. By fixing discourse, a text "destroys" the event of discourse, according to Ricoeur. This destruction, however, is not a negative but a positive phenomenon. It completes the first distanciation in the sense that the text's detachment from any actual speech gives it free to be transferred to other worlds and other speech communities. The second distanciation detaches the text from any particular addressee: by addressing no one in particular, the text addresses everyone who can read. Thus, meaning comes to its true ideality in writing.[54] In contrast to Plato, Ricoeur argues that the text's decontextualization does not rob it of its truth, as Plato feared, but opens up the possibility of recontextualization and thus frees the text for an endless unfolding of its meaning in endless appropriations. This has important implications for the relation between disclosure and displacement: "[The] link between disclosure and appropriation is, to my mind, the cornerstone of a hermeneutic which would claim both to overcome the shortcomings of historicism and to remain faithful to the original intention of Schleiermacher's hermeneutics. To understand an author better than he could understand himself is to display *the power of disclosure implied in his discourse beyond the limited horizon of his own existential situation.*"[55] This quote tells us that displacement as distanciation allows "the power of disclosure" of a particular discourse to come to a full bloom beyond the limits of its event. Apparently, the disclosure of a discourse does not coincide with its event, as Heidegger and, in the wake of his thought, Nancy argues. Ricoeur does not restrict disclosure to a singular event. By means of the dialectic between disclosure and appropriation, the disclosive power of a particular discourse comprises many events: the original event of its saying but also "beyond the limited horizon" of this original event, the multiple events in which its meaning is appropriated. In this way, displacement as distanciation is explained as a feature of discourse that allows us to *deepen* the first disclosure. As a consequence, this also means that displacement as distanciation is in the service of the unfolding of the power of disclosure.

In relation to Plato, the *coup de génie* of hermeneutics is thus to have exchanged Plato's father of the *logos* for the meaning and signification of discourse. The text repeats this signification without any loss. Moreover, since the original situation is in itself limited, the transgression of these limits in *gramme* does not rob the *logos* of its truth, but rather allows this *logos* to extend and deepen its power of disclosure.

This leads to a somewhat problematic and odd conception of the text. On the one hand, the repeatability of meaning depends on writing. It is the materiality of writing that grants the text its *persisting existence*. This persisting existence, as already Husserl noted, enables the transference of a text to other generations.[56] In this materiality, meaning seems to be outside itself. Gadamer acknowledges this when he speaks about the alienation of speech and meaning in written signs, but also Ricoeur needs a moment of appropriation as an eventful counterpart of distanciation in which meaning reappears. As such, the transference of meaning is indebted to a vehicle that does not coincide with it. On the other hand, however, hermeneutics insists that the repeatability of writing is the repeatability of meaning. This is the only way to overcome variants of the Platonic objections to writing. Since it allows discourse to unfold its full power of disclosure, Gadamer and Ricoeur claim that language gains its true ideality or spirituality (*Geistigkeit*) in writing. This line of thought implies that the transmission of the text is completely in the service of meaning and its unfolding and even coincides with it. Ricoeur writes, "Because discourse is now linked to a material support, it becomes more spiritual in the sense that it is liberated from the narrowness of the face-to-face situation."[57] Apparently, to interpret the repeatability of writing as the repeatability of meaning implies that the ideality of meaning *coincides* with the materiality of the text! In contrast to the tension between writing and its eventful appropriation, this line of thought implies that this tension can be completely reconciled and that displacement as the distanciation of discourse is a purely profitable and productive enterprise in which meaning is gained without any loss. Though lacking disclosure, displacement is understood here as being integrated in a dialectic dynamic serving the unfolding of the disclosure of discourse.

With respect to this hermeneutic position, the question remains whether it is adequate to approach the transference from one context to another as well as the traversal of differences that takes place in this transition from the point of view of the power of disclosure. The notions of meaning, signification, and subject matter (Gadamer) as well as the idea of the disclosive power of discourse seem to be regulative ideas that orient and guide this transference. Of course, this hermeneutic conception is probably right in claiming that the interpretation of a text and the appropriation of its meaning is a process guided by these regulative ideas. It is difficult if not impossible to think interpretation and appropriation without these regulative notions. However, it remains to be seen whether the transference of writing as such is adequately discussed when treated in the light of interpretation and appropriation solely. As we shall see later on, Derrida will insist on the transference of writing as a traversal of differences.[58] His point of departure is not the interpretation or appropriation of a text's meaning, but rather the linguistic movement that allows writing to decontextualize and to recontextualize. If every context or every event of dialogue is singular then this decontextualization and recontextualization presupposes a traversal of differences that cannot be manifested in either context and cannot be understood as meaning in either context. If this is true, this process cannot be approached from within the realm of disclosure. Yet, since this traversal of differences is a condition of possibility of interpretation, and of the further unfolding of the power of disclosure, does this not imply that the relation between displacement, now thought as the traversal of differences, and disclosure should be put upside down? Does it not imply that the hermeneutic experience, in which a text is experienced as meaningful and interpretable, refers back to another experience in which the dissemination or proliferation of writing, which Plato already feared, is experienced?[59]

Distanciation and World

The power of disclosure is not only deepened by distanciation in the sense that it provides the possibility of multiple interpretations. Distanciation also deepens it by allowing different dimensions of language to be broached. In a normal conversation we do not hear signs or words. Instead, we immediately hear and understand meaning. The text, however, by destroying the event, disrupts this immediate showing of speech. By this disruption, the text also suspends the immediate reference to a world. This particular suspension has two consequences involving the explanation of the composition and the world of the text.

By suspending the world, distanciation suspends the *disclosure of meaning*. This is not only a negative phenomenon, but a positive, productive one as well: thanks to this suspension, it allows us to approach different aspects of the text to which we pay no attention in an actual dialogue. It allows us to address the text's structure, its composition, the laws of the genre to which it belongs, the binary oppositions it employs, the characteristics of the author's style, and so on.[60] This third form of distanciation allows the development of an *explanatory* dimension of hermeneutics. It strives to give structuralism and other human sciences their proper place in this theory of discourse. Hermeneutics is not only devoted to understanding (*Verstehen*), but the study of discourse has a proper place for explanation (*Erklären*) as well. In opposition to Dilthey, for whom explanation belonged solely to the natural sciences, Ricoeur maintains that the text as the object of study of the human sciences requires an explanatory approach as well. Especially structuralism and semiotics have demonstrated that such an explanatory approach to the text is very fruitful and corresponds to fundamental dimensions of the text as text. However, Ricoeur also insists that these explanatory approaches to the text have their proper place in the hermeneutic enterprise. Perhaps contrary to their self-understanding, these approaches are completely in the service of the kingdom of meaning: they criticize the primacy of the disclosure of meaning in one singular event by examining the structure of the text, but this critique is nothing but a deepening of our understanding of the text. It sharpens and clarifies the disclosure of meaning beyond the naivety of a first disclosure. Thus, to explain is to understand better, as Ricoeur often notes.

Clearly, this form of distanciation is nothing but the methodical distance Gadamer attacks in *Wahrheit und Methode*. As such, Ricoeur's account of this distanciation implies an important critique of Heidegger and Gadamer. Their exclusion of the human sciences from the descriptions of the understanding is based on the bias that a methodological, scientific approach leads to an alienation of the original belonging to language of human beings.[61] According to Ricoeur, however, the possibility of scientific explanation is not only part and parcel of the distanciation of the text itself—and thus of language as discourse—but it also introduces the possibility of a critical stance toward the language we speak. Language is not only the realm of a pure eventful disclosure. Every immediate disclosure is marked by distortions. Only the mediate way of distanciation allows us to purify the power of disclosure and to distinguish the concealing and the unconcealing elements that always play together in every appearance. Immediate disclosure involves *pseudos* in Heidegger's sense of the word.[62] In order to tackle this concealment, a scientific, critical distance can be beneficial. Therefore, explanation does not lead understanding astray, but complements it. In fact, it is a way to validate the guesses of understanding, as Ricoeur also puts it. Therefore, it allows us to proceed from naive interpretations, not validated by explanation, to informed and critical ones.[63]

Along this line of thought Ricoeur incorporates the insights of structuralism, psychoanalysis, and the Habermasian critique of ideologies into a more developed hermeneutics. This incorporation is not simply an adaptation: its aim is to show how these dimensions can be subsumed under the primacy of meaning and understanding.[64] However, it remains to be seen whether the critical force of structuralism and psychoanalysis can be dealt with in this way. Is it not possible that their critical force undermines the very kingdom of meaning that Ricoeur wants to maintain? Could it not be possible that they refer to a displacement that does not allow a renewed disclosure and appropriation of meaning? All revolves around one issue: can we understand the suspension of meaning as a moment in the hermeneutic circle? Is the suspension of meaning always already in the service of a practice of deciphering, or might it be an irrecoverable interruption of this practice and a genuine disruption of the hermeneutic circle, as Derrida suggests in *Béliers*?[65]

The suspension of our everyday world has yet another consequence, which for Ricoeur is the culmination point of distanciation.

The suspension of the everyday world forms the condition of possibility of disclosing another world. This aspect of distanciation is of huge importance for his account of fiction, literature, and narrative. By opening up the possibility to configure a poetic world, this third form of distanciation inaugurates the poetic dimension of language: The suspension of the (everyday) world allows the text to create and present (*présentifier*) an "imaginary" world.[66] It is important to note that "imaginary" or "fictive" should not be understood in a pejorative sense of the word. In fact, Ricoeur relates these worlds created and discovered in literature and poetics to Heidegger's enterprise in *Sein und Zeit.* Although the world of a given literary text is a world of fiction and is therefore distinct from our everyday world, it is definitely not without relation to our being. Ricoeur claims that literature "reaches the world" at a more profound level. He relates this level to Husserl's notion of the life-world (*Lebenswelt*) and to Heidegger's conception of being-in-the-world. Coming from his analyses of the symbol in the 1960s in which the symbol expresses life, we see that fiction takes on the disclosive role in his work from the 1970s onward. It is by means of fiction that our own mode of being is disclosed to us. In this sense, Ricoeur furthers Gadamer's claim that language is the medium of understanding. *Poetic* language is the medium of understanding our being-in-the-world *par excellence.*

The world of the literary text is a double of the world we inhabit: it resembles the world we inhabit. With an expression borrowed from Aristotle, Ricoeur calls the world of fiction a mimesis of reality.[67] Consequently, the world of fiction *is* and *is not* our world. This particular formulation, to which we will return in the next chapters, implies that distanciation inscribes itself in this ontological postulate of fiction: due to distanciation, fiction presents a mimesis of the world and presents something that *is as* our world, but this "to be as" includes both to be and to be not. Such an imaginary world is the greatest gift a text can bestow upon us. The interpretation of such a text wants "to explicate the type of being-in-the-world unfolded *in front of* the text."[68] By the detour of distanciation, Ricoeur can rejoin Heidegger's conception of understanding (*Verstehen*) in *Sein und Zeit* with some modifications. Understanding a literary text is similar to Heidegger's account of understanding: it is a way of discovering our own mode of being-in-the-world. In Ricoeur's case, it is the text, rather than Dasein itself, that projects these new possibilities of being-in-the-world.[69] To understand these possibilities to exist is the genuine task of hermeneutic understanding. In this light, Ricoeur reinterprets the dialectic between throwness and projection from *Sein und Zeit* as the dialectic between the everyday world to which we always already belong and the possibilities projected in the fictional world of a novel or a narrative. This poetic project of possibilities reveals the true *destination* of discourse: to discover new ways of being-in-the-world. Fiction is therefore the privileged way to refigure and redescribe the world we inhabit.[70]

Despite these similarities, one might also sense a particular difference with respect to *Sein und Zeit*. Why does Ricoeur talk about "our most proper possibilities" if the world of the text "is and is not" our world? Due to distanciation the "is not"-part marks the discovery and the disclosure of our being-in-the-world. For Heidegger, the project of possibilities is a dimension of Dasein's own disclosedness. In this sense, properness or authenticity (*Eigentlichkeit*) is an adequate term: these possibilities are grounded in Dasein's openness itself. In contrast to Heidegger, the "is not" of the text's possibilities implies that the notion of proper or ownmost is a bit out of place here. Ricoeur tries to solve this in his account of appropriation. Appropriation means that we *make* the world of the text *our own*. Hence, we understand the world of fiction *as resembling* the world we inhabit. Therefore, we understand the text *as proposing possibilities* that might also be found in our world. Making a text our own is thus a way of seeing the possibilities proposed by the text as our own possibilities.[71] Hence, what is called "our own" is nothing but a product of our confrontation with an other, a text, which is not truly possessed by us and to which we do not belong. This also means that the question still stands: Does it make sense to talk about "proper" and "own" here, and what exactly does the "is not" in "being as" imply for the relation between Heidegger and Ricoeur? These two questions will be discussed extensively in the next chapters.

Distanciation in Appropriation

Our discussion has already brought us to the fourth and final form of distanciation: self-understanding through loss of the self. Self-understanding is not immediate. It requires the detour through the expressions of human life. Already in 1960s, in his confrontation with the hermeneutics of suspicion, Ricoeur argues that self-understanding implies a loss of the self.[72] This theme returns in the 1970s and 1980s. This loss of the self in the reading of a text is the fourth distanciation. To mark once more Ricoeur's place among the other thinkers we discuss in this chapter, let me note that this self-loss implies a particular difference to Gadamer's account of reading and interpretation. For Gadamer, every understanding presupposes *Vor-urteile*—prejudgments or prejudices. If we approach a text in light of these prejudgments, we impose ourselves and our perspective on the text. If this is the case, does this not imply that we merely find ourselves and our prejudices in the text? How can we learn something new about the text if we impose ourselves and our prejudices on it? Triggered by these questions, Ricoeur argues that what is to be interpreted can only be found in the text itself. The text brings its own, autonomous world with it. Instead of *imposing* him or herself *on* the text, Ricoeur suggests that the interpreter *exposes* him or herself *to* the text.[73] This may mean that the interpretation of the text improves and deepens the interpreter's understanding of the world he or she inhabits: the text opens up a new being-in-the-world. But it may also mean that the text *exposes* the illusions of the interpreter. Therefore, understanding a text is both an *appropriation* and a *dispossession* of one's self. This dialectic between appropriation and dispossession is the final form the dialectic between event and meaning assumes. In interpretation, the text is brought back to the event of disclosure, which takes place as self-understanding through self-loss in being exposed to other, unheard possibilities disclosed in the text.[74]

Distanciation and the Question of Transference

Looking back on Ricoeur's account of displacement as distanciation, one might wonder what has happened to the Platonic and Heideggerian problem of the *pseudos* of writing. In passing, I have already mentioned how Ricoeur deals with a number of aspects of the Platonic "attack against writing." I do not want to repeat them here; I want to elaborate only one question we encountered in the previous discussion. This question is not so much concerned with the way Ricoeur dismisses and tries to resolve the problem of the falsity of writing, but rather with an aspect of his work on distanciation that might reintroduce the problem of *pseudos,* of a possible treacherous appearance.

Ricoeur finds the destination of discourse in the invention of the world of fiction, which deserves to be called a "disclosure" since it is the privileged way in which our being-in-the-world is opened up to us. Although it deserves to be called disclosure, it is a typical kind of disclosure. I have emphasized a number of times that Ricoeur's interpretation of displacement as distanciation is always in the service of the power of disclosure of discourse. Yet, at this culmination point, the relation between displacement and disclosure is almost overturned. Displacement does not simply support the unfolding of the power of disclosure, but the third displacement leaves its traces on the particular disclosure at work in the world of fiction. These traces can most clearly be found in its ontological characterization: the world of fiction is a mimesis of reality; its ontological status is "being as," that is, it *is* and *is not* the world we inhabit. This "is not" implies that the disclosure of this most profound dimension of our existence is always marked by mediation and distanciation.

Since "being as" involves "being not," one question needs to be raised: is it not possible that the disclosure of our existence by means of fiction leads to a distorted understanding of our being-in-the-world? In fact, since Ricoeur emphasizes that the interpreter does not impose him or herself on the text, but is exposed to the text, this possibility of distortion should be taken very seriously: the interpreter places him or herself in light of the text and makes the text his or her own. Could it not be possible that instead of unmasking the illusions of the self, a text introduces and produces illusions? This possibility is entirely due to the "is not" that characterizes the disclosure of fiction: if the text could disclose the modes of being as they are, this distortion would only be relative. Against the background of this possibility, we see the advantages of Heidegger's position—Dasein can understand his ownmost modes of being without mediation or distortion—and we understand why Heidegger can never be satisfied with a disclosure that is only mimetic: how can disclosure fight against and rob from the phenomenon of *pseudos* if it is *identical* to this phenomenon?!

How to deal with the possibility of distortion in poetic disclosure? As opposed to the poetic configuration that gathers and assembles the world of the text, the possibility of distortion requires a disfiguration (*défiguration*) in Lacoue-Labarthe's sense of the word. He introduces this notion in a discussion of the weakness of fables (*défaillance du mythe*).[75] The identification by means of narrative might be indispensable, but the possibility of distortion points us to the weakness of fables and narratives. Ricoeur's analysis of mimesis is so caught up in the configuration that discloses unheard-of and unthought-of aspects of the world that it lacks the attention to this weakness. Ricoeur seems to have so much faith in the disclosive dimension of the text that he forgets this weakness of the text altogether as well as the necessity to think disfiguration as an antidote for the distorting disclosure of poetics. Chapter 4 will deal with these issues.

Moreover, although Ricoeur explains the third distanciation in terms of the disclosure of another world, it seems that distanciation has a more original function as well. Without the suspension of our everyday world, the imagination would have *no margin* and *no room to play*. Radicalizing this idea, one could say that distanciation itself has an opening dimension. A work of fiction discloses an imaginary world, but distanciation provides the room to play for the imagination before and beyond its disclosive power. By withdrawing the immediate presence of the everyday world, distanciation does not provide an immediate replacement for this loss of the world. It only inaugurates the space for literature to occur. Ricoeur, then, proposes to understand the play in this space as a play that compensates the loss of the presence of the everyday world by providing a deeper understanding of the world. But despite this interpretation, one could wonder whether this moment of distanciation preceding the compensating gesture, is not very close to a Derridean conception of *différance* as the originary displacement at the heart of every disclosure. This consideration suggests that Ricoeur's explicit elaborations of distanciation underestimate the possibility of a more originary role played by concealment in writing and in fiction. In the following section, we turn to the work of Derrida for whom this phenomenon of concealment is crucial to understand writing, disclosure, and transference.

DERRIDA ON WRITING AND DISPLACEMENT

By turning to Derrida's thought, we enter the realm of a different experience. Hermeneutics arises from the experience that a text speaks to us and has something meaningful to say. This hermeneutic experience always moves within the horizon of meaning and aims accordingly at the decipherment of the sense that promises itself in this experience. In distinction to this hermeneutic experience, Derrida describes in *Béliers* the experience to which his own thought belongs as a disseminal one.[76] Hence, in 2003 he still uses the term "dissemination" to describe the dimension of writing that attracts his interest: the unbounded proliferation of writing. Unlike Ricoeur and Gadamer who try to overcome Plato's objections to writing by showing its fertility for hermeneutic understanding, Derrida's choice of terms—dissemination and proliferation—demonstrates that according to him the problematic status of writing cannot be overcome, but rather reflects an inescapable and fundamental dimension of language, which moreover contaminates thought. This marks the difference between a hermeneutic and a deconstructive thought on writing. In relation to the problem of concealment, we already saw that the former thought tends to efface or at least relativize the distorting quality of writing. The latter, in contrast, does not efface this distortion but rather effaces the idea of an origin: the interrupting distortions and the disseminating displacements do not refer back to an origin but are original themselves.

Because of this particular perspective on writing, Derrida challenges Heidegger's work from an entirely different angle. He does not try to show how the text might be a productive element in the disclosure of discourse. As I noted in the previous chapter, Heidegger's idea of *pseudos* can be understood from the model of the trace. For him, however, a trace refers back to a more original realm of the open that makes the trace possible in the first place. Derrida, on the other hand, insists that writing as a trace is originary. Hence, Heidegger's work is not challenged from the perspective of the truth of writing, but from its untruth. To develop this perspective, I will first introduce some famous aspects of Derrida's account of writing and show how these mark an important difference with hermeneutic strands of thought. The second part of this section then deals with the main ingredients of Derrida's questions with regard to Heidegger's account of language.

Writing as Supplement and Concealment

Derrida's critique of metaphysics, though clearly indebted to Heidegger's, is in a few important aspects different from the latter's critique. The main point of Derrida's critique is that metaphysics tends to describe notions such as "sign," "representation," "repetition," "trace," or "writing" as secondary with respect to a present origin. However, as his careful analyses of multiple philosophical texts show, this claim can never be accounted for fully. In fact, Derrida argues that these secondary notions are primary and that the presence of what is usually understood as origin is secondary.[77] This approach allows him to rethink the relation between presentation and representation. Unlike Heidegger, Derrida does not describe representation in the first place as a form of *Vorstellung*. As *Vorstellung*, as Heidegger argues in multiple texts, representation is the metaphysical idea of modern philosophy *par excellence*. For Derrida, however, representation is first and foremost re-presentation, that is, that which forms the condition of possibility of the repetition of presentation.[78] According to Ricoeur, as we saw above, no power of disclosure is exhausted by one of its event; it requires multiple events to unfold itself. Derrida's attention to re-presentation affirms the idea of Ricoeur that no actual presentation is self-sufficient since it is in need of its repetition in other contexts. However, unlike Ricoeur, Derrida emphasizes that no presentation—past, present, or future—can manifest these repetitions all at once or on its own. Therefore, it is premature to approach this complex of presentations and their references to as-yet concealed and always displacing representation as the process of the unfolding of discourse's power of disclosure. The only conclusion that can be drawn is that representations as displacing repetitions are presupposed by every presentation. Derrida elaborates this idea in many of his texts. I will focus on two exemplary early texts: his account of writing in his reading of Husserl's *Der Ursprung der Geometrie* allows me to discuss his critique of Ricoeur's and Gadamer's hermeneutics, and his account of "the original double" in his reading of Plato's *Phaedrus* allows me to show how he interprets the concealment intrinsic to writing.[79]

Husserl and the Supplement of Writing

Throughout the history of philosophy, writing is understood as a supplement. Being supplementary, writing would be external to the presentation of meaning and to the understanding. At best, writing would be helpful for educational purposes. At worst, writing would be a dangerous supplement threatening memory and understanding, as King Thamus stresses in his response to Theuth, as Rousseau repeats in his *Confessions,* and as Husserl fears in *Die Krisis der europäischen Wissenschaften.*[80] Derrida does not deny that writing is supplementary, but he adds that writing is a *necessary* supplement, and that supplementarity is characteristic of language as such. Writing is thus not simply *external* to what it supplements, but writing is a *placeholder* of consciousness, of meaning, of the event of speech, that is, of all kinds of presence: It supplements a certain lack of presence.

The transference of a text provides a beautiful example of this supplementarity. Writing is not simply the absence of meaning. It is rather the condition of possibility for the repetition of the manifestation of meaning. In the intermediary moments when a text is transferred from one context to another—for instance, when a book rests on its shelf in a library—no meaning is present. Only its material supplement traverses the differences between these contexts. Thus, it allows another interpretation of the text to take place.

In his reading of *Der Ursprung der Geometrie,* this idea of supplementarity already plays a huge role.[81] In this text, Husserl confronts the problem of the constitution of geometrical objects and the constitution of a scientific tradition of geometry. He refuses to think a Platonic realm of forms in which geometrical objects would always already exist. Instead, he wants to think the discovery of a geometrical object by its inventor as a genuine creation or *institution*. This institution is characterized by a process of infinitization. This latter activity of human consciousness is required since the ideal objects of geometry cannot be found in the perception. Perception does not offer us a circle; at best, it offers us circle-like shapes. Hence, the existence of these objects depends purely upon consciousness and its presence for consciousness. Yet, this act of institution is not enough since Husserl wants to think the *ideality* of these objects as well: once instituted for the first time, a geometrical object should be repeatable identically by other geometers. In particular, Husserl wants to think the *continuing-to-be* of geometrical objects. This persistence of the existence of these objects implies that their constitution involves more than consciousness alone since, as Husserl notes, their inventor is not always conscious of it—he or she might be asleep, for instance, and what secures the existence of these objects at that time? Because he rejects the eternal presence of a geometrical object in a Platonic realm of forms, he has to account for this continuing-to-be in another way. To this end, he takes his recourse to language. Spoken language is not enough, as Husserl writes: "What is lacking [in spoken language] is the *persisting existence* of the 'ideal objects' even during the periods in which the inventor and his fellows are no longer wakefully so related or even are no longer alive. What is lacking is their continuing-to-be even when no one has (consciously) realized them in self-evidence."[82] Therefore, Husserl turns to written language. The persistent existence of writing should supplement the inventor's institution of the geometrical object in order to account for the object's ideality. Thus, the materiality of writing should lend the object its ideality—to some extent, although in an entirely different field of problems, Husserl's thinking on the ideality of the geometrical object in relation to written language is very close to Gadamer's articulation of the ideality of language and to Ricoeur's claim that the materiality of writing makes discourse more spiritual.

At this point, Derrida's analysis intervenes. He notes that writing is a necessary supplement in Husserl's proposal. It is not simply external to, but it is a condition of the object's repeatability and ideality. The presence of a geometrical object for the inventor's consciousness is not enough to constitute this object as an ideal object. Its constitution requires a supplement to this presence to consciousness.[83] Hence, writing is not simply a repetition of an object that is originally given for consciousness alone, but the constitution of this object itself requires and presupposes its re-presentation in writing. Already in the constitution of this object, writing is the placeholder of a consciousness that will sleep and will die.

This has important implications for the status of the tradition or the history of, in this case, geometry. A tradition is not opened up by a pure presence for consciousness, but by a difficult interplay between the inventor's act of institution and the dependence of this institution on that which allows the object to be repeated in a tradition, namely, writing. Writing is indispensable for the object's ideality, but this robs the ideality of presence. Husserl acknowledges this when he argues that a text is a *passive* signification. As a passive signification, a text does not simply present a geometrical object when it is read by someone. Instead, it may lead to careless associations that obstruct a genuine reactivation; this is what Husserl calls the "seduction of language." Therefore, writing is a supplement that still requires a complement of consciousness to reactivate (*Reaktivierung*) the object for consciousness. This reactivation would repeat the ideal object identically. It is quite remarkable that Husserl simply posits the possibility of such a reactivation. It would be an intrinsic possibility of everyone who can speak—again one might note the parallel with Gadamer's expression that the subject matter of the text is available to everyone who can read.[84] However, one could wonder, as Derrida does, how we can make a strict distinction between a genuine reactivation and a passive association if the origin itself is always already given in and by means of its supplement, and requires its supplement for its constitution as an ideal object. The ultimate measure to which this reactivation should aim, an original presence of the ideal object, has never been and will never be present for consciousness. In this way, coming back to a remark I made in the first section of this chapter, Derrida affirms Gadamer's idea that language is the medium of understanding. However, he adds that we can never return to the original as such because the ideal object is always already given as its double: repetition as a doubling founds this ideality. To be in the medium of language means that we are always already dealing with doubles and supplements of an origin. These two forms of displacements, doubling and supplementing, are conditions of possibility of any renewed disclosure.

I noted that Husserl's account of the ideality of a geometrical object shares a remarkable resemblance (despite some other differences) with Ricoeur's and Gadamer's understanding of the ideality of meaning. In both cases, the materiality of a text accounts for the ideality or spirituality of meaning. At the same time, Husserl as well as Gadamer and Ricoeur maintain that something identical guides the repetition enabled by writing. In Husserl's case, although this identical object is constituted by writing as well, it should nevertheless be purified from writing. This idea can be found in Gadamer's and Ricoeur's thought as well. The text is marked by an absence of meaning. Therefore, Gadamer determines writing as alienated speech and describes the task of hermeneutic consciousness as changing signs back into speech and meaning: it is the same subject matter that is understood in each interpretation of the text. Like Husserl, Ricoeur subsumes transference under *that which* is transmitted. Discourse can be identified and reidentified as the same: the repeatability at stake in Ricoeur's account of the text concerns the repeatability of the same meaning.[85] With these similarities in mind, Derrida's questions with respect to Husserl become questions with respect to Gadamer and Ricoeur as well: Are they capable of doing justice to the primordial contamination of writing and meaning if they consider interpretation as a process that aims at the manifestation of the same meaning or subject matter?

In Ricoeur's and Gadamer's understanding, interpretations take place, as Lawlor calls it, in a "regulative horizon of identity."[86] The meaning of the regulative character of this horizon will be discussed more carefully in chapter 4. At this point, I only want to raise the question whether Ricoeur's and Gadamer's insistence on the sameness of meaning and subject matter does not imply that these notions work as a "transcendental signified" (*signifié transcendental*) in Derrida's sense of the word.[87] Meaning and subject matter function in Gadamer's and Ricoeur's thought as entities beyond any particular context or situation that attract and orient interpretation. They form the end of interpretation in the double sense of the word: they are both its goal and ending. This leads to a conception of interpretation as the decipherment of meaning. In 1967, Derrida characterizes this conception as a nostalgic quest for an origin that tries to escape the play of differences: this latter play is subsumed under the transcendental signified.[88] In 2003, he still insists on this description of hermeneutics as a decipherment of meaning, and he opposes it to his own conception of dissemination. Dissemination then refers to the interruptions and undecidables that every decipherment presupposes and which problematize this decipherment as an endless, continuous process attracted by a meaning given beyond this context.[89] The notion of the *undecidable* can perfectly be described in terms of the problem of writing: if the constitution of meaning indeed presupposes a moment of writing and, hence, is not founded in a full presence, the constituted object itself refers back to something that cannot be fully accounted for. Consequently, the object itself escapes pure calculability and is marked by undecidables. Interpretation as decipherment tends to forget that these elements of unaccountability or undecidability interrupt the process of decipherment: there is no present being or meaning to be deciphered in the first place. In *Béliers,* Derrida notes how Gadamer, in his reading of Celan, "acknowledges very quickly, and explicitly, that his interpretive reading must take more than one interruption into account." And he adds, "His reading must also leave in suspense a series of questions that are so many interruptions in the decipherment of meaning."[90] Consequently, decipherment of meaning is only possible when we suspend these unaccountable elements in a reading, that is, when we read as if a transcendental signified attracts our interpretation. Also with respect to Ricoeur, it can be said that Derrida understands his hermeneutics as an exponent of a hermeneutics that does not take the moment of dissemination into account.[91]

Clearly, in his account of writing as an integral part of the constitution of a geometrical object, and of meaning for that matter, Derrida wants to maintain that the "seduction of language" is not an external problem but rather concerns a fundamental problem of language as such. Every reinterpretation or reactivation of a text has to deal with unaccountabilities and undecidables. These elements are indeed added by language as writing, but they cannot be opposed to a language devoid of these elements: a language purified by a philosophical *logos* or a hermeneutic decipherment might be the dream of (hermeneutic) philosophy but is never a present actuality. Consequently, the ruptures and interruptions we encounter in a text are not relative to a horizon of meaning. They rather form the blind spots and the vanishing points of this horizon. Yet, this also means that the concealment of writing has its own particular movement: displacement. Playing with the word "sense," which means both meaning and direction, one could say that the hermeneutics of Gadamer and Ricoeur always moves within the boundaries of the horizon of sense, that is, in the horizon of a particular direction that orients every reading. The focal point of this horizon is the subject matter or the world of the text that is read. Derrida's conception of dissemination and displacement tries to show that writing means that such a direction and orientation is never absolute. In fact, the experience of dissemination in reading allows the reader to experience a movement in the text that goes against the grain of a given sense or direction. The attention to interruptions and undecidables in a reading means that the reader is always ready "to embark on a wholly other path" and thus to move in wholly different direction.[92] In distinction to the hermeneutic movement within a horizon of sense, and the Heideggerian movement "on the way" to that which is one's own, the movement of language to which Derrida pays attention is a "passage beyond" a given horizon and toward that which is other.[93]

Plato and the Concealment of Writing

> Only hidden letters can thus get Socrates moving [*faire marcher*]. If a speech could be purely present, unveiled, naked, offered up in person in its truth, without the detours of a signifier foreign to it, if at the limit an undeferred *logos* were possible, it would not seduce anyone. It would not draw Socrates, as if under the effects of a *pharmakon,* out of its way.[94]

This quote from "*La pharmacie de Platon*" demonstrates Derrida's particular attention to the relation between the *seduction* of writing and its *concealment.* In the opening scene of the *Phaedrus,* Phaedrus seduces Socrates to leave his ordinary dwelling place in Athens in order to come with him to Ilisus. Phaedrus has this seductive power over Socrates because he hides a written speech of Lysias under his cloak. Socrates loves to hear speeches more than anything else. In its concealment, the text promises to speak. Here, in the context of Plato's work we know from the first section of this chapter that the promise of the text is to be distrusted. The text promises a better memory but provides only an external memory. The text promises knowledge, but turns out to be without any knowledge. As in the case of memory and understanding, the promise of the text to say something can lead us astray—and it does so in the case of Socrates. Feeling the appeal of the text, he exclaims: "But you seem to have discovered a drug [*pharmakon*] to entice me into walking outside the city. Just like dangling green branches or fruit of some kind in front of a hungry animal to lead him on, so you are likely to lead me through all of Attica or anywhere you want, simply by holding words in a book in front of my nose."[95] Derrida uses the expression "*faire marcher*" to describe how the text makes Socrates move. This expression means both to lead someone as a puppeteer does, but also to lead someone astray.[96] Indeed, the hidden text moves Socrates in the wrong direction: he belongs in the city and with his fellow men whom he interrogates; hence, the movement out of the city is a movement that leads Socrates astray.

In the dialogue, Phaedrus leads Socrates to Ilisus, the place where the myth of Pharmaceia occurred. This myth tells the story of the maiden Oreithuia, who was killed while she was playing with Pharmaceia.[97] The message is clear. Socrates should take care not to expose himself to the dangers and the seduction of writing. When asked by Phaedrus what the myth of Pharmaceia means and whether it is true, Socrates remarks that he is not interested in the question of the truth of myths because he follows the Delphic inscription "Know thyself."[98] Yet, in his circumstances, Socrates's remarks seem quite careless and seem to indicate that he definitely does not know himself. Not only is he seduced by writing to leave the city where he finds himself in a similar situation to Oreithuia playing a dangerous game, but his brief explanation of the myth—it would concern a gust of the North Wind—indicates that he does not realize at this point that the myth is about him and in this sense has something to contribute to his self-knowledge.[99]

This brief introduction already shows that Derrida reads Plato's concerns regarding writing in a different way than Ricoeur and Gadamer do. The latter two argue that Plato has not seen the productive contribution of the text to the meaning and understanding. They efface the Platonic dangers of the text as dangers. Derrida does something else. He emphasizes that which Plato considers to be the most important danger of writing, namely, its capacity to seduce to go into another direction, to promise and not to give. Rather than trying to overcome this danger, he extends it to every form of language. If Derrida criticizes Plato he does not criticize him for having overestimated the dangers of writing, but rather for having underestimated them: the difference between speech and writing allocates the dangers of language to writing and reserves a demarcated space in language where this danger can be overcome or avoided.

For Plato, speech is to be privileged over writing since it is closer to the understanding of the soul turned toward the truth. Both *logos* and writing are forms of representation, but what distinguishes them is the presence and the absence of the *father*, namely, the one who speaks with understanding. As we have seen, Gadamer's and Ricoeur's hermeneutics overcomes the Platonic problems by dropping the idea of the father of language and by letting the meaning of an expression or a text take the place of the father. Derrida also problematizes the role of the father, but he does so in a different way. He tries to show that in Plato's account of language as a representation of an origin, Plato can never get past the possibility that *this origin is concealed*. From time to time, Plato seems to be saying that this origin is only given in its representation. Derrida aims to show that, in its most radical sense, this implies that the origin of language has never been present and never will be present, but that the representation of language is an original double of this origin and introduces an inescapable detour to come to this origin. In this sense, *every* language and not only writing is of the order of the trace. The origin is only given in and as a trace.[100]

As an example, Derrida refers to the famous passage from the *Phaedo*. The origin of language is often compared to the sun, the most shining and present being. In the *Phaedo*, Plato emphasizes that the sun cannot be seen: whence we look into the sun we are blinded. Consequently, the concealment of this source of *logos* is required for us to be able to see. Instead of looking directly into the sun, Socrates suggests that we take a detour along *logos* to understand how things are. Hence, this *logos* is illuminated by a sun that conceals itself. In this sense, the origin illuminates the derived *logos* by concealing itself. This particular absence of the origin turns the relation between origin and *logos* into a problematic one. In absence of the origin, its representation is needed to disclose this origin. Thus, although the origin is the source, the *logos* is the necessary resource (*ressource*).[101] Derrida's choice of words is excellent here since it shows the fundamental ambiguity of *logos*. *Logos* as *ressource* means that *logos* is at the same time a representation or a double of its source—its re-source—and the indispensable, necessary resource for the truth of this origin.

In this way, the concealment of the origin disrupts Plato's hierarchy of truth and language as well as Plato's hierarchy of living speech and dead writing. If the distinction between *logos* and writing runs parallel to the presence and the absence of the father, then the primary absence of the father complicates and effaces this distinction. Up to now we noted that writing is a danger for Plato since it presents itself as something it is not. Here we see how this appearance of writing goes at the heart of the hierarchy between truth and language. Truth cannot be approached in its simple presence but requires the detour of language for its disclosure. Consequently, writing and *logos* are marked by the *same* absence of the father. Now we see why the capacity of writing to lead in a different direction is in fact, for Plato, a form of leading astray: unlike *logos*, writing does not move *toward* the origin, but embarks on another path. Writing leads to a detour without return to the origin. Hence, the difference between *logos* and writing is imperative for Plato. However, if the origin has never been present, how do we know that *logos* is indeed turned toward the truth? Is *logos* not in the same situation as writing? Is it not likewise a representation of something that still is in need of disclosure? If this is the case, Derrida's conclusions make sense: the originary concealment of the truth of *logos* conditions disclosure as such. Due to this primary disappearance of "the good-sun-father-capital," language is always in the first place writing, that is, a supplement that promises an origin without being able to present it:

> The disappearance of truth as presence, the withdrawal of the present origin of presence, is the condition of all (manifestation of) truth. Nontruth is the truth. Nonpresence is presence. *Différance*, the disappearance of any originary presence, is *at once* the condition of possibility

> *and* the condition of impossibility of truth. At once. "At once" means that the being-present (*on*) in its truth, in the presence of its identity and in the identity of its presence, *is doubled* as soon as it appears, as soon as it presents itself. *It appears, in its essence, as* the possibility of its own most proper non-truth, of its pseudo-truth reflected in the icon, the phantasm, or the simulacrum.[102]

As soon as an origin appears, it appears in the form of its double. Language is the medium of truth, and language indeed brings beings to presence but always on the basis of displacement: language does not show a being as it is, but always in displacement. This displacement is due to the fact that language is supplementary: *it is added to a being in order to let this being appear*. Thus, Derrida agrees with Heidegger that no being is or appears without language, and he agrees that language concerns bringing to presence out of concealment, but he adds that no expression coincides with its event of manifestation. Every presencing or truth is a "pseudo-truth," a truth that is conditioned by displacement and *pseudos*. Language is first and foremost trace. The primacy of writing is nothing but the primacy of concealment as *pseudos*. In this sense, Derrida and Heidegger differ. Heidegger remains Platonic in the sense that the concealment of writing remains a secondary form of concealment: for him, *pseudos* is always secondary in contrast to *lēthē*. The essence of *lēthē* can be kept in what is experienced as unconcealment as such: saying as showing. In this way, the original concealment and the original unconcealment are purified from any representation. For Derrida, however, the question of the essence is always already problematized since every essence is only given as and in a representation. Displacement precedes disclosure because no expressing is a simple bringing to presence of a being; every expressing is always also a supplement.[103]

Transference as Grafting and Quoting

In the discussion of the notion of the text in Ricoeur's work, I noted that for Ricoeur the decontextualization and the recontextualization of the text were essential features. To understand this recontextualization, Ricoeur takes the autonomy and the integral character of the text—the world of the text, its plot, and so on—as his point of departure: the whole of the text can be recontextualized because it is independent of any particular context. For Derrida, the idea of recontextualization is also important, but he approaches it in a different way. The main models he uses to describe how a text can be decontextualized and recontextualized are the models of quoting and grafting.[104] By proposing quoting as a model for recontextualization, he stresses that recontextualization involves an intrinsic violation of the whole of the text and introduces necessarily heterogeneous elements (the inscription of references to other texts) that disrupt the supposed integral character of a text. A quote isolates a part of a text and incorporates it into another context. If a quote is inscribed in another text, then its original context is lost. This loss is typical for the repeatability of language understood as citation: "This citationality, duplication, or duplicity, this iterability of the mark is not an accident of an anomaly, but is that (normal/abnormal) without which a mark could no longer even have a so-called 'normal' functioning. What would a mark be that one could not cite? And whose origin could not be lost on the way."[105] As a consequence of this loss, the meaning of the quote can be altered considerably; a quote may mislead us with respect to the original meaning. Even if an author tries to avoid any form of manipulation as he or she quotes, he or she nevertheless changes its meaning because of its changed context. By placing it into another context, the original text relates to different topics and refers to new texts. Therefore, every quotation or citation is a violent operation that displaces the text and its meaning by disrupting the original composition of the text.

This latter point shows why, for Ricoeur, Derrida's model of quoting misses the importance of semantics and discourse in his attention to writing. In his brief comments on Derrida, Ricoeur insists on the difference between semantics and semiotics. He argues that Derrida has missed this difference in his attention to *différance,* which would belong to the domain of semiotics.[106] To formulate Ricoeur's objections in terms of quoting, we could say that from his perspective, quoting belongs to the level of semiotics—it incorporates signs in a new complex of signs—and misses the realm of meaning because meaning itself *belongs only to the whole of discourse*—to the whole of the text in this case. Meaning belongs to the unity of a text and does not belong to one of its parts. Because quoting does not respect this whole, Derrida's model would miss the semantic level altogether.

To respond to Ricoeur's objection, one should note that Derrida's descriptions of quotations do not simply concern parts of particular texts. It is a model that describes what happens when a text is transferred from one context to another. Such a transference is like quoting. Behind this conception lies the idea that the meaning of a text *depends* on the context in which it is understood. Transmitting a text has drastic consequences because it *exscribes* a text from an old context: a text *loses* meaning in transference. Consequently, a text does not simply *have* a meaning in Derrida's conception. Its meaning is an effect of the text *and* the context in which it is inscribed. Thus, transference as exscription and inscription implies both a loss and a gain of meaning. Moreover, this loss and gain are not compatible, but disproportionate. They cannot be computed in terms of each other. The recontextualization of a quote brings into play other references to other texts, which were not given in the old context. These new references displace the original text, but also create a new, unheard-of context for the quote, thus allowing the citation to speak in unthought-of ways.

The displacement and distortion at the heart of quoting might give the impression that quoting is always concerned with a certain lack of loyalty or fidelity to the text and its meaning. Especially from the perspective of Ricoeur's idea of the integrality of the text, this impression might impose itself on us. However, Derrida claims the opposite. In *Mémoires pour Paul de Man*, he notes that, after the death of one's conversation partner, the possibility to remember and to speak in the memory of the one who has departed us involves quoting. In fact, the fidelity to a text, to an author or to a deceased conversation partner *requires* that one quotes. As he writes,

> Ultimately, at the very extremity of the most ambiguous fidelity, a discourse "in memory of" might even wish only to quote, always supposing that one knows where a quotation begins and where to end it. Fidelity requires that one quote, in the desire to let the other speak; and fidelity requires that one not just quote, not restrict oneself to quoting. It is with the law of this double law that we are here engaged, and this is also the double law of Mnemosyne—unless it is the common law of the double source, Mnemosyne/Lethe: source of memory, source of forgetting.[107]

Quotation allows for the survival of someone else's utterances beyond the context and the life in which he or she uttered them. In this sense, quotation precedes interpretation. Moreover, a quote is always concerned with the effort to let someone else speak. In this sense, a quote is always a work of remembrance: we quote in order not to forget. One might think that, ideally, such a remembrance in which we let the other speak requires that we *only* quote. If we would only quote the words of the other, only the other would speak. However, quotation as a model of the text and of remembrance problematizes this ideal situation in a double sense: first, a quote is always only a fragment; and secondly, a quote always implies contamination. When Derrida writes, "a discourse 'in memory of' might even wish only to quote, always supposing that one knows where a quotation begins and where to end it," he states these two problems at once.

Since a quote is only a fragment one does not know "where to end it"; that is to say, one could always supplement this quote with other words of the other. Since the speech of the other, like writing, lacks any ultimate integrality, it also lacks clear boundaries telling us where to begin and where to end. Since these supplements might give rise to different readings and different interpretations of the words of the other we never know when we have quoted enough. In fact, the addition of the supplement is that which gives to read, as Derrida writes, "Adding, here, is nothing other than giving to read."[108] The model of quotation implies that we lack any measure that would allow us to conclude at some point that our quotations have done justice to what the other has to say. Consequently, quoting is never simply quoting. In remembering, one cannot "restrict oneself to quoting" since in addition one has to decide the undecidable, namely where to begin and where to end the quote. This problem of having to decide where to begin and where to end is also part of a reconstruction of Derrida's possible response to Ricoeur. Since for Derrida the meaning of a text is always the effect of an interplay between text and context, the boundaries of the semantic whole of a text always still need to be determined. Hence the question of the semantic integrality of the text is marked by the problem of having to decide where to begin and where to end this whole.

Something else is also at stake when Derrida suggests that we do not know "where a quotation begins." This beginning concerns the demarcation of a quote in a text or a speech in which it is quoted. One might object to Derrida's suggestion by saying that it is perfectly clear, especially in a text, where a quotation begins, namely with the quotation marks. However, to capture what he means here we need to inquire into the meaning and the consequences of the decision involved in quoting. By the decision where to begin and to end the quote—that is to say, by the decision where to put the quotation marks—the one who quotes leaves its traces on the quote. The one who quotes codetermines how the other speaks in this effort to let the other speak. Therefore, this letting is not identical to the Heideggerian letting of *lassen* and *Gelassenheit*. Heidegger notes in "*Der Spruch des Anaximander*," when he interprets the Greek notion of *dikē*, that *dikē* implies that we give to the other what properly belongs to him or her.[109] For Derrida, however, this letting in letting the other speak does not simply give to the other that which is proper to him or her: it gives only by a contamination. Consequently, this desire to let the other speak never leads to mere quotation: it is never simply the other who speaks in quotations. In this sense, the work of remembrance as the presencing of the voice of the other is at the same time a work of forgetting that displaces and distorts this voice. This risk cannot be avoided. We can only avoid it by keeping silent. However, if we keep silent and do not quote we do not let the other speak at all.

This difficult relationship between memory and forgetting is related by Derrida to the notions of Mnemosyne as *alētheia* and of forgetting as *lēthē*. In this sense, the model of quoting and quotation does not only provide us with his response to Ricoeur's emphasis on the semantic unity of a text, but it is also Derrida's entrance to a discussion of the Heideggerian notions of *alētheia* and *lēthē*.

Derrida's Critique of Heidegger's Account of Language

Derrida's well-known notion of *logocentrism* can be defined as the tendency in the history of philosophy to think writing as a derivative of *logos* or speech. He reckons Heidegger as one of the many philosophers—such as Plato, Husserl, and Rousseau—in whose work this logocentric motive can be discerned.[110] In light of our explication of Heidegger's account of *logos* in the previous chapter, it will come as no surprise that logocentrism concerns *logos* as saying and showing as well as *logos* as *legein* and gathering.

Showing, Sign, and Writing

To show how the account of language as showing creates a hierarchy between speech and writing in Heidegger's thought, Derrida finds an important clue in his description of the sign. Both in *Sein und Zeit* and *Unterwegs zur Sprache,* Heidegger argues that the notion of the sign (*Zeichen*) should be interpreted in light of its etymological relation to showing (*Zeigen*).[111] In *Unterwegs zur Sprache,* he is very clear about this relation: "*The essential being of language is Saying as Showing.* Its showing character is not based on signs of any kind; rather, all signs arise from a showing within whose realm and for whose purposes they can be signs."[112] From a Derridean point of view, this quote manifests a logocentrism beyond any doubt. Every sign is grounded in a showing that precedes it, and every sign merely serves showing. In this sense, the sign is indeed a mere derivative. Moreover, since this showing arises in and as saying, it is clear that writing and written signs can only be accounted for as derivatives from speech.

Before penetrating more deeply into Derrida's concerns, let me recall that for Heidegger this account of sign, saying, and showing is not metaphysical in nature. On the contrary, for him this account arises in a *critique* of an instrumental, metaphysical understanding of language as *representation*. In fact, in *Unterwegs zur Sprache*, Heidegger notes that the Stoic account of language as an instrument for signification implies a rupture with Aristotle's account of language that would still experience language as letting appear.[113] The change the Stoics brought about in their account of language coincides with the change in the essence of truth that takes place in the history of metaphysics. As such, Heidegger's analysis of the sign as a derivative of showing concerns his critique of metaphysics as well as the metaphysical conception of truth as agreement.

Considered from this point of view, Derrida's tendency to regard Heidegger's conception of the sign as a form of logocentrism and of metaphysics of presence is at least somewhat misleading: it tends to conceal the particular difference between Heidegger's thought and traditional metaphysics, which Heidegger articulates precisely as the relation between sign and showing.[114] Nevertheless, Derrida's distortion clarifies Heidegger's thought as well. Heidegger's dismissal of the sign is not an incidental case. Rather, it is a symptom of a more general tendency in his thought to subsume writing under saying. Let me point out a few important passages in his work where we can clearly find this subsumption.

In the first place, in his *Parmenides* lectures, Heidegger remarks that Plato's dialogues complete and mark the end of the fundamental Greek experience of saying as showing. Thinking saying (*das denkende Sagen*) would get the form of dialogue in Plato's thought. Plato's attention to dialogue would affirm the primacy (*Vorrang*) of immediately spoken words over written words.[115]

In the second place, in *Was heißt Denken?* Heidegger argues that Socrates is the most pure thinker of Western philosophy *because* he did not write.[116] With a play on the different meanings of the German verb *ziehen*, Heidegger notes that Socrates placed himself in the draft (*Zugwind*) of the draw (*Zug*) that relates (*Bezug*) us to what withdraws (*Entziehen*) itself. That which withdraws itself—the as yet unthought—is for Heidegger that which remains to be thought.

Thinking as thinking being relates always to being as that which withdraws itself. Therefore, only someone who places himself in the draft that draws to this unthought can genuinely be called a thinker. As opposed to Socrates, Heidegger describes the thinkers in Western philosophy that wrote as people who are no longer placed within this wind that carries the destiny of being. Instead, by writing they fled out of the wind into a protective shelter (*Windschatten*).[117] The problem with writing is thus that it flees from thinking: "For anyone who begins to write out of thoughtfulness must inevitably be like those people who run to seek refuge from any draft too strong for them."[118]

Since writing is fleeing from thinking, the distinction between writing and thinking runs parallel to another distinction in *Was heißt Denken?*[119] In our time, according to Heidegger, we tend to read the texts of ancient philosophers as an expression of their points of view. As opposed to this conception of language as communication, which is the model of writing and of fleeing for thinking, he describes the language of the genuine thinker as showing: a thinker *says* what is. Reading a philosophical text is not only repeating the points of view of this thinker, but it is accompanied by its own task: it requires that we think what remains *unthought* in the work of a philosopher. According to Heidegger, "The unthought is the greatest gift that thinking can bestow."[120] The unthought is the greatest gift because it cannot be recapitulated as the points of view of a philosopher. Rather, it opens up the task of thinking, namely, to be drawn to what withdraws itself.

Heidegger's attention to the unthought of a *text* shows that his remarks on writing as fleeing from thinking are at least somewhat ambiguous: a text is not a mere loss, it also gives much to think. Yet, this does not mean that this gift is grounded in the textuality of the text. On the contrary. Heidegger notes, "Plato and Aristotle speak in what is still our language of today. Parmenides and Heraclitus, too, think in what is still our realm of ideas."[121] Thus, Plato's and Aristotle's texts give to think their unthought since Plato and Aristotle still *speak* in our language. Since we belong to the same language and the same realm of thought as our tradition, we are capable of thinking its unthought. This shows that Heidegger develops in *Was heißt Denken?* a contrast between the triple saying, thinking, and belonging (to a language or a history) and the triple writing, fleeing from thought, and a conception of history that approaches history as something that has passed and that is of no concern to our present, historical situation. This contrast is in fact a contrast between disclosure and displacement, between truth and (secondary) untruth: Each term of the latter triple is a displacement and a concealment of the primordial task of thinking to bring into presence, that is, to disclose out of a belonging.

To grasp what is at stake in this passage of *Was heißt Denken?* and to show that it is indeed this belonging that accounts for the possibility of thinking, let me recall how Heidegger describes the transition from Greek to Latin in his *Parmenides* lectures: the Latin translations of Greek thought do not give rise to thinking since Latin is a language in which the unthought possibilities of the Greek cannot be thought.[122] Hence, displacement in the form of translation threatens the possibility of thinking since it might disseminate an original thinking in a sterile environment, that is, an environment that does not give to think. Hence we see how thinking as the disclosure of the unthought is distinguished in Heidegger's thought from the displacements involved in writing and other forms of transference.

Clearly, it is exactly the possibility of a dissemination in a sterile context that marks Derrida's *l'écriture*. Hence, even though Derrida is as intrigued by the primacy of concealment and of the unthought of a text as Heidegger is, he insists that our relation to this unthought can never be separated from dangers of dissemination at the heart of displacement. In fact, Derrida emphasizes the problem of the double bind here. For Heidegger, thinking is only possible in fertile environment; hence, it is necessary to tame the dissemination of writing. At the same time, thinking depends on that which is handed over to us. Yet, handing down implies displacement, and displacement necessarily carries with it the possibility of a dissemination to a sterile place. For Derrida, the history of philosophy is not a continuity of language and thought; it is a history of ruptures, cross-fertilizations, sterilities, and discontinuities.[123] The supplement of writing and of representation is a necessary supplement to showing and presencing.

In the third place, to see how Heidegger indeed tries to tame writing, Derrida points to yet another example of the hierarchy between sign and showing. For Heidegger, writing is essentially handwriting.[124] This means that he understands writing under the aspect of the hand, and he explicates this as follows: "There is a 'hand' only where beings as such appear in unconcealedness and man comports himself in a disclosing way toward beings." In this way, the essence of writing as handwriting refers us back to truth as unconcealment and to the disclosive character of the word. He adds, "In handwriting the relation [*Bezug*] of Being to man, namely the word, is inscribed in beings themselves."[125] This relation of being to the human being marks the draw (*Zug*) and the drawing (*Zeichnung*) of handwriting.

This foundation of handwriting as drawing in truth is transformed by the development of writing machines (typewriters and so on). The typewriter, Heidegger claims, is without sign and without signification because it conceals the relation of man and being through the disclosing word.[126] Here we see a more or less Platonic movement where the difference between speech and writing leads to a fundamental difference between two forms of writing: handwriting and typewriting. The first writing reflects the essence of writing and affirms once more the intrinsic relation between sign, signification, and showing. The second writing conceals this intrinsic relation. Since it obstructs the reference to an original saying and showing, Heidegger even claims that this writing is without sign (*zeichenlos*). Yet, with Derrida, one might wonder whether it makes sense to speak of the essence of writing when this essence *excludes* particular forms of writing. According to Derrida, the typewriter is merely a modern aggravation of a more encompassing *evil* of writing for Heidegger that already resounds in his account of writing as a flight from thinking: The typewriter obscures the relation between being and humans in disclosive saying.[127]

To move toward an alternative account of language, Derrida makes two important suggestions. The first stems from *La main de Heidegger* and the second from *Mémoires pour Paul de Man*. With a play on the word "*monstre*," which in the French can mean sign but is also related to the verb *montre*, to show, Derrida characterizes the Heideggerian sign as monstrous: every sign is marked by its reference to an original showing.[128] He shows in *La main de Heidegger* how this showing determines the essence of man in relation to his hand and to the essence of writing as handwriting, as I noted above. However, in the margin of this text, Derrida also uses this *monstre* in another sense—this second meaning imposes itself only in the French. Monstrous also refers to that which is beyond normality. In this second sense, a sign is monstrous if it does not refer back to an original showing. Derrida shows that Heidegger's work contains a monstrous sign in this second sense. Obviously, such a monstrous sign is unique and an exception since it is a deviation from what is normal and general. The occurrence of this unique, monstrous sign brings us back to *Mnemosyne* and in particular to Heidegger's reading of Hölderlin's poem that carries this name. After his claim in *Was heißt Denken?* that Socrates is the purest thinker because he did not write, Heidegger gives a description of how the human being relates *as a sign* to what withdraws itself. In reference to Hölderlin's phrase "*Ein Zeichen sind wir, deutungslos*" he writes, "When man is drawing into what withdraws, he points into what withdraws. As we are drawing that way we are a sign, a pointer. But we are pointing then at something that has not, not yet, been transposed [*übersetzt*] into the language of our speech. We are a sign that is not read [*deutungsloses Zeichen*]."[129] In this passage, Heidegger points to the limit situation in which thinking occurs: the human being as a thinking being points to a realm that has not yet been thought or spoken; it points to a realm that is as yet concealed. Hence, it is a sign that does not refer back to an original showing.[130] It indicates that the human being is first a sign, a trace, and a displacement of that which withdraws itself. As this monstrous sign, the human being refers to that which has never been present. Even within the realm of the disclosive capacity of human language, the draw to what withdraws itself never results in a complete presence. The movement of disclosure and presencing is at the same time a movement of concealment and absencing. As such, this sign also refers to that which will never be present. As this monstrous sign, the human being originally has the structure of the trace. This trace is the condition of possibility of disclosure: it is only as this trace that the human being can think, that is, can be drawn to what withdraws itself.

Strictly speaking, this monstrous sign also leaves its traces on the appropriate word that Heidegger longs for in his quest for the essence of language. If speaking indeed depends on the human being as a monstrous sign, then appropriation also always implies expropriation, as Heidegger sometimes admits.[131] In this case, the appropriateness of the word that is spoken and that would disclose the essence of language becomes highly problematic: the linguistic movement (*Be-wëgung*) that discloses and renders the appropriate word, is the same movement that conceals and expropriates the word. It is the ambiguity of the French notion of the monstrous that allows Derrida to argue that this reversal of the order between sign and showing does not only empirically take place at certain points in Heidegger's work, but concerns the very displacing movement at the heart of disclosure.

A second alternative or displacement in Heidegger's emphasis on showing is developed by Derrida in dialogue with Paul de Man. Remarkably, also here the alternative stems from a discussion of the problem of memory and Hölderlin's poem *Mnemosyne*.[132] Clearly, a Heideggerian concept of memory can be found in notions such as *Andenken* and *Gedächtnis*. In each of these terms, he relates memory or commemoration to the thinking of an original realm of disclosure to which all thinking and speaking belongs. Therefore, Derrida writes, "Can memory without anteriority, that is to say, without origin, become a Heideggerian theme? I do not believe so."[133] For Heidegger, Derrida argues, memory is a form of re-collection, that is, a gathering that discloses an original word or an original realm of showing. Although this realm is as yet unthought, it is of crucial importance to Heidegger's thinking since it directs thought. The important phrase "on the way" (*Unterwegs*) reflects this orientation: To be on the way to language or to thought always means to be on the way to the most original realm from which we always already speak and think. At the same time, to be on the way means that this origin is always pending: it is an origin that *has never been present and will never be given in the present*. It is never actually given to thought: it is only given in its trace.

This particular givenness of the origin intrigues Derrida. In his comments on the notion of the gift, he describes the implications of this givenness: "There is Being, but this '*es gibt*' never gives anything that is a 'present' or that is gathered in a present; it calls [*heißen*] as a promise, it calls itself a promise, a commitment, an invitation."[134] Heidegger's gift, which he thinks in the expression "*es gibt*" is not a gift that is given in a present. Rather, the gift itself is a promise; it is a "promised memory" of the original givenness of being. Usually, promise and gift are clearly separated. In the promise, a gift is not given but only promised. The promise defers the actual gift of what is promised, and when the gift is actually given, it is no longer promised to us. Of course, this is very obvious, but it raises the question of what happens in Heidegger's thought when he conflates gift and promise, when the gift is only given as a promise.

According to Derrida, a similar difficulty arises in Heidegger's notion of language: also in relation to language and in Heidegger's quest for the essence of language, the appropriate word that would grant us this essence, and thus a memory of the original realm out of which we always already speak, is never simply given as such but always in and as a promise. In fact, following de Man's explication of the infamous Heideggerian phrase *Die Sprache spricht* (Speech speaks, language speaks), Derrida notes, "Now what does Paul de Man do here? He takes note of this necessity that *Die Sprache spricht*. He takes it with a certain measure of seriousness. But in miming it, in *its* language, in German, he replaces *spricht* with *verspricht*, 'speaks' with 'promises.' This is another way of saying that the essence of speech is the promise, that there is no speaking that does not promise."¹³⁵ In light of our discussion of the relation between gift and promise, de Man's displacement of speaking (*sprechen*) to promising (*versprechen*) is not simply a distortion of Heidegger's conception of language. It rather shows an element in this thinking that escapes the primacy of showing and appropriation. Since the essence of language is never given as such, it is only present as a promise and as a trace. This has consequences for the Heideggerian quest for an appropriate word. A word in its proper place is a word that says and shows exactly what it says and shows. This is the word Heidegger is looking for in *Unterwegs zur Sprache* when he writes: "But when the issue is to put into language something which has never yet been spoken, then everything depends on whether language gives or withholds [*versagen*] the appropriate word."¹³⁶ However, when this word is a promising word as well, it cannot be called "appropriate" as such since it refers beyond that which is disclosed in the present to a future that it cannot show or say but only promise. In this sense, the word, even the appropriate one, is a promise and a trace of a future that will never be present. Differently put, as a promise, this word says more than it says; it promises beyond that which it shows.

This latter dimension brings us to another aspect of de Man's reinterpretation of the essence of language. If we say more than we want to say, we "made a slip of the tongue" or we "let our tongue run away with us." In German, we can say the same thing in such a simple way that the relation to the previous discussion is immediately clear: the verb *sich versprechen* exactly says that we say more than we want to say or made a slip of the tongue. When Paul de Man replaces Heidegger's *die Sprache spricht* with *die Sprache verspricht sich,* he refers to this meaning of *sich versprechen,* as Derrida notes, "[Paul de Man] implies that when the *sprechen* of speech is affected by a 'ver-,' it not only becomes a promisor, but it also becomes unsettled, disturbed, corrupted, perverted, affected by a kind of fatal drift. You know that in German the prefix 'ver-' very often has this meaning."¹³⁷ This quote tells us that the promising character of language relates every word to a corruption, a contamination, and a distortion. Clearly, the corruption at stake here is the corruption of the disclosure of language by a displacement toward the future that it cannot account for and that it cannot manifest. I have already mentioned a few times the relation between *pseudos* and trace. Heidegger translates *pseudos* often as *verstellen*. This word is also marked by the prefix "ver-," and it also refers to the disturbing, distorting, and displacing character of *pseudos*. But also the term *versprechen* itself is used in this sense by Heidegger. He uses it in his reading of Trakl where, as Derrida notes, it refers to the corruption of the essence: this verb *versprechen* expresses here the *Verwesung*, the decay of the human species (*Geschlecht*).[138] Hence, Heidegger explicates in a number of ways how this prefix "ver-" indeed refers to a corruption of the essence. In this sense, *versprechen* and *sich versprechen* refer to such a displacement of the essence of language as *Sprache*.

Yet, in distinction to Derrida and de Man, Heidegger maintains a hierarchy between this essence of language and its decaying non-essence (*Unwesen*). Consequently, the corruption and the displacement always refer back to an original showing, as we noted before. Therefore Derrida notes, as I quoted above, that the Heideggerian memory always refers to an origin. Derrida and de Man, however, encounter this displacing quality of language in the very essence of language itself since no language merely says and shows but also always promises to show and thus displaces the actual showing toward the announcement of a future that will never be given in the present. What is actually shown by Heidegger is only a trace of that which is promised to be shown. Since the promised gift can only be related to by means of a promising trace, the trace affects the gift and upsets and corrupts the essence of language as *Sage*.[139] This promising displacement, this *pseudos* at the heart of the disclosure of language has fundamental implications for Derrida's assessment of the relation between truth and untruth, as we shall see below, but before we discuss this we first need to come to terms with Heidegger's understanding of the orientation of thinking and Derrida's interpretation of it.

Gathering Places and Idioms

The orientation and direction of thinking can only be understood if we interpret it in relation to the notion of gathering, this other crucial dimension of Heidegger's conception of language. It is this gathering that provides an orientation to the Heideggerian being on the way and that distinguishes this being on the way from what Derrida calls "*errance*" or wandering: "It must gather itself in the One, carry and carry itself towards the essence assigned to it, migration—but not wandering (*errance*)."[140]

In "*La main de Heidegger*" Derrida does not only note how Heidegger relates the human hand to showing (*monstration*); he also argues that this co-belonging of hand and language refers back to Heidegger's account of the gathering of language.[141] The place and the role of this gathering lead to a particular difference between Heidegger's and Derrida's thought on language. To some extent, Derrida's critique of this theme is similar to the critique he develops in the 1970s of Ricoeur's thought. Although Ricoeur is attentive to the multiplicity of interpretations and meanings, the notion of polysemy is a multiplicity that is regulated by a certain unity of meaning, as Derrida notes, and therefore different from dissemination since this term "marks an irreducible and *generative* multiplicity."[142] Also in his critique on Heidegger's gathering, Derrida insists on this productive character of multiplicity that is excluded by the motive of gathering: although Heidegger allows for and even insists on a certain multiplicity and polysemy, the Heideggerian "'good' polysemy" implies a plurality that lets itself be gathered in a "'higher' univocity." Derrida claims, "On several occasions, Heidegger shows himself receptive to what could be called a 'good' polysemy, that of poetic language and of the 'great poet.' This polysemy must let itself be *gathered* in a 'higher' univocity and in the oneness of a harmony (*Einklang*)."[143] This difference between a good and a bad polysemy repeats the Platonic distinction between a good and a bad writing. In Heidegger's work, it appears in light of language as gathering, and it results in a distinction between a writing that serves the gathering corresponding to the poeticizing of a great poet and a writing that merely disseminates, which is the writing of those who poeticize poorly. To trace this motive in Heidegger's work, Derrida focuses in "*La main de Heidegger*" as well as in *De l'esprit* on "*Die Sprache im*

Gedicht." In the former paper, which bears the subtitle *Geschlecht II*, he shows in multiple ways how Heidegger's discussion of the word *Geschlecht* in Trakl's poetry indeed pays attention to the polysemy of this word, but also that it concerns here a polysemy "towards a certain unity that gathers this multiplicity." In *De l'esprit,* Derrida demonstrates that in the same reading of Trakl a similar emphasis on the primacy of gathering can be found in Heidegger's interpretation of the word *Geist.*[144]

Rather than repeating this reading, I want to point out that Derrida has indeed captured three crucial motives of Heidegger's essay on Trakl. These motives can already be found on the very first pages of this essay. Here, Heidegger explains that he will undertake an explication (*Erörterung*) of Trakl's poems (*Dichtungen*). Such an explication, as the German word indicates, aims to arrive at the place (*Ort*) out of which the poet and each of the poems speak; as such, the place is a place of gathering.[145] Thus, the task of the *Erörterung* is to explicate the place that gathers Georg Trakl's poetic Saying into his poetic work [*Gedicht*].[146] Usually, one would translate *Gedicht* also as poem. However, to emphasize the crucial difference between the multiplicity of poems (*Dichtungen*) and this poem (*Gedicht*), I will leave the word *Gedicht* untranslated.

What exactly is this *Gedicht* in relation to the poems? Heidegger tells us that every genuinely great poet has a unique *Gedicht* out of which he or she poeticizes. In this sense, the *Gedicht* is the *origin* of a poet's poeticizing. Moreover, it is a unique and *singular* origin: the *Gedicht* is the proper, idiomatic language of this poet. In relation to the actual poems, Heidegger notes that neither actual poem nor the collection of all poems coincides with the poet's *Gedicht*. He claims, "The *Gedicht* of a poet remains unspoken."[147] Nevertheless, each and every poem speaks out of this *Gedicht* and is moved by it. As such, the *Gedicht* is the unthought, singular place that *gathers* all the poems of a great poet in their origin.[148]

These three motives—the *Gedicht* as an origin of a poet's work, the *Gedicht* as the singular place of the poet's idiom, and the *Gedicht* as the unthought gathering place of the poet's poems—determine

Heidegger's explication of Trakl's poetry as *Erörterung*. The *Gedicht* as the as yet unthought attracts the thinker in its dialogue with the poetry of Trakl. To be on the way to the poet's language and to make an experience with this poetic language coincides with such an explication of the *Gedicht*.[149] Thus, Heidegger's explication of Trakl does not approach this poetry neutrally. These three motives shape or inform this explication and provide it with its typical orientation: it is a quest for an original place that gathers the idiom and the singular saying out of which all of the great poet's poems speak.

Derrida emphasizes these three motives. The motive of gathering tames the reading of this poetry since it prescribes that to which the thinker is on its way as a "gathering in the one." The migration at work in this being on the way to the poet's language is not carried away in the "wandering" (*errance*) that marks writing but is rather carried toward an origin.[150] To understand the nature of this origin, the third motive of the idiomatic character of the *Gedicht* is crucial. Derrida gives numerous examples that show how Heidegger's explication is idiomatic in character. For instance, he notes how Heidegger's account of *Geschlecht* and *Geist* is built upon the specific meanings of these words and its derivatives in the depths of the German language. Apparently, explication presupposes the rootedness in this singular, German language. It is this particular idiom that orients the entire explication and renders it untranslatable.[151] This implies also that the explication is a form of purification that wards off any contamination from the outside. Instead of affirming the multiplicity of languages, it gathers itself toward the unique idiom of the German language. If one asks what would happen if this idiom is transformed, if the context of a word is altered, or if these words are uprooted from this particular German context and transferred to another one, Heidegger's response would be that such a transition may of course happen and has often happened, but that it only results in an obstruction for thinking since it robs thinking of the unique possibilities that are to be found in the German language. For Heidegger, the difference between gathering and multiplication is the difference between a fruitful explication that gives rise to thought and a sterile transference that leads to the decay of thinking. As Derrida notes, the privilege of the Greek and the German language with regard to thinking are "absolute."[152] In fact, in Heidegger's reading of Trakl and especially in his interpretation of the word *Geist,* it turns out that even the Greek language is not capable of disclosing the unheard-of possibilities of the word *Geist* that the German language holds in store. At any rate, in his interview with *Der Spiegel,* Heidegger leaves no doubts as to the primacy of the German language over any Roman one in relation to thinking: The French would have told him again and again that once they start thinking, they start speaking German.[153] In sum, explication as *Erörterung* as well as thinking can only mean going more deeply into the unique idiom of the German language.

This primacy of the German language and the movement of explication as a movement into the roots of this unique idiom are typical for Heidegger. In fact, he uses at several occasions the figure of a tree that is nourished by the soil in which it is rooted and which can only grow by getting rooted more deeply into this soil. This figure prescribes his method, his being on the way as an appropriation of the place (*Ort*) out of which we speak, poeticize, or think. In contrast to this image that depends on the fertility of rootedness, Derrida employs a powerful counter-image that is the botanical variant of quoting: the figure of *grafting.* Transference is like grafting a branch onto another rootstock.[154] In this sense, a text or a word is never at home or in its proper environment: it is always already a grafted branch that could be grafted onto another rootstock as well. Therefore, it is always foreign to and different from the context in which it is embedded. In the model of grafting, generative multiplicity by means of transference cannot be reduced to a movement of gathering, according to Derrida.

His attention to transference and grafting does not mean that Derrida would not be interested in the idiomatic character of language. Quite the contrary: a genuine multiplicity presupposes the idiomatic character of language. However, the idea of a unique idiom or a unique language for thinking is problematic. Instead, Derrida tries to relate thinking to the multiplicity of idioms. It is not the task of thinking to keep a particular idiom pure and to go more deeply into the roots and origins of this idiom. Rather, the chance of thinking consists in risking the transition from one idiom to another. This particular approach to the multiplicity of idioms plays a huge role in Derrida's own reading of poetry, in particular in his reading of Paul Celan's poetry. In the interview *La Langue n'appartient pas* on Celan's poetry, he asks, "how can one be in favor of the greatest idiomaticity—which one must be, I think—while resisting nationalist ideology?" He answers his own question by pointing to the task of those he calls not simply the poets, but the *translator*-poets: "It is their task to explain, to teach, that one can cultivate and invent an idiom, because it is not a matter of cultivating a given idiom but of producing the idiom." Hence, rather than trying to appropriate an idiom or poeticize an already given *Gedicht* in each poem, it is the task of the poet to invent and produce a new idiom. This is also the task of translation: rather than simply affirming the untranslatability of certain idioms, the translator has the poetic task to translate beyond the interruption between two idioms and to invent a new idiom in a given language, even though the resulting idiom will never be identical to the original idiom from which it stems. This task or chance of the translator is also the chance of thinking. In *Béliers,* Derrida writes, "*I must* translate, transfer, transport (*übertragen*) the untranslatable in another turn even where, translated, it remains untranslatable."[155]

If this is the chance for thinking, neither philosophy nor thinking can be aligned with one unique language or one unique idiom since the transference between multiple, singular languages is the realm of the philosophic itself, as Derrida writes in "*Envoi*": "The philosophical . . . can no longer in this case allow itself to be shut up within the closure of a single idiom, without thereby being set afloat, neutral and disembodied, far from every body of language. The simply philosophical finds itself caught up in advance in a multiple body, a linguistic duality or duel, in the zone of a bilingualism that it can no longer efface without effacing itself."[156] This transference between languages, as he adds in *Mémoires pour Paul de Man,* is the proper place for deconstruction, and, if we can put it like this, the unique phenomenon to which his account of language pays tribute. He writes, "If I had to risk a single definition of deconstruction, one as brief, elliptical, and economical as a password, I would say simply and without overstatement: *plus d'une langue*—both more than a language and no more of *a* language."[157] Derrida's deconstruction is thus different from a Heideggerian dismantling that dismantles in the name of something, which is a more primordial experience of being and thinking. Deconstruction as the experience of dissemination aims rather at the phenomenon of transference and differentiation itself: it is a way or a passage that coincides with the transference of language in the experience of a *plus d'une langue*. It is not a migration toward the unique language of thinking but rather a wandering in which the multiplicity of languages provides the chance for thinking.

Mnemosyne / *Lēthē*

To keep my promise to show the implications of Derrida's reading for the themes of truth and untruth, let me return to *Mémoires pour Paul de Man*. We have already seen that for Derrida memory is always of the order of the distorting promise. As such, it problematizes the relation between gathering and thinking memory (*Gedächtnis*) to which Heidegger points in *Was heißt Denken?* As Derrida writes, "Its memory will promise but never provide a chance for re-collecting itself, for the *Versammlung* in which a thinking of being could collect itself."[158] Moreover, as I already noted, memory as Mnemosyne is a name for *alētheia*. What does this tell us about Derrida's understanding of the relation between *alētheia, pseudos,* and *lēthē*?

To answer this question, let me first sketch a particular difficulty that arises out of Derrida's comments on Heidegger in *Mémoires pour Paul de Man*. To introduce it, I quote once more a conclusion from "*Actes*": "Can memory without anteriority, that is to say, without origin, become a Heideggerian theme? I do not believe so." A "memory without origin" refers to an account of memory in which that which is commemorated cannot be presented and has never been present. One of the examples Derrida mentions, the commemoration of those who have deceased, show that memory is marked by a particular finitude: memory is "the trace of the other in us." As such, memory confronts us with an absence that cannot be recuperated in a presence. In this sense, true memory is always a memory marked by a double law, namely the law of Mnemosyne and *Lēthē*: this memory commemorates that it can never compensate for the loss of the other. It is a memory that remembers forgetting, and as such a work of mourning: "We recalled ourselves to the name Mnemosyne, and we recalled, in the name of Mnemosyne, that *one must not forget Lethe.*"[159] This latter comment can be translated in more Heideggerian terms. If we do so, Derrida suggests in this quote that a "memory without origin" can be thought as a form of truth as unconcealment (*alētheia*) that remembers untruth as simple concealment (*lēthē*). This leads to our problem. If this translation makes sense, then we have to conclude that Heidegger *does* think such a "memory without origin." In the previous chapter, I demonstrated that Heidegger's explication of Plato's myth of the river *Lēthē,* interprets this *muthos* as a locus of *alētheia* where the essence of simple concealment, *lēthē,* is preserved and remembered as the provenance of the essence of the human being. Is this not a "memory without origin" in Derrida's sense of the word?

To understand what is at stake here, we need to be aware of the true scope of this problem. Derrida notes at the end of "*Actes*" that he has focused "a certain voice of the Heideggerian text," and that Heidegger's text has more than one voice. Nevertheless, "the voice in question often appears dominant."[160] This applies to Heidegger's comments in his *Parmenides* lectures. Even though he clearly attempts to think a memory without origin in the discussed passages, it remains to be seen whether his attempt does run aground due to the particular account of *muthos* that accompanies it. He interprets *muthos* as a form of disclosive saying thanks to which the essence of simple concealment can be preserved. For Derrida, however, the language that corresponds to a memory without origin cannot be understood as disclosive saying.

In his account of Paul de Man's understanding of mourning, he indicates the kind of language involved in this memory: "True 'mourning' seems to dictate only a tendency: the tendency to accept incomprehension, to leave a place for it, and to enumerate coldly, almost like death itself, those modes of language which, in short, deny the whole rhetoricity of the true." Why is this denial necessary? Derrida argues that the language of mourning and memory is of the order of a trace. This means the following: "This trace results in speech always saying something other than what it says: it says the other who speaks 'before' and 'outside' it." Hence, the language of memory is a language that does not bring to presence—it is not involved in presencing as such—but is a saying that refers back to something that cannot be presented. Memory as a form of truth that truly remembers a forgetting, a *lēthē*, requires a language that adopts the form of "traces which themselves never occupy the form of presence." Consequently, this language can never be a language that says or discloses the essence of simple concealment. It needs to be a language that is neither pure truth nor pure lack of truth since it needs to keep the difference between truth and untruth, between *alētheia* and *lēthē* in memory: "We must think at the same time the two sources: Mnemosyne, Lethe. Translate this, if you like, as: we must keep in memory the difference of Lethe from Memory, which we may call *aletheia*."[161] Thus, to account for myth as a disclosive saying would ultimately efface the remembrance of forgetting. Hence, Heidegger's account of *muthos* contradicts that which this *muthos* should achieve in relation to *lēthē*, namely preserve its remembrance. To be able to be a "memory without origin," myth should not be a disclosive saying such but should have, like allegory and, as we shall see in the next chapter, like metaphor, a different truth value: Only a contamination of concealment and unconcealment can keep in memory the difference "Mnemosyne, Lethe." The truth value of this difference is the truth value corresponding to a language that traces an absence that it cannot present: the dangerous and distorting untruth of *pseudos*. For Derrida, the trace does not distort the realm of presencing that would precede it, as Heidegger argues. For Derrida, the trace as *pseudos* differentiates *alētheia* and *lēthē* and thus refers the realm of disclosure back to its unheard-of and unsaid provenance in displacement.

THREE

Inventions of Metaphor

Mockingbirds are the true artists of the bird kingdom. Which is to say, although they're born with a song of their own, an innate riff that happens to be one of the most versatile of all ornithological expressions, mockingbirds aren't content to merely play the hand that is dealt them. Like all artists, they are out to *rearrange* reality. Innovative, willful, daring, not bound by the rules to which others may blindly adhere, the mockingbird collects snatches of birdsong from this tree and that field, appropriates them, places them in new and unexpected contexts, recreates the world from the world.

—Tom Robbins, *Skinny Legs and All*

But the greatest thing by far is to be a master of metaphor. It is the only thing that cannot be learnt from others; and it is also a sign of genius, since a good metaphor implies an intuitive perception of the similarity in dissimilars.

—Aristotle, *Poetics*

In Heidegger's work, poetic language plays a crucial role to think the essence of language as the disclosure of being. In the wake of his work, contemporary hermeneutics and deconstruction have developed a keen interest in poetics. In particular, much attention has been paid to the use of metaphor and mimesis as important elements of the innovative and disclosive aspects of the poetic dimension of language. However, although these developments are indebted to Heidegger, for him neither metaphor nor mimesis are examples of language as saying. This confronts us with a particular problem: How to relate

Heidegger's tendency to interpret metaphor and mimesis as metaphysical notions to the way his thought is inherited by the work of Ricoeur and Derrida on poetics?

The key to answering this question can be found in the particular nature of metaphor and mimesis. This key also demonstrates why these phenomena are of high interest to the present study. Metaphor, even in its most general sense, is understood as revealing a resemblance by its deviation from our common, everyday use of language. Thus, the disclosure of metaphor occurs as a displacement of common language. Similarly, the complex notion of mimesis always involves both representation and presentation. For Aristotle, human action is imitated in a tragedy, but it is also shown and presented in an elevated way. Thus, mimesis requires a displacement from everyday reality in order to disclose this reality on another level. Consequently, both metaphor and mimesis are located at the intersection of disclosure and displacement. This basic insight will guide me through this and the next chapter to understand why Heidegger dismisses metaphor and mimesis as belonging to metaphysics and how Ricoeur and Derrida aim at more positive, though mutually distinct appreciations of these notions and how they assess Heidegger's critique of them.

HEIDEGGER'S CRITIQUE OF METAPHOR

The hermeneutic conception of metaphor in the work of Gadamer and Ricoeur is inspired by Heidegger's understanding of language as disclosure. Against this background, Heidegger's dismissal of metaphor might be quite unsettling for a hermeneutic conception of metaphor. The common way to neutralize Heidegger's dismissal is to make the following two claims. First, Heidegger's *frequent use of metaphors* in his own work would contradict his dismissal of metaphor. Secondly, Heidegger's dismissal of metaphor would be confined to a particular Platonic conception of metaphor aligned to a metaphysical distinction between the sensible and the intelligible. By confining himself to this concept of metaphor, Heidegger would have missed the opportunity to discuss metaphor from a more Aristotelian point of view. From such a point of view, the disclosure of resemblance would be the defining characteristic of metaphor.[1]

It remains to be seen to what extent this strategy is helpful. In this section, I want to discuss Heidegger's comments on metaphor along three lines of thought. First I will discuss his claim that metaphor belongs to metaphysics. This is a well-known discussion. Nevertheless, I incorporate it not only for completeness' sake but also to show how other elements, irreducible to a Platonic metaphysics, are also part of Heidegger's critique of metaphor. The second and third line of thought will explore two of those elements. The second line examines Heidegger's famous claim that the expression "language is the house of being" should not be understood as a metaphor.[2] The third line analyzes Heidegger's comments on metaphor in *Unterwegs zur Sprache* as comments on an Aristotelian conception of the liveliness of metaphor rather than on a Platonic one.

Heidegger on the Metaphysics Intrinsic to Metaphor

One of the most famous comments on metaphor can be found in *Der Satz vom Grund,* where Heidegger writes,

> The idea of "transposing" and of metaphor is based upon the distinguishing, if not complete separation, of the sensible and the nonsensible as two realms that subsist on their own. The setting up of this partition between the sensible and the nonsensible, between the physical and the nonphysical is a basic trait of what is called metaphysics and which normatively determines Western thinking. Metaphysics loses the rank of the normative mode of thinking when one gains the insight that the above-mentioned partitioning of the sensible and nonsensible is insufficient. When one gains the insight into the limitations of metaphysics, "metaphor" as a normative conception also becomes untenable—that is to say that metaphor is the norm for our conception of the essence of language.... The metaphorical exists only within metaphysics.[3]

This quote beautifully summarizes Heidegger's critique of metaphysics. In its many appearances, metaphysics is fundamentally Platonic in nature. The dualism of the sensible and the intelligible characterizes

Western thinking throughout its history. Due to the insufficiency of this dualism, however, metaphysics "loses the rank of the normative mode of thinking." At the same time, this quote is a quote on language. Heidegger claims that metaphor marks the metaphysical determination of the essence of language. To see this relation between metaphor and metaphysics, Heidegger draws upon the Greek original *metapherein*, which means transference or transposition. A metaphor transposes a word from the domain in which it is commonly used to a domain in which it is not commonly used. For instance, Homer's metaphor "Achilles leapt on the foe as a lion" transposes the word "lion" from the animal kingdom to the domain of human warriors in order to express that Achilles fights as courageously as a lion.[4] Due to this transference, we no longer understand "lion" in its ordinary or literal sense, but in its metaphorical sense. As a transposition of meaning, every metaphor presupposes such a division of domains: a literal or common domain from which the word is borrowed and a metaphorical domain to which the word is applied.

For Heidegger, however, metaphor fundamentally involves a particular transference, namely the transference from the sensible to the intelligible.[5] This distinction forms the metaphysical presupposition of metaphor. To understand what he means here, it is not very illuminating to consider a metaphor such as "Achilles is a lion." It is more appropriate to think of *philosophical* metaphors, such as Plato's metaphor of the sun in his allegory of the cave or Hegel's metaphor of *begreifen* (grasping or apprehending). In his allegory, Plato compares the sun, which belongs to the sensible domain, to the Idea of the Good, which belongs to the intelligible domain. In his explanation of metaphor, Hegel gives the metaphor of *begreifen* as an example. The sensible grasping with our hands, *greifen,* can become a metaphor for the spiritual phenomenon of understanding, *begreifen.*[6]

Heidegger's comments concerning metaphor relate first and foremost to these philosophical metaphors that derive from the (Platonic) metaphysical distinction between the intelligible and the sensible. Now we can understand his claim that metaphor is the norm for a metaphysical conception of language: to enter the domain of the intelligible, the metaphysician borrows language that is used in the domain of the sensible, and by deviating from this use he or she may apply it to the domain of the intelligible. Hence, the language of the metaphysician is necessarily metaphorical. Hence, in this metaphysical framework, philosophy and philosophical language is only possible thanks to metaphor. At these points, Heidegger protests. In the first place, transference *presupposes* a division. A metaphor adds a relation between two distinct and already given domains. Since the two *relata* are prior to the relation, the relation is ontologically secondary. In the case of metaphor, this relation is usually called "resemblance" (*homoiōsis*): a metaphor shows what two beings have in common. Yet, because the distinction of these domains is prior, these domains have their essence in themselves, and a metaphor can only show the *properties* these domains have in common. A metaphor can perhaps help us to become acquainted with the realm of the intelligible by using sensible images, but it can never say or show the intelligible *as it is.* That is to say, by adding something, the metaphor displaces the intelligible domain. By not saying the essence of this domain, a metaphorical expression misses the proper word. For instance, the metaphysical distinction between the sensible (the sun) and the intelligible (the Idea) implies a distinction between proper expressions saying the essence of beings and metaphorical expressions that do not say what a being is. Clearly, Heidegger cannot take this perspective as a point of departure for his understanding of language or poetry. For him, (poetic) language as saying means showing things as they are and in their being and not showing them in a deviated, distorted or displaced way.

In the context of the above quote, Heidegger illustrates this by his expressions thinking as listening (*Er-hören*) and thinking as bringing-into-view (*Er-blicken*). From a metaphysical concept of language, these expressions are understood as "mere" metaphors. However, Heidegger explicitly denies that they are metaphors. They do not transfer something sensible to something intelligible. Instead, thinking as listening and as bringing-into-view intends to say thinking *as it is.* It discloses the essence of thinking and not a mere resemblance between thinking and some sensible activities.[7] To conclude this discussion of the above quote, let me finally point out the role played by resemblance in this conception of metaphor. In Greek, resemblance is *homoiōsis*. Consequently, like truth as *homoiōsis*, metaphor is reigned over by *homoiōsis*. In metaphysics, both truth and metaphor are understood from the perspective of this word. In the context of truth, *homoiōsis* obstructs the possibility to think truth as disclosure. Similarly, in the context of language, *homoiōsis* obstructs the possibility of thinking the disclosure of language.

Distinguishing Distinctions

To prepare for the discussion of Ricoeur and Derrida in later sections of this chapter, let me make a few comments on Heidegger's use of terms. Some are only instructive to readers not familiar with Heidegger's work on poetry whereas others serve as reading marks for the rest of this chapter.

Heidegger argues in his discussion of metaphor that metaphysics is marked by a specific hierarchical relation between *concept* and *metaphor*. Often, the difference between concept and metaphor runs parallel to the difference between *philosophy* and *poetry*. It is important, however, to note that Heidegger's famous pairing of *Denken* and *Dichten* (thinking and poeticizing, or thought and poetry) is *not* homologous to either of these two (metaphysical) distinctions.

In this chapter, we shall see that both Gadamer and Ricoeur try to give another account of metaphor than Heidegger. To overcome the metaphysical origin of metaphor, they privilege Aristotle's attention to resemblance in his definition of metaphor. In the *Poetics* Aristotle writes, "a good metaphor implies an intuitive perception of the similarity in dissimilars."[8] In this way, they try to relate metaphor to Heidegger's conception of language as both showing and gathering. A metaphor gathers two heterogeneous elements and manifests a resemblance between them that has not yet been said or seen.

However, Gadamer's and Ricoeur's definitions of metaphor do not simply mean that Heidegger has failed to find a definition of metaphor that would relate this concept to his own conception of the essence of language. I already noted Heidegger's attention to resemblance as *homoiōsis* and its relation to the problem of truth as *homoiōsis*. More generally, we shall see that Heidegger is concerned with the question of being and its relation to disclosure. The difference between essence and property indicates that this problem is not overcome if we simply shift our attention from transference to resemblance: resemblance is usually understood as showing similarities between two beings and not as showing their essence. Therefore, one should still inquire into the difference between *legein* and *metapherein* in the wake of this redefinition of metaphor. In the section on Ricoeur's conception of metaphor, I will show that exactly this problem reoccurs: according to Ricoeur, a resemblance between, say, X and Y always implies that X *is* and *is not* Y. This "is not" is highly problematic from a Heideggerian point of view because it implies that a metaphor (at least partially) shows something *as it is not*. To show something as it is not is in Heidegger's view a form of concealment (disguise and displacement). Therefore, one may begin to suspect that the distinction between metaphor conceived from a Platonic distinction and metaphor conceived from Aristotle's attention to resemblance is not as absolute as one might believe; at least not from a Heideggerian perspective, in which they both involve the idea of metaphor as disguise and displacement.

Heidegger's depiction of metaphor as disguise also implies a renewal of the distinction between the *proper* and the *metaphorical* in his thought. If we want to trace such a distinction in his thought, then we should take notice of the fact that it is neither equivalent to the metaphysical distinction between concept and metaphor, nor to the Heideggerian pair "thought and poetry." Instead, it relates to what I have discussed in the second chapter as Heidegger's reappropriation of the notions of the proper and appropriation. In Derrida's reading of Heidegger's rejection of metaphor, this distinction will play an important role.

Heidegger on Thought and Poetry

Let me conclude these considerations with a brief discussion of Heidegger's description of the relation between *Denken* and *Dichten* in *Unterwegs zur Sprache*.[9] He describes the relation between thought and poetry as a nearness (*Nähe*). In order to think its "nearness" to poetic language, thought needs to pay special attention to the poetic experience of language.[10] At no point does Heidegger describe this relation as a transference; at no point are poetic expressions *transferred* to thought. The "nearness" of poetry and thought is never a euphemism for confusion, mixture, or contamination. Despite their proximity, poetry and thought are distinct and are separated by a cleft: they live on "the most separated mountains," as Heidegger claims, in yet another expression that one would be tempted to call metaphorical.[11]

It is clear why this proximity between thought and poetry is important. The realm of thought depends on language as saying. Thought is near to poetry since poetry speaks out of an experience of language *as saying*. Thus, poetry and thought share the same source: saying. In fact, despite the image of the separated mountain tops, they are not separate domains that exist in themselves. They only reach into their essence and only receive their essence once they think their co-belonging. Heidegger uses the verb *aufreissen* to suggest how poetry and thought "burst" and "tear" at each other at their point of intersection at infinity.[12] Hence, rather than describing thinking as a realm on its own, Heidegger argues that thinking can only reach its essence if it is torn by a mode of language that is usually opposed to philosophy, namely poetics. In this way, we see that it is necessary to overcome the opposition between philosophy and poetry or between *logos* and myth to arrive at the essence of thinking.

It will come as no surprise that Heidegger determines this moment of tearing that allows thinking to reach its essence as *Ereignis:* it is the event that discloses the essence of thought and thus lets thought appropriate its essence and thus arrive at what is proper to it. At the same time, this appropriation is never an appropriation in which this essence becomes the possession of thought. Here the theme of the promise, which we discussed in the previous chapter, returns: the *Ereignis* only occurs as a saying in which language promises (*zusagen*) thought its essence.[13] Hence, by drawing near to poetry, thought receives *its own essence* as a promised gift.

In fact, this promise is essential for Heidegger to maintain the cleft between thought and poetry. The nearness of thought and poetry stems from the co-belonging to language as saying. Yet, this shared root of thought and poetry is never given as such. It is only given as a promise *in* two different languages *as their nearness.* By postponing the gift of this root that gathers thought and poetry, Heidegger can maintain the multiplicity of thought and poetry and their fundamental cleft. This, of course, gives rise to one of Derrida's questions that we encountered in the previous chapter and that will return in this one: What does it mean for the essence of saying that it is never presented as such but only disclosed in *multiple* tongues and languages by means of displacing promises?

The Direction of Transference

Though the Platonic distinction between the sensible and the intelligible is an important ingredient of Heidegger's account of metaphor, it is, contrary to what is often noted in the literature, not fully exhausted by this distinction. In this and the following section, I will show which other aspects of the ancient definition of metaphor are of importance here. To show this, let me recall first one basic aspect of Aristotle's definition of metaphor.

A (living) metaphor has always been understood as a deviation from ordinary language. Aristotle writes in the *Poetics,* "Metaphor consists in giving the thing a name that belongs to something else." A common name for a thing *familiar to us,* say Y, is transposed to another thing, say X. This transposition is guided by resemblance: the familiar thing has certain properties in common with the other thing. In the *Rhetoric,* Aristotle specifies this transposition as a transposition that provides us with certain knowledge. In fact, a metaphor is agreeable because we learn something from it: "Ordinary words convey only what we know already; it is from metaphor that we can best get hold of something fresh."[14] The difference between an ordinary word and a metaphor is that a metaphor shows us something (of X) *that we did not yet know.* A metaphor is capable of showing this unfamiliar aspect of X because X shares this aspect with Y of which this aspect is known. For instance, if we did not know that a lion is an animal that fights courageously, the metaphorical expression "Achilles fights like a lion" would make no sense to us. But because we know that a lion is courageous, a metaphor can borrow this aspect of a lion to say something about Achilles' behavior in combat.

This aspect of Aristotle's definition amounts to the following. The transference of a metaphor has a specific direction. It moves from what is familiar to what is unfamiliar, and its gain in knowledge is indebted to the similarities it discloses as well as to our knowledge of the similar properties in familiar cases. By expressing similarities, metaphor expresses the extension of our experience and draws the unfamiliar near on the basis of its resemblance with what is familiar. This dimension of metaphor cannot be derived from the perspective of the metaphysical distinction between the sensible and the intelligible. Rather, the metaphysical use of metaphor *presupposes* this direction: going from the well-known sensible domain to the lesser known intelligible domain is a particular case of this movement. This direction of metaphor brings us rather close toward Gadamar's and Ricoeur's concept of metaphor for whom this direction is important to explain how a metaphor can extend human experience.

Derrida points out that Heidegger's objection to metaphor in his explanation of the expression "the house of being" is concerned with this directionality of metaphor. This expression might seem to be a perfect example of a metaphor in Heidegger's work.[15] Because language is not actually a house—at least not in our everyday understanding—it might seem that this expression applies our familiar conception of house and dwelling to language in order to say something about language and about being: being dwells in language as we dwell in our houses. Yet, Heidegger rejects this interpretation: this expression is *not a transference* of the image of a house to being. Rather, the essence of being one day will provide thinking with what "house" means and what "living" is in a sense prior to our ordinary understanding of the home and what it means to live somewhere.[16] Hence, that which is most unfamiliar comes first: the essence of being. In sum, a metaphor discloses an unfamiliar being in the light

of a familiar being, but Heidegger wants to leave this ordinary meaning of dwelling behind in order to open up the possibility of *another*
meaning of dwelling and another sense or direction than the one of
metaphor to understand the dwelling that is promised to us in this
expression.

This rejection of metaphor repeats a gesture that we already
encountered in *Sein und Zeit*. It continues his general mistrust of
ordinary language and everyday familiar notions and meanings.[17]
In *Sein und Zeit*, Heidegger argues that the disclosedness of beings
can obscure the possibility of disclosure grounded in understanding.
Thus, *our familiarity with particular beings disguises the possibility of
understanding*.[18] In *Unterwegs zur Sprache*, we encountered a similar
distrust: in ordinary language, the essence of language never comes
to language, but is forgotten.[19] Heidegger's remarks on "the house of
being" move within the realm of this distrust: to understand language
as metaphorical will obstruct the thought of language as saying and
showing.

In addition, this rejection of the ordinary logic of metaphor demonstrates a particular dimension of Heidegger's strategy of his critique
of metaphysics, as Derrida argues in "*Le retrait de la métaphore*." The
logic of metaphorical transference implies that we disclose a being
in the light of another being — *not in the light of how this being is
from itself*. Strictly speaking, this implies that a metaphor displaces
how and what a being is. In fact, if we stress this aspect of the logic
of metaphorical transference — to see a being in the light of another
being — then we see once more the intrinsic relation between metaphor and the onto-theological character of metaphysics. Heidegger
argues that metaphysics determines the beingness (*Seiendheit*) of a
being in light of one highest being. It determines beings on the basis
of their correspondence to a highest being, such as the Platonic Idea.
In fact, metaphysics even discusses being itself as a highest being:
metaphysics confuses a most evident being with being *as* shining; it
understands the essence of being from this most evident being. For
Heidegger, this is the ultimate disguise and distortion of the question
of being. *The metaphysical tendency to approach being from the point of*

view of its familiarity with a particular highest being is the forgetfulness of being itself.

Derrida argues that this aspect of the logic of metaphorical transference moves beyond the typical relation between metaphor and metaphysics.[20] The concept of metaphor, developed and *presented within* the realm of metaphysics, would be different from this (quasi-)metaphorical approach of being that *opens up* the realm of metaphysics and is *effaced and concealed within* this realm. Whether the distinction between concept of metaphor and quasi-metaphor that Derrida makes here is accurate is a question to be discussed. Nevertheless, he shows that in Heidegger's thought, this quasi-metaphor is distinguished from what I propose to call, for reasons of symmetry, a *quasi-proper,* which is to be found in Heidegger's quest for the essence of being, thought, and language. This essence is not somewhere present, but is marked by a fundamental withdrawal: Heidegger's use of words such as *zusagen* and *Vermutung* in his discussion of the "nearness" of thought and poetry indicates such a fundamental withdrawal. It also expresses the fact that this essence is *to come* and is *to occur,* and that this occurrence is a form of disclosing appropriation (*Ereignis*). However, this withdrawal is veiled by the inaugurating metaphoricity of metaphysics, which approaches being as *a* being. Thus, the metaphoricity of metaphysics disguises a fundamental withdrawal; it is a concealment of concealment. This reading shows that Heidegger's analysis of metaphor is not so much a dismissal of one metaphysical distinction—namely the sensible versus the intelligible—and one metaphysical position (namely Plato's), but concerns the question of the concealment and displacement intrinsic to metaphor and metaphysics, as opposed to the disclosure of saying (*Sage*).

Heidegger on Aristotle's Metaphor

To capture a third dimension of Heidegger's account of metaphor, let us turn to *Unterwegs zur Sprache.*[21] Once more, Heidegger relates metaphor to the realm of metaphysics. This time, however, the realm of metaphysics is explicitly related to Aristotle's *On Interpretation.* He invokes the opening passage of *On Interpretation* in which

Aristotle describes language as a sign or a symbol and as vocal sounds (*stimmliche Verlautbarung*). In this way, language would be classified under the metaphysical notion of the sensible.[22] In what follows, Heidegger invokes the poetic experience of Hölderlin as an alternative to this Aristotelian approach to language. Hölderlin describes language as the bloom of the mouth (*Blüte des Mundes*) and he describes words as flowers (*Worte, wie Blumen*). According to Heidegger, Hölderlin's descriptions would pull language out of the physiologic-physical realm of phonetics and draw it closer to the letting-appear-of-world.[23]

In this context, Heidegger remarks that we remain within metaphysics if we take Hölderlin's words — *Worte, wie Blumen* — to be a simple metaphor.[24] Because he mentions the sensible domain and because Aristotle's opening passage of *On Interpretation* seems to be derived from the distinction between sensible and intelligible, one might argue that this comment relates to the same metaphysical distinction as was mentioned in *Der Satz vom Grund*. However, the expression "words like flowers" cannot be read as a transference from the sensible to the intelligible domain. If read as a transference in this context, then it would be a transference from the realm of the organic and the living to the realm of sounds. This metaphor does not present something intelligible as something sensible, but *it presents a sound as something alive*. Given this specific dimension, it is more reasonable to consult Aristotle's account of metaphor once more in which this liveliness is essential. This seems to have escaped the literature on Heidegger's account of metaphor so far.

To some extent, this is odd, since there are good reasons to read Heidegger's comment on metaphor in this context as a reference to Aristotle. He cites Gottfried Benn's reading of Hölderlin's "*Worte, wie Blumen*" who is not so much interested in metaphor as a reference to a physiologic-physical entity. Rather, Benn's comments relate to Hölderlin's "comparison" in a different way. The key to Benn's critique of Hölderlin concerns the *wie* in the phrase *Worte, wie Blumen*. According to Benn, this *wie* would be a rift in the vision of the poem; Hölderlin's phrase would merely be a simile. This would reduce the tension of language, and it would imply a weakness of the creative transformation involved in this phrase.[25] If we want to understand Heidegger's remark on metaphor better, we need to understand it in the context of Benn's remarks on the *wie*. In particular, we need to understand how Benn can understand this *wie* as a metaphorical weakness. How can this *wie* weaken an image? To understand this, the distinction between sensible and intelligible does not help. However, if we consider it from the perspective of Aristotle's analysis of the relation between metaphor and simile in his *Rhetoric*, it makes sense.

In the third book of the *Rhetoric*, Aristotle indicates a close proximity between metaphors and similes. In chapter 4, he argues that they are more or less the same: "The simile is also a metaphor; the difference is but slight."[26] However, though slight, the difference between a simile and a metaphor is exactly the "as," "like," or "*wie*": "The lion leapt on the foe" is a metaphor and the corresponding simile is "Achilles leapt on the foe *as* a lion." Further on, in chapter 10, Aristotle discusses the relation between simile and metaphor in the context of his discussion of the "liveliness" of speech. Here, the "as" obtains a particular meaning. Living speech is agreeable to us because we learn something from it, Aristotle claims, and a metaphor is especially agreeable because it allows us to get hold of such a new idea: "ordinary words convey only what we know already; it is from metaphor that we can best get hold of something fresh."[27] The best metaphors are those metaphors that depict something as alive. This liveliness is especially present in a metaphor, while it is present *in a lesser way* in a simile. Because a simile is longer, it evokes a less attractive idea. As Ricoeur points out, this means that a metaphor is not an abbreviated simile, but a simile is an extended metaphor.[28] Aristotle writes, "[the simile] does not say outright that 'this' *is* 'that,' and therefore the hearer is less interested in the idea. We see then, that both speech and reasoning are lively in proportion as they make us seize a new idea promptly."[29] Hence, the degree of liveliness depends on how promptly an expression makes us seize a new idea and transforms reality for us.

Aristotle invokes the word *energeia* to describe what it means that something is shown as alive. He explains that the liveliness of speech in metaphor makes us see things, and he continues that he means "by 'making see things' using expressions that represent things as in a state of activity [*energeia*]." A good metaphor is one that suggests this very activity. The effect of activity can especially be reached if poets give "metaphorical life to lifeless things."[30] Aristotle provides an example borrowed from Homer: an arrow is depicted as an animal hungry for its prey. Due to this activity, the metaphor strikes us, and this lively image presents the arrow in its full vividness before our eyes.

We may conclude that Aristotle introduces exactly those aspects of the weakness of the *wie* that Benn invokes and to which Heidegger objects: Hölderlin's "*Worte, wie Blumen*" would break up the vision, that is, it does not allow a prompt seizure of a new idea and therefore it does not agree to us as much as the metaphor. It reduces the tension of language, that is, it reduces the liveliness of speech; it would be a weakening of the creative transformation given that it does not show promptly a lifeless thing (word) as alive (a flower). Benn's comments thus affirm the higher degree of liveliness in metaphor as opposed to the less "active" simile. Instead of the metaphysical distinction between the sensible and intelligible, Aristotle introduces another metaphysical distinction in his explanation of the liveliness of metaphor, as Ricoeur explains, namely the distinction between actuality and potentiality. According to Ricoeur, Aristotle describes the liveliness of a good metaphor as showing something's potential (what it can be) as if it were already actual. If the relation I seek between Benn's attention to Hölderlin's *wie* and Aristotle's analysis of metaphor in the *Rhetoric* is right, then Heidegger's comment on metaphor concerns this metaphysical view rather than Plato's.

Can this latter conclusion be attributed to Heidegger and may we say that Heidegger dismisses metaphor because he rejects *this* metaphysics? I admit that the textual basis of *Unterwegs zur Sprache* is too feeble to draw such a firm conclusion. However, it is justified to say that Heidegger protests against the implications of Benn's comment that Hölderlin should have depicted language *as if* it were energetic and active, and that Hölderlin should have used the full resources of his vivid image in order to reveal language as if it were active and alive. Heidegger is not interested in this metaphorical "as if." He is interested in Hölderlin because his poetry says language *as it is;* it *says* the essence of language, that is, it lets it occur and brings it forth into unconcealment. In this way, Hölderlin provides a poetic experience of language. Therefore, thought can draw near to this kind of poetry while it is on the way to the essence of language. Thought, however, cannot draw near to a metaphorical poetry that merely creates striking images. Diametrically opposed to Aristotle's conception of metaphor as a lively word that is rich in imagery, Heidegger writes at the end of his *Logos* essay, "The word of thinking is without image and without charm. The word of thinking rests in a sobriety to that what it says. Nonetheless, thinking changes the world."[31] Once more, Heidegger objects to conceptions of metaphor as an "as if." How striking it may be, the "as if" implies that metaphor shows something as it is not. Moreover, this striking "as if" derives from metaphor's transference. In contrast to this metaphorical displacement, Heidegger points in his discussion of Hölderlin to the bringing forth of the word out of its beginning.[32] Poetry can disclose the word as saying and *therefore* genuine poetry is not metaphorical.

RICOEUR ON LIVING METAPHOR

In the previous chapter, we noted that for Ricoeur, the ultimate task of hermeneutics is to understand the being-in-the-world opened up by literature. This disclosure of the literary text is described as "the *creative* dimension of distanciation."[33] Unlike Heidegger, Ricoeur insists that the poetic disclosure of literature is the positive counterpart of distanciation in discourse. In this and the next chapter, we shall discuss Ricoeur's analysis of poetic disclosure more carefully by studying two major examples: metaphor and narrative. Metaphor and narrative both invent our being-in-the-world and our self in the double sense of the word: "to invent" (*inventer*) means both "to create" and "to discover" in the French.[34] In his theory of metaphor, he stresses that a new *resemblance* between beings is shown in a metaphorical expression. In his theory of narrative, the work of the imagination consists of the creation of an unheard-of *plot* or configuration. In *Du texte à l'action,* he summarizes, "In both cases, the novel—the not-yet-said, the unheard-of—suddenly arises in language: here, *living* metaphor, that is to say, a *new* relevance in predication; there, wholly *invented* plot, that is to say, a *new* congruence in the emplotment." The inventions of poetics are not imaginary in the pejorative sense of the word. As discovering, both metaphor and narrative refer to and disclose the world. The postulate that poetics has such a reference is called "the ontological postulate of poetics." It says that poetic language is not closed in on itself: the genuine concern of poetics is not language as such but rather the disclosure of our own existence. As such, poetics has its own poetic truth. The affinity with Heidegger's conception of truth as disclosure is acknowledged by Ricoeur. He writes, "The Heideggerian tone of these remarks is undeniable; the opposition between truth-as-manifestation and truth-as-agreement...is easily recognized here."[35] Nevertheless, despite this proximity, I will focus on the difference between Ricoeur's and Heidegger's account of disclosure and in particular on the assessment of the "as if" in Ricoeur's account of metaphor's disclosive dimension.

The Semantics and Ontology of Metaphor

The conception of metaphor as a word-figure goes all the way back to Aristotle's definition. In the *Poetics* he writes, "Metaphor consists in giving the thing a name that belongs to something else; the transference being either from genus to species, or from species to genus, or from species to species, or on grounds of analogy." Hence, metaphor is a transference of a word to a thing of which it is not the name in common language. In this way, metaphor uses a word in a deviated way and borrows the meaning of its common use in a different context or semantic field.[36]

In line with his discourse theory, in which the unities of meaning are not words but rather sentences or even larger groups of words, Ricoeur doubts whether the classification of metaphor as a word-figure is accurate. Although we can identify a metaphor in a word—we can say that "lion" is the place where the metaphor occurs in the simile "[Achilles] leapt on the foe as a lion"—the word alone is not enough to understand a metaphor.[37] To some extent, this is already implied in the idea of transference. As a transference, the metaphorical use of the word "lion" refers back to its common use. If we do not know this ordinary use of "lion," we will not perceive its derived and deviated use in a metaphor. Moreover, to recognize the deviation and the borrowing of metaphor, it is not enough to say "lion" and to know its ordinary meaning. We also need to see that "lion" is somehow connected to "Achilles" in the simile.[38]

These circumstances indicate that a metaphor presupposes a specific relation to the context in which it is uttered. Without this context, a metaphor simply cannot be understood. Therefore, Ricoeur proposes to understand metaphor not as a word-figure, but as an expression, and more precisely as a peculiar kind of *predication*.[39] The predication implied in "the lion leapt on the foe" is "Achilles is a lion." This predication is "peculiar" since Achilles is a human being and not a lion. It cannot be taken literally. This shows, according to Ricoeur, that against the background of the context in which it is uttered, a metaphor stands out as a peculiar predication that truly *gathers* two heterogeneous elements in one sentence—a human being, Achilles, and an animal, a lion—in such a way that the predication cannot be taken to be a literal description. This does not mean that this predication does not predicate at all since the failure of a literal description is merely the back side of a positive phenomenon. A metaphor does not describe Achilles in the strict sense of the word but suggests to see Achilles *as* a lion. As such, a metaphor predicates something positive: it predicates a resemblance between Achilles and the lion: they both fight courageously. Moreover, since Achilles and the lion belong to two heterogeneous domains—they are distant in logical space, as Ricoeur writes—the metaphorical predicate is synthetic in a special sense: it gathers two heterogeneous elements together by showing a new idea, namely their resemblance. Due to this specific synthesis, a metaphor can be called a *semantic innovation:* by predicating a resemblance between two distant words, it allows the emergence of new meaning: it shows a certain homogeneity between heterogeneous elements.[40] To understand a metaphor is to understand this emergence of meaning: the deviation, borrowing, and transference of metaphor are indispensable but only secondary to this semantic innovation.

At the same time, Ricoeur insists that this semantic innovation has ontological significance. Although the nonsense of a literal reading of a metaphor implies that a metaphor *suspends* the reference to our common, everyday world, this suspension does not abolish the referential function of language altogether. In addition, metaphorical language has another reference: the resemblance it shows says something about the beings that are gathered together in a metaphor. To predicate the metaphor "X is Y" means to say "X is as Y." The metaphorical "being" is actually "*being-as*," that is, "*being*" and "*being-not.*"

This "being-as" has an ambiguous status in Ricoeur's work. On the one hand, it is the *appropriate* ontological form of poetics. Unlike a philosophical analogy, Ricoeur argues that a poetic resemblance is not subsumed under the requirement of identity. Thus, "being-as" is not subsumed under being, at least not in poetics. On the other hand, only ontology and the speculative discourse of metaphysics have a sense for this ontological postulate of metaphor. In this sense, "being-as" concerns only an *implicit* form of being in poetic language. That is to say, it is implicit in poetics and can only be explicated in a discourse on being, that is ontology, which is a conceptual language marked by the primacy of identity. However, if we can only *grasp* this metaphorical reference through the conceptual language of philosophy, which necessarily subsumes being-as *under* being and resemblance *under* identity, does this not mean that we always lose the particular and appropriate ontological dimension of poetics and determine it in a way it is not? This is the question that guides me through the rest of this section, and I want to explicate it by means of a confrontation with Heidegger.

Let me recall that Aristotle argues that a (good) metaphor allows us to seize a new idea promptly. Ricoeur's elaboration of metaphor identifies this new idea as the sudden emergence of a resemblance. Therefore, *understanding* a metaphor means to seize immediately the resemblance and its corresponding semantic innovation.[41] Understanding needs to be distinguished from identification. Our understanding of a metaphor "X is as Y" moves back and forth between the identity "X is Y" and the negation "X is not Y." Understanding a metaphor is exactly understanding this tension and its corresponding dynamic. Identification, on the other hand, is the *redescription* of X as Y on the basis of what we learn from X in light of its resemblance with Y.[42] As soon as we interpret, that is, go from poetics to ontology in order to explicate the ontological dimension of a metaphor, we redescribe the metaphorized being. As we shall see, Ricoeur locates interpretation between poetics and speculative discourse. As such, it is only in interpretation that we can address the ontological implications of poetics. At the same time, an interpretation conceptualizes the being-as of metaphor and identifies X by identifying the similarities between X and Y. In sum, interpretation attempts to overcome the dynamic of metaphor. Apparently, only by losing the liveliness of metaphor's disclosure in a conceptual explication, we arrive at the question of ontology.

The Metaphorical "As"

To capture the difference with Heidegger, I propose to call the "as" of Ricoeur's metaphor the *metaphorical "as"* in order to distinguish it from Heidegger's hermeneutic and apophantic "as." Heidegger's hermeneutic "as" concerns an interpretation that takes place within the realm opened up by the gathering of understanding. This gathering is not marked or characterized by a tension with ordinary language or common understanding. Heidegger's apophantic "as" concerns the showing of a being, but it shows a being *as it is* and *lets itself be seen out of itself.* It does not show it "as it is and is not" or lets it be seen from its resemblance with another being, as a metaphor does. Hence, Heidegger's conception of the hermeneutic and the apophantic "as" lacks the "is not" involved in the metaphorical "as." This "is not" is derived from the tension with everyday language and our everyday world. Of course, Heidegger pays attention to our everyday existence, but he qualifies it as *pseudos* or concealment.

Heidegger understands "is not" as concealment and displacement and not as disclosure. *Pseudos* involves a being that is shown *as it is not*. Disclosure, however, only concerns what is. Only in disclosure can we conceive how a being is. In Heidegger's thought, the distinction between "to appear as it is" and "to appear as it is not" runs parallel to the distinction between disclosure and concealment, between opening and closure.

In his elucidation of metaphor as predication, Ricoeur explicitly relates metaphor to Heidegger's analysis of *Aussage* (assertion or predication). He does this in terms of Aristotle by describing metaphorical predication as a form of *apophansis*. Yet, in his use of this term he also shows the difference with Heidegger's analysis by describing the metaphorical "as" as the apophantic *is/is not*.[43] For Heidegger, this would be a contradiction in terms. This indicates that for Ricoeur the disclosure of poetics does not concern being, but only being-as. Metaphor does not disclose the essence of a being. The main reason for this difference is that Ricoeur discusses being always from the perspective of identity because the question of being is addressed in the conceptual discourse of metaphysics. The question of the ontological dimension of metaphor has to be treated within the conceptual framework of philosophy, which subsumes resemblance under identity. This leads to the question of whether this does not destroy the typical disclosure of metaphor marked by resemblance. It also leads to the question of whether poetic disclosure requires a transformation of the speculative discourse and its understanding of being. To respond to these questions, we first need to understand how Ricoeur explains the "ontological postulate" of metaphorical language.

Disclosure as the Life of Metaphor

For such an explanation, Ricoeur turns to Aristotle. In the *Rhetoric*, Aristotle writes that a metaphor makes people see things "as in a state of activity." This activity of metaphor is the heart of its "life." Aristotle points to Homer who gives "metaphorical life to lifeless things: all such passages are distinguished by the effect of activity they convey." Following Aristotle, Ricoeur describes the task of poetics in general and of metaphor in particular as "signifying things in act" (*signifier l'acte*).[44]

Ricoeur argues that Aristotle uses the metaphysical distinction between *dunamis* and *energeia,* potentiality and actuality, to explicate the ontological dimension of metaphorical expressions.[45] The specific quality of poetics seems to be its capacity to transgress and trespass this metaphysical distinction. A good metaphor does not merely describe what is lifeless *as* lifeless and what is potential *as* potential. A good metaphor transgresses the distinction between actuality and potentiality and describes what is potential as if it is actual; it describes the lifeless as alive. The image of the arrow as an animal panting for its prey, which Aristotle borrows from Homer, is a typical example in this respect: it depicts a lifeless arrow as alive. Ricoeur explains this as follows. A dormant possibility, for instance, of an arrow is actualized metaphorically. This "as in actuality" is the main ontological quality of metaphor. Metaphor depicts the dormant possibilities of our being-in-the-world *as if they are active.* By disclosing the concealed possibilities of our world, metaphor acts as the opening and the budding of the appearance (*l'éclosion de l'apparaître*) of our being-in-the-world. By awakening these possibilities, metaphor does not simply open up the real of our reality; it elevates it and shows it as actual. It elevates our reality to the level of its genuine and most proper possibilities.[46] Thus, we can conclude that Ricoeur understands the being-as of metaphor from the perspective of its disclosure: the disclosure of metaphor *depicts the potential as if in act.*

In his comments on Heidegger's remarks on Hölderlin's "*Worte, wie Blumen,*" Ricoeur explicitly relates this "opening" aspect of metaphor to Heidegger's attention to the opening of language. Metaphorical language, which discloses reality, is like the opening up of a flower: it brings our world to presence. At the beginning of *La métaphore vive,* Ricoeur remarks that his study on Aristotle's concept of metaphor is a continual struggle with metaphors that define the concept of metaphor, namely the transference of (physical) movement to a linguistic phenomenon. It seems that Ricoeur has found in Hölderlin's metaphor "*Worte, wie Blumen*" an alternative metaphor of metaphor. Metaphor is the flower of our language; it is the semantic event in which dormant possibilities emerge as actual.[47]

Despite this affinity to Heidegger, there seems to be a difference between Ricoeur and Heidegger in their evaluation of Hölderlin's "*Worte, wie Blumen*" as well. According to Heidegger, Hölderlin says the essence of language as it is. For Ricoeur, however, "*Worte, wie Blumen*" is a metaphor of metaphor. Aristotle's formulation, on the other hand, would be a more proper and metaphysical formulation of metaphor's liveliness: a metaphor shows possibilities as actual. To understand what this difference between Heidegger and Ricoeur exactly means and to prepare the following section, I want to make two remarks.

First, in Ricoeur's understanding, it seems that metaphor's disclosure can only be explained as what must appear as a confusion of categories in metaphysics. From within metaphysics, there can only be one conclusion: poetics does not show something as it is; it does not show the essence of something, but it confuses potentiality and actuality, *dunamis* and *energeia*. It lacks a proper speaking about potentiality as potentiality and actuality as actuality. The task of (philosophical) interpretation is then well-defined: it should identify possibilities *as* possibilities.[48] Thus, for instance, it should explicate that an arrow is not actually a bird or a panting animal, but that an arrow has the possibility to vibrate heavily and that this possibility is actualized if it hits the ground. This implies that metaphor is always a veiled speech. It provides much to thought and it discloses something about being, but it never discloses something *as it is*. It discloses always by concealing. Consequently, metaphysics is needed in addition to poetry to complete and purify the ontological contribution of a metaphor.

In Aristotle's conception of metaphor, it is not difficult to trace this concealing aspect of metaphor. For him, metaphor is always a *veiled* speech as opposed to the proper speech of philosophy. In his *Topics*, Aristotle remarks that one of the ways to find the obscurities in a speaker's or a writer's expressions is to see whether he or she has used metaphors: "Another rule [to discern obscurity] is to see if he [i.e. the speaker] has used a metaphorical expression...For a metaphorical expression is always obscure." This concealment intrinsic to Aristotle's understanding of metaphor implies that Ricoeur's being-as is always related to *missing* the essence of a thing. Metaphor can at best be helpful *on our way* to understanding something properly. In the same passage, Aristotle writes, "For a metaphor does make what it signifies to some extent familiar because of the likeness it involves (for those who use metaphors do so always in view of some likeness)."[49] The resemblance of metaphor is better than other obscure phrases because it is involved in making something familiar. Yet, despite its liveliness, metaphor is an obscure rather than a proper utterance. Heidegger objects to this derived status of metaphorical language since he is interested in poetic language as disclosing reality *as it is*. Ricoeur's approach to metaphor seems to be rather ambiguous. On the one hand, he affirms the opening value of metaphor as having an ontological status. On the other hand, he claims that metaphysics is the proper discourse in which this ontological status needs to be explicated. This discourse, however, emphasizes that identification is the *telos* of the discourse on being. In such a way, the disclosure of resemblances in metaphor can only be an intermediary moment on its way to a higher truth.

Secondly, one may also be surprised that Ricoeur does not follow another line of thought. In line with Aristotle's definition of metaphor, Ricoeur suggests that metaphors transgress categories. Thanks to this transgression, a metaphor gives rise to a redescription and a reinvention of the conceptual order. Applied to the basic conceptual order of metaphysics, it would imply that the disclosure of metaphor, which appears in metaphysics as a confusion of categories, is a transgression in order to reinvent metaphysics as a discourse on being. Would this not imply that the metaphorical confusion of potentiality and actuality proposes thinking something like "potentiality as actuality" as more fundamental than the distinction between actuality and potentiality? Would it not imply thinking of resemblance as the basic category of ontology instead of identity? But this is not the way Ricoeur proceeds, probably for the following reason: a transgression of the metaphysical categories that explicate the ontological postulate of metaphorical language would imply the dissolution of his explication of the ontological postulate as we will discuss below.

Philosophy and Poetry

Ricoeur argues that *poetic* discourse "opens up and regains" an immediate experience of belonging to a world.[50] This immediacy is reflected in the metaphor as a semantic event and as an immediate, unreflected tension giving rise to its dynamics. This immediate saying of poetry is indeed a *semantic* gain, but it is not yet a *conceptual* gain: we still do not know exactly what its referent is since it is marked by the tension of "is" and "is not." This implies that the ontological dimension remains *implicit* in a metaphorical expression. Both the semantic gain and the implicitness of its referent demand an additional discourse that allows us to elaborate the conceptual gain.[51] This is the task of *speculative* discourse. Speculative discourse is marked by distanciation. Thanks to this distanciation, it can explicate the metaphorical referent and fix it by identifying the referent. This identification leaves the realm of resemblance behind and moves toward the conceptual realm, which is characterized by univocity and identity. Hence, the explication of the metaphorical referent coincides with a conceptualization, as Ricoeur writes, "the passage to the explicit ontology called for by the postulate of reference is inseparable from the passage to the concept called for by the structure of meaning found in the metaphorical statement."[52] Hence, the ontological dimension of metaphor is not so much found in the metaphorical disclosure itself, which only discloses a resemblance between two beings X and Y, but rather in the conceptual explication and redescription of X. Consequently, ontology is ultimately only interested in the being X as such rather than the resemblance between X and Y. This implies that the metaphorical "as" is different from Heidegger's hermeneutic "as" in yet another perspective. For Heidegger, the explication of X as Y implies that X is never disclosed as such, but always out of its co-belonging and "togetherness" with Y. This co-belonging is the ontological ground of any interpretation. The notion of resemblance could have played a similar role. However, according to Ricoeur resemblance is merely implicitly ontological; only in the process of identification, the explicit and genuine ontological implications of the metaphorical predication become clear. Apparently, only when X is explicated in its independent, substantial-like nature, we arrive at an ontological viewpoint.

Poetic discourse is thus a *source* from which the dormant possibilities of reality are disclosed and brought to presence. Without the semantic innovation of poetic discourse, these possibilities would be hidden from our view. Therefore, poetics is indeed the domain of disclosure and manifestation. However, given the ontological postulate and since poetic discourse does not manifest its ontological gain as such, poetic disclosure is at the same time incomplete and in need of an explication in order to develop this ontological gain. This is what Ricoeur means when he calls poetic discourse the *possibility* of speculative discourse.[53] It provides speculative discourse with material to think and with the task to conceptualize the semantic gain of poetic disclosure. However, although metaphor enables the formation of new concepts, it does not form conceptuality as such. The primacy of identity and its conceptual nature are not derived from poetry, but are grounded in speculative discourse itself. Hence, speculative discourse has its own internal *necessity,* as Ricoeur puts it.[54]

The difference between these two discourses reflects the difference between two languages and two concepts of truth. The proper language of philosophy is conceptual, whereas the proper language of poetics is metaphorical. Truth as disclosure reigns in poetic discourse, whereas truth as correspondence reigns in philosophical discourse due to its conceptual nature. At the same time, since truth is concerned with being, truth as poetic disclosure is completed in truth as correspondence. Here we see that Ricoeur's account of poetry is much more classical in nature than Heidegger's.

Ricoeur emphasizes the asymmetry between philosophy and poetry along three lines of thought. The asymmetry concerns (a) *equivocalness:* philosophical discourse masters the equivocalness of being whereas poetic discourse is marked by a proliferation of poetic equivocalness or plurivocity; (b) *resemblance:* philosophy subsumes resemblance under identity whereas poetics discloses a resemblance without identity; (c) *being:* philosophy is concerned with being and identity, whereas poetry contains an implicit form of being, which metaphysics identifies as a form of being-as. These disproportions mark the difference between philosophy and poetry, and they emphasize that philosophy finds its necessity in itself.

To capture how these three lines are related, let me highlight one typical difference between poetic and philosophical discourse, which Ricoeur discusses in the final study of *La métaphore vive:* the difference between metaphor and analogy. Analogy refers here to notions such as the *analogia entis* from Thomas Aquinas and the *pros hen* relation discussed by Aristotle in book 4 of his *Metaphysics* when he argues that though being is said in multiple ways, each of these ways are directed to one focal meaning, namely being as substance. Ricoeur emphasizes that one should not confuse the plurality at work in metaphorical resemblance with the plurality of the ontological notion of analogy. Aristotle's *pros hen* indicates that the plurality of analogy is directed toward a unity and Thomas's account of the *analogia entis* indicates that this plurality of being is always a regulated plurality. As opposed to this regulated plurality, poetic plurality is fundamental. Resemblance is not subsumed under or directed to a unity in poetic discourse. Ricoeur writes, "The ordered plurivocity of being and poetic plurivocity move on radically distinct levels. Philosophical discourse sets itself up as the vigilant watchman overseeing the ordered extensions of meaning; against this background, the unfettered extensions of meaning in poetic discourse spring free." In light of this explication, it is clear that Lawlor's claim that "a live metaphor is regulated by univocity" is not true taken in its generality: metaphor is not regulated by univocity if we take it as a proper ingredient of poetic language.[55] The multiplicity of poetic language is not regulated at all. However, if we adopt an ontological perspective, Lawlor's claim is correct: as far as poetic discourse has something to tell us about reality, the explication of this ontological implication requires a transition from poetic to philosophical discourse. This transition transfers the "unfettered" plurality of poetic discourse to the regulated plurality of ontology. As soon as the question of being comes into play, the primacy of unity is established via the classical way of analogy.

It is the task of interpretation to enable the transition between poetry and philosophy. As an intermediary, interpretation responds to the demands of the concept as well as the metaphor. It needs the clarity of the concept as well as the semantic innovation of the metaphor.[56] To understand the movement of interpretation between poetic and speculative discourse, Ricoeur describes living metaphor as a Kantian aesthetic Idea. By producing a metaphor, the imagination produces an Idea to which no concept responds adequately. Because no concept corresponds to an aesthetic Idea, this Idea always demands us to think more (*penser plus*).[57] As such, poetic discourse inspires the philosophical conceptualization and at the same time, no concept is capable of exhausting the semantic innovation of a living metaphor.

From a semantic point of view, the incapacity of the concept to exhaust the metaphor is utterly trivial: since a concept subsumes a plurality under a general unity and since a living metaphor proposes an unregulated plurality, it is obvious from the outset that no concept can do justice to this plurality. However, from an ontological point of view, it is not entirely clear what this semantic incapacity exactly implies. The combination of the radical plurality of poetic discourse with the ontological postulate of poetry gives rise to serious problems and ambiguities when Ricoeur tries to think the intersection between poetry and philosophy. Since speculative discourse is interested in explicating the ontological dimensions of poetic discourse, the incapacity to capture the metaphor is an incapacity to capture its ontological implications. Since this incapacity is related to a fundamental unregulated or irregular plurality of metaphor, one might wonder whether this does not imply that being as such is plural in an unregulated or irregular sense of the word. Yet, this is in flagrant contradiction to Ricoeur's guiding idea that the notion of being needs to be thought as one—even if this unity is only understood as a Kantian regulative idea rather than as something we can experience.

Ricoeur's remarks on ontology and speculative discourse imply that resemblance, being-as, and poetics' awakening of dormant possibilities are always metaphysically understood as referring back to an identity and an essence. However, poetic discourse does not "allow" an identity over the resemblances it discloses. Would this disproportion between philosophy and poetics not also apply to poetics' ontological dimension, to its *being-as?* In fact, if being is indeed affected by a radical plurality, this would imply, in Ricoeur's vocabulary that poetics' being-as does *not* allow a more primordial identity. On the other hand, if the explication of poetry's ontology is always already a conceptualization, how can we ever discern this disproportion ontologically? Does this not imply that poetry's ontological dimension might transgress metaphysical discourse and is actually missed by metaphysics because it relates poetics back to a given essence? Finally, does this not open up the question of whether the ontology of poetry does not require another thought of being? We may admire Ricoeur's insistence on the distinction between philosophy and poetry, which allows him to stress the radical plurivocity of poetic discourse. Nevertheless, his account of metaphorical reference lacks a thought on truth as disclosure and on emerging being *that does not try to relate this emergence back to a metaphysical ontology of identity.* Is this not a return to an onto-theo-logical conception of being that determines being by means of the effects of its emergence—that is, the identification of beings—and not from this emergence itself?

To explore this latter suggestion, let me recall that Ricoeur understands poetic disclosure in Aristotelian terms: poetic disclosure shows the potentiality of beings as actual. In this way, metaphysics identifies the being disclosed in poetry as being-as in the pejorative sense. More precisely, the "is not" at work in the being-as of poetics is due to poetics' reversal of the metaphysical order of actuality and potentiality. Given this consequence of Ricoeur's explanation of the ontological postulate of poetics, two possibilities are open. On the one hand, we can stick to the primacy of the metaphysical distinction between actuality and potentiality as a framework to interpret poetic disclosure as the disclosure of being-as. In that case, the disclosure of metaphorical language conceals as well: at the heart of poetic *disclosure,* we find the *confusion* of one of the basic ontological distinctions. In this case, the task of metaphysics is to *destroy* this disclosure by restoring the ancient order between actuality and potentiality, which metaphor transgresses. On the other hand, we can apply Ricoeur's suggestion that metaphor transgresses a logical order to reinvent this order at the ontological level. In this case, it is clear that poetic disclosure cannot and should not be accounted for in terms of these concepts since this disclosure opens up the way to a new logical order. Hence, rather than destroying this disclosure one should follow up on this disclosure and try to create a new logical order out of it. The either/ or of these two possibilities is not meant to proclaim the priority of poetry over philosophy or vice versa. Rather, it points to a problem in Ricoeur's discussion of the speculative considerations involved in his ontology of poetics.

In light of these problems, we may understand better what is at stake in Heidegger's efforts to approach the disclosure of poetics not from the conceptual framework of metaphysics, but from the mutual *nearness* of thought and poetry. In Heidegger's conception, thought does not yet know its essence and has no fixed conceptual framework such as metaphysics has. In fact, this metaphysical framework leads to a concealment of the essence of thought itself since thinking this essence requires thinking poetic disclosure. From this Heideggerian point of view, Ricoeur's account of poetic disclosure is highly problematic: by approaching poetic disclosure in metaphysical terms it misses the opportunity to receive a new way of thinking about this disclosure. According to Heidegger this even means missing the opportunity to think the essence of thought itself as a discourse on being. By emphasizing that thinking receives its own essence from its nearness with poeticizing, Heidegger takes the implications of the ontology implicit in the poetic experience of language much more seriously than Ricoeur does. Indeed, poetry is a "gift" to thought, but this gift is an ontological problem itself. Thought no longer thinks poetic disclosure in terms of the concepts inherited and adopted from metaphysics, but it seeks the appropriate word to think this disclosure.

Regarding the problem of poetic disclosure, there are two main points of divergence between Ricoeur and Heidegger. In our examination of Ricoeur's metaphorical "as" and his explanation of the ontological dimension of metaphor as being-as, we saw how Ricoeur and Heidegger part ways in their understanding of poetic disclosure. Being-as as both being and being-not implies in a traditional way that metaphor is also a veiled speech that disguises how a being is. Ricoeur would probably deny this, but it is clear from his account that poetic disclosure requires a complement in the conceptual identification of being in this being-as. Heidegger, on the other hand, claims that poetic language says, discloses, what is. No displacement is involved in this disclosure.

By leaving the question of being to the conceptual discourse of metaphysics, it seems that Ricoeur does not recognize the intricate relation between metaphysics' conceptual approach of being and what Heidegger calls the onto-theo-logical constitution of metaphysics. The conceptual discourse of metaphysics privileges the identity of beings and approaches being under the aspect of this identity. It is exactly this aspect of metaphysics that conceals the question of being in the history of metaphysics. By privileging the traditional discourse of metaphysics in his account of the ontological postulate of poetics, Ricoeur runs the risk of losing the positive account of the disclosure of poetic language and its full ontological implications.

DERRIDA ON THE EFFACEMENT AND WITHDRAWAL OF METAPHOR

With the following words, Derrida comments on Anatole France's dialogue "*Ariste et Polyphile, ou le langage métaphysique*": "White mythology—metaphysics has erased within itself the fabulous scene that has produced it, the scene that nevertheless remains active and stirring, inscribed in white ink, an invisible design covered over in the palimpsest."⁵⁸ In this dialogue, Polyphile argues that the language of metaphysics is originally a metaphorical language. Terms such as "*soul*" originally had a purely sensible meaning. According to Polyphile, these terms have become metaphysical because of their metaphorical use. However, the metaphysician does not treat these terms as metaphors: the metaphysician has forgotten the metaphorical origin of the terms he or she considers to be his or her essential concepts. Therefore, Polyphile describes the language of the metaphysician as white mythology. It is a metaphorical language, but this metaphoricity is forgotten and effaced: it is written in white ink. The metaphysical text is thus a palimpsest: it hides its metaphorical origin. At the same time, the effacement of this metaphorical origin is not complete: although effaced and disguised, "the fabulous scene that has produced it," as Derrida writes, "remains active and stirring."

Derrida is clearly intrigued by Polyphile's description of the relation between metaphoricity and metaphysical language. Yet, he does not simply adopt Polyphile's archeological account, since Polyphile remains indebted to certain metaphysical presuppositions; he maintains the perspective of a purely sensible, physical language to which we would return if we could restore the original meanings underlying the metaphysical metaphors. Nevertheless, it is not difficult to see what attracts Derrida beyond these metaphysical presuppositions in Polyphile's claims. In contrast to Heidegger's claim that metaphor remains within metaphysics, Polyphile suggests that metaphors are at the hidden center of metaphysical language and form the unreflected orientation and direction of metaphysics: metaphor is the "*sens*" of metaphysics. Metaphor does not belong to metaphysics, but, on the contrary, metaphysical language stems from an original metaphoricity that metaphysics has effaced from the very moment of its beginning: "It becomes a metaphor when philosophical discourse puts it into circulation. Simultaneously, the first meaning and the first displacement are then forgotten. The metaphor is no longer noticed, and it is taken for the proper meaning.... Constitutionally, philosophical culture will always have been an obliterating one." This quote marks both the similarity and difference between Heidegger and Derrida.

Derrida follows Heidegger in his idea that philosophy is marked by a fundamental forgetting. Yet, following Polyphile, he insists that this forgetting is due to a certain metaphorical movement. It is this aspect of Polyphile's account that Derrida wants to affirm and that he tries "to reinscribe…otherwise," that is to say beyond its metaphysical presuppositions.[59] This opening passage of "*La mythologie blanche*" already shows that Derrida neither approaches the question of metaphor from the perspective of disclosure, as Ricoeur does, nor from the perspective of metaphor's belonging to metaphysical discourse, as Heidegger does. Instead, Derrida approaches metaphor under the aspect of a generative concealment and a forgotten displacement. Since philosophy begins with and as this forgetting, this displacement and its intrinsic metaphoricity cannot be recuperated by the conceptual language of philosophy.

The Question of Usury

As the essay's subtitle indicates—"Metaphor in the Philosophical Text"—Derrida addresses the question of the use of metaphors in philosophical texts in "*La mythologie blanche.*" Unlike Ricoeur, he is not so much interested in giving an elaborate understanding of poetic metaphors, such as "Achilles leapt on the foe as a lion." Rather, in line with Heidegger's comments on metaphor, the examples of metaphor are first and foremost *philosophical metaphors,* such as the sun and its light in Plato's allegory of the cave as well as Hegel's understanding of *Sinn.* He is concerned with the questions of how philosophy deals with the metaphoricity of its own texts and whether philosophy can succeed in grasping this metaphoricity of its own texts under a concept of metaphor.

Metaphors pose a particular problem for philosophy since the presence of metaphors in philosophical texts—they are present everywhere—upsets and threatens the univocity that the conceptual discourse of philosophy aims at. Ricoeur, as we saw, proceeds from an ideal distinction between poetics and philosophy.[60] This allows him to presuppose that as soon as a metaphor enters philosophy, properly speaking, it would be mastered by conceptual discourse and its equivocality would be regulated. Derrida contests this ideal distinction because we cannot say that we *first* have philosophy and *subsequently* compose philosophical texts guided by its ideal of conceptuality. For instance, metaphors found in Hegel's work, such as *begreifen* and *Sinn,* show that metaphoricity *precedes* conceptualization. Moreover, philosophy cannot sidestep this problem because this metaphoricity opens up philosophy and is never fully mastered within philosophy. For instance, the metaphor of grasping opens up the possibility of thinking "understanding" (*begreifen*) and "concept" (*Begriff*) in Hegel's thought. As a consequence, Hegel cannot but think thought as a form of grasping. This metaphor overtakes his entire discourse: it opens and orients it, but it is no longer present in this discourse *as metaphor.*

Because of this concealed metaphorical surplus of philosophical discourse, its univocity is not a given property of a philosophical text, but it is at best a *telos* to which philosophy strives in order to attain the identity of beings. Therefore, in order for philosophy to conceptualize its own discourse, it first needs to conceptualize its own metaphoricity. That is to say, philosophy needs to master its metaphors and to that end it tries to develop a *concept of metaphor.* It is exactly the impossibility of this concept of metaphor to which Derrida devotes his entire essay and by that very gesture undermines Ricoeur's enterprise.

The Impossibility of a Concept of Metaphor

Since metaphors are at work in philosophical texts from the outset, a concept of metaphor to master the metaphoricity of philosophical discourse can only be developed *après coup,* afterward. Thus, according to Derrida, the concept of metaphor is preceded by metaphoricity, and it is produced as an effect within a field in which this metaphoricity is always already active. Therefore, the important question is: Is it possible for philosophy to produce within its own field a concept that completely masters the metaphoricity that has produced or has helped to produce this field? From this perspective, it is clear that the aim of the concept of metaphor is not so much an element of a poetic or rhetoric theory, but rather concerns a reflection of philosophy on its own textuality. This concept should provide us with the law or the structuring principle of this metaphoricity. In this way, it would describe the metaphorical origin of philosophy as such, and master it. As a consequence, philosophy and its genesis would become completely transparent to philosophy. These are the stakes of the concept of metaphor.

Obviously, Derrida's answer to the above question is negative from the outset; he does not even try to produce such a concept or risk an introduction to such this project, as he writes, "Here, instead of venturing into the [prolegomena] to some future metaphorics, let us rather attempt to recognize in principle the *condition of impossibility* of such a project."[61] This particular impossibility is grounded in the following paradox.[62] On the one hand, to construct a metaphorics that could oversee the entirety of the metaphoricity at work in philosophical texts, we would need to have a point of view *exterior* to philosophical discourse. The law of a discourse and the principles of its structuration can only be discovered if we step *outside* this discourse and place it opposite to us. On the other hand, this metaphorics depends on a *concept* of metaphor, which means that it is a fundamentally philosophical enterprise that can only be carried out by and in philosophy. Hence, we can only attain such a law *within* philosophy.

The necessity of stepping outside of philosophy in order to determine a metaphorics and the impossibility of doing so determine the particular blindness of the concept of metaphor. To relate the problem of the concept of metaphor to problems I have previously described, it can be helpful to keep in mind that in Derrida's essay on metaphor, the *concept of metaphor* plays the role of a *transcendental signified*. It is philosophy's presupposition that its metaphoricity can be determined in a concept of metaphor. However, because of the above paradox, no metaphorics can attain this transcendental signified in its pure form. This lack of a transcendental signified is interpreted as a productive space by Derrida. That is to say, the creation of the concept of metaphor will itself involve the use of metaphor.

Hence, philosophical discourse cannot help itself: in its attempt to *create* a concept of metaphor, it uses metaphors that go unnoticed by this concept.[63] As a consequence, no concept of metaphor is adequate to the ideal of a metaphorics because every concept involves new metaphors.

The Disproportion between Concept and Metaphor

In "*La mythologie blanche*," Derrida approaches the relation between metaphor and concept from the perspective of the effacement and the usage (*usure*) of metaphor. This "usage" is a common theme in a major line of thought on metaphor: a philosophical concept would be generated on the basis of a worn-out metaphor. According to Derrida, this complementary relation between metaphor and concept is typical of both a teleological and an archeological account. In a teleological account, the loss of metaphor is determined as a conceptual gain. The discontinuity between metaphor and concept is solved by the hierarchy between concept and metaphor. In Hegelian terms, a concept is an elevated metaphor. In an archeological account, the concept that arises on the basis of an effaced metaphor has lost its original liveliness and does not know by which metaphorical figures it is determined. As a consequence, the effacement of metaphor points to a certain naiveté in the concept, which should be overcome in a deciphering of the concept. However, this account assumes a continuity between metaphor and concept that allows us to go back to and revive the original metaphor.

Although Derrida is inspired by this archeological account, the presupposed continuity and the resulting possibility of returning to an original metaphor from which a concept would stem, is an assumption too metaphysical for his taste. Instead, he adapts it as follows: Because the concept does not complement the effacement of metaphor, a disproportion and a discontinuity between concept and metaphor exists. Since this discontinuity is never resolved by a hierarchy between concept and metaphor, the disproportion can still be traced in the philosophical text. This tracing is not an archeological movement back to an original metaphor, but it is rather an active supplementing of this effacement. It is this *extra supplement* that both displaces (or deconstructs) the concept of metaphor and traces the effacement of metaphor in such a concept. Hence, this additional supplement does not suffer from the metaphysical presuppositions of the common archeological accounts, and it can demonstrate that the developed concept of metaphor is not able to capture this newly traced metaphorical movement in the philosophical text.

Hence, Derrida refuses to reduce the concept to a metaphor and he refuses the idea that the effacement of a metaphor would lead to a pure conceptual gain. Rather, he merely wishes to show that against the philosophical claim that philosophical discourse is purely conceptual, this discourse cannot get rid of its own metaphoricity. In this way, Derrida starts questioning at those points that Ricoeur seems to take for granted, namely that we could determine the language of a discourse as conceptual or as metaphorical. His aim is to show that such a discourse is never purely one language but is composed of multiple languages that speak in it. This multiplicity in a language or a discourse threatens the unity of this discourse. In particular, metaphor threatens philosophical discourse. At the same time, the surplus value of *usure* itself—the possibility to create new concepts—depends on this contamination of philosophical discourse by metaphor.

Derrida's critique of both archeology and teleology shows that he aims at the explosion of "the reassuring opposition of the metaphorical and the proper"[64] *without wiping out the very difference between concept and metaphor.* Instead, *différance* is exactly the disproportion between multiple languages such as a metaphorical and a conceptual language. Their difference cannot be identified but it can also not be reduced to an identity. Derrida's attempt to think the effacement of metaphor from the logic of supplementarity and from the multiplicity of languages has important consequences for our understanding of the task of philosophy. The logic of supplementarity opens up the possibility to think the forgetfulness of conceptual thought by displacing philosophy's conceptualization of its other. This means that the task of thinking does not coincide with *conceptualizing* the other of philosophy—in this case, metaphoricity as a concept of metaphor—because this conceptualization remains blind to the supplementarity at work in the transition, transference, and translation of the other of philosophy into philosophy.[65] Derrida's work shows that it is the task of thinking to trace this work of *différance* by displacing philosophical discourse.

Thus, thinking the other can no longer mean *conceptualizing* the other. Rather, thinking the other means tracing what happens and what is missed in the translation and the transition of what is other to philosophy. This transference between multiple languages is the realm of the philosophical itself as "a duel of language."[66] This duel or this incapacity to speak with one voice or out of one genre is exactly the problem of metaphor because a metaphor always already employs two semantic fields and contaminates them. Along these lines of thought, Derrida's thought is perhaps the most metaphorical of the three. Philosophy and poetics neither have their essence in themselves, as Ricoeur seems to argue, nor do they retrieve their essence from an encompassing whole in which they both would have their appropriate place, as Heidegger argues. Rather, the poetic and the philosophical discourses contaminate each other.

Ricoeur and "La Mythologie Blanche"

With this analysis of "*La mythologie blanche*," we are ready to turn to Ricoeur's comments on this essay in the final study of *La métaphore vive*. To some extent, these comments are disappointing since they fail to address the real thrust of Derrida's essay. Derrida also notes this in his brief, somewhat indignant response in "*Le retrait de la métaphore*."[67]

Ricoeur argues that Derrida's essay contains two major assertions. In the first place, Derrida is said to enter the scene from the perspective of dead, worn-out metaphors that would somehow be active behind our (metaphysical) backs in some secretive dimension of metaphysics. As a consequence, "a simple inspection of discourse in its explicit intention, a simple interpretation through a game of question and answer is no longer sufficient." Instead of a simple, semantic inspection, Derrida would approach metaphor armed with the critical weapons of the masters of suspicion: "Armed in this way, the critique is capable of unmasking the *unthought* conjunction of *hidden* metaphysics and *worn-out* metaphor."[68] In the *second* place, Derrida is said to repeat Heidegger's arguments with regard to metaphor. Like Heidegger, Derrida would affirm the metaphysical distinction between sensible and intelligible in his treatment of metaphor.

Most of Ricoeur's discussion rests on these two claims. Yet, these two claims miss Derrida's actual arguments. The first claim misses the point that Derrida does not embrace the usage of metaphor as worn-out metaphor. Although he does pay attention to the notion of concealment and the unthought, he does not do this from the distinction between living and dead metaphor. This distinction is not Derrida's; it is Hegel's. Derrida contests it.[69] Moreover, Derrida does not claim that metaphysics is guided by some hidden metaphor. Polyphile claims this in his dialogue with Ariste. Also with regard to this claim, Derrida is very cautious and spells out all the metaphysical presuppositions of Polyphile's comments. In his analysis of *usure* as usury, he points to a surplus value of metaphor. This surplus value is not the surplus value of a concealed, original metaphor, but it concerns an extra supplement that needs to be brought into play. Hence, rather than referring back to an original, worn-out metaphor, Derrida wants to show that despite philosophy's claim or goal of being a purely conceptual discourse, it always contains metaphorical potential by which a philosophical expression turns out to be "saying something other than what it says."[70] In this sense, his attention to the fundamental metaphoricity of philosophical discourse moves in the same direction as his attention to the *sich versprechen,* the slip of the tongue, in his account of de Man's critique of Heidegger. Philosophy says more and says something beyond the scope of the univocity to which it wants to limit itself. For Derrida, metaphoricity concerns this possibility intrinsic to philosophical discourse to bring an unforeseeable, additional metaphorical turn into play. His only claim is that this possibility is indeed intrinsic to philosophy as a discourse, despite philosophy's teleological self-understanding. Ricoeur's second claim is simply wrong. In fact, Derrida tries to show the untenability of the distinction between sensible and intelligible if we want to understand the metaphoricity of philosophy.[71]

The Multiplicity of Philosophy and Poetics

The outlines of the first discussion have already been given: Ricoeur delimits philosophy and poetry as two separate discourses, whereas Derrida pays attention to the inescapable contamination of philosophy by metaphors. Rather than repeating this issue, let me give one more additional proof of this fundamental difference. In "*La mythologie blanche,*" Derrida argues that the (sole) thesis of philosophy is that the (conceptual) meaning aimed at through the figures at work in certain philosophical concepts is rigorously independent of the figures that transport meaning. Ricoeur explicitly rejects this. He argues that without this philosophical thesis, philosophy would not be possible.[72] Philosophy must maintain itself as a distinct discourse. Derrida, however, argues that philosophy cannot succeed in excluding its original metaphoricity. It is always affected by it.

Despite this very important difference, Derrida's questions are not entirely foreign to Ricoeur's analysis. One of the problems Derrida finds in conceptualization is that it cannot achieve the totality and generality it claims for itself.[73] In his understanding of interpretation, Ricoeur notes that interpretation leads to a conceptual representation of the resemblance disclosed by a metaphor. By its conceptual nature, this representation necessarily misses the metaphorical resemblance and its matching equivocality because it approaches them both from the perspective of univocity and identity. This particular loss implies that no concept provides an adequate representation of a metaphor. Ricoeur conceptualizes this by describing metaphor as a Kantian aesthetic Idea.

This conceptual inadequacy can perhaps be extended to every intersection between philosophy and a discourse heterogeneous to it. In his thought, Derrida extends this problem of heterogeneity to the practice of philosophy as such. Philosophy always tries to subsume what is other than philosophy under a concept. This is the genuinely philosophical movement. Philosophy is always related to what is other than itself and is always trying to reduce this otherness by representing it within conceptual discourse. This fundamental relation of philosophy to what is other than itself is also affirmed by Ricoeur when he argues that poetics is the *possibility* of philosophy. Without a relation to what is other than itself, without something that provokes thought, philosophy would not think. And within this relation to what provokes thought, conceptual discourse is always inadequate. This points to a particular dependency of philosophy on what is other and to a particular threat to philosophy by this other. Ricoeur, however, does not take the final step that Derrida does take. Derrida traces this dependency and this threat *within* the conceptuality of philosophical discourse itself. Within its own texts, philosophy finds a metaphoricity that provokes thought and opens up concepts, but these cannot be mastered in an encompassing concept of metaphor. Therefore, the metaphoricity of philosophy itself remains a question even if we have tried to conceptualize it or to regulate its equivocality.

The Question of Transference

Another important difference between Ricoeur and Derrida concerns the question of whether it is fruitful to develop a concept of metaphor. Ricoeur's *La métaphore vive* proposes a new theory of metaphor. Derrida argues that such a theory might be very interesting but will never be able to control the metaphoricity of the philosophical text itself.[74] In this sense, his critique of the concept of metaphor concerns Ricoeur's enterprise as whole. This might be the reason why Ricoeur is so critical of "*La mythologie blanche*." How could Derrida's critique of the concept of metaphor affect Ricoeur's analysis?

Ricoeur can only determine philosophy and poetics as two *separate* discourses by his own conceptual determination of metaphor. Without this conceptual determination, it would not be clear that a metaphorical discourse is strictly distinct from a conceptual discourse. The concept of metaphor operates as a means for excluding the metaphorical from the philosophical. Thus, if there is any truth to Derrida's considerations about metaphoricity in philosophical texts,

Ricoeur has effaced the possibility of such a metaphoricity in his definition of metaphor.

Ricoeur determines metaphor from the perspective of resemblance and he does so following Aristotle. In his analysis of Aristotle's concept of metaphor, Derrida indicates that the Greek word Aristotle uses for resemblance, *homoiōsis,* is the same word that he uses to describe the condition of truth as correspondence. This indicates that metaphor is the condition of truth.[75] This is indeed the case, but in a particular sense: metaphor is supposed to be in the service of truth and knowledge. It is a means to bring something to knowledge, as we have seen in Aristotle's description of the agreeability of metaphor. This agreeability corresponds to the fact that metaphor lets us seize a new idea promptly. This insertion of metaphor within the philosophical enterprise of understanding also implies that metaphorical language itself is only secondary to the metaphysical discourse of full truth.[76] According to Derrida, this determination of metaphor as being in the service of truth already effaces the dissemination of metaphoricity. This dissemination does not restrict itself to a resemblance that can be accounted for conceptually and that increases our knowledge or our experience of the world.

It is obvious that the relation between metaphor and understanding is very important for Ricoeur. Against this background, the difference between Ricoeur's analysis of the suspension of the literal sense and reference of metaphor and Derrida's analysis of a similar suspension is striking. According to Ricoeur, this suspension is merely the flip side of a more positive phenomenon. This positive phenomenon concerns a semantic and ontological gain that gives itself to be understood in metaphor. Derrida, however, approaches this suspension as the deferral of the truth of language. A metaphorically used word is detached from its common referent. This means that metaphorical language does not simply efface itself for the presentation of its true referent, but begins as a *transference,* as a "wandering" (*errance*) of the semantic. Hence, this transference begins by *deferring* the truth of language, in the Aristotelian sense of correspondence and univocity.[77]

From this Derridean perspective, it is telling that Ricoeur argues that the ontological gain of poetics is only implicit and can only be explicated *afterward* by metaphysics. Ricoeur claims that metaphor discloses and discovers a deeper level of reality, but this discovery is only established and unfolded *afterward in a discourse that allows no metaphors.* Does this not indicate that the semantic innovation of metaphor is more like a wandering of the semantic than an implicit disclosure of reality? Like Ricoeur, Derrida argues that metaphor is an intermediary stage, and that metaphorical transference is a transgression of conceptual space. However, Derrida, pace Ricoeur, does not argue that the goal of this transgressing transference lies in a reformulation of this conceptual space and in a newly discovered truth. Instead, he claims that the possibility of meaning employed in metaphor's "wandering" is the possibility of untruth. Metaphor is a detour in which truth can lose itself.[78] Differently put, the displacement of metaphor does not only precede and condition its disclosure but it also threatens its disclosive dimension. Therefore, metaphor is not simply in the service of truth, as Aristotle would like to have it, but it is a danger to the metaphysical discourse of truth.

According to Ricoeur, Derrida would equate the distinction between sensible and intelligible to the distinction between proper and metaphorical. However, Derrida's discussion of the "proper" in Aristotle's philosophy shows that his attention to this notion has nothing to do with such an equation. He points out three characteristics of this notion, and I want to pay attention to the first two.[79] First, Derrida argues that Aristotle determines proper language as a *univocal* language. Univocity is the *telos* of language for Aristotle. As a consequence, metaphor is not a proper language; it is equivocal and plurivocal. Obviously, this nonproperness of metaphor is not the same as being a sensory figure in distinction to its intelligible meaning. This nonproperness indicates that in metaphorical language we have not yet reached the true goal of language. With respect to truth, a metaphor is always obscure and a veiling speech, as we have seen in a passage from Aristotle's *Topics* we discussed above and which is quoted by Derrida.

Secondly, Derrida argues that although "proper" is related to essence, a metaphor does not disclose the essence of a thing; it merely transposes properties. A metaphor shows that an unfamiliar thing shares certain properties with a familiar thing, but it does not disclose a thing simply and fully *as it is*.[80] Therefore, metaphor can only be a mediated speech and needs to be supplemented by a full, proper speech that addresses the essence of beings. It is this aspect of non-being in metaphor that reoccurs in Ricoeur's conception of resemblance. In Derrida's analysis, this non-being of metaphor shows that it cannot be fully in the service of the discourse on truth and continually threatens this discourse. Hence, Derrida paints a picture of effaced metaphoricity as a metaphoricity that disrupts the discourse of truth due to its transference. Both aspects of the Aristotelian notion of the proper to which Derrida points are lacking in Ricoeur's analysis of metaphor. It is remarkable that exactly these two aspects indicate the problem of concealment and veiling in the concept of metaphor that Ricoeur refrains from addressing.

The Withdrawal of Metaphor

"*Le retrait de la métaphore*" is Derrida's second important essay on metaphor. In this essay, he approaches the question of metaphor from the perspective of Heidegger's concept of withdrawal (*Entziehung*), which he translates as *retrait*. Derrida plays with this word by showing its relation to *re-trait*, which he explicates as a supplementary trait, or another characteristic. Throughout his essay, he develops what we could call a logic of the *retrait/re-trait*. According to this logic, withdrawal only takes place by the addition of some supplementary trait. This logic implies (1) that without such a supplementary trait we cannot trace withdrawal, and (2) that every withdrawal introduces a supplementary trait of what is withdrawn. Both implications play a role in his essay. The second implication plays a role in his understanding of Heidegger's critique of metaphor. According to Derrida, this critique involves a *withdrawal* of the *concept* of metaphor. By this withdrawal, Heidegger opens up a space in which other characteristics (*re-trait*) of metaphoricity can be marked; sometimes Derrida calls this other metaphoricity "*quasi-metaphoricity.*"

In this section, I want to argue that the genuine import of Derrida's reading of Heidegger's conception of *Entziehung* from the logic of *retrait/re-trait* can be found in the first implication stating that withdrawal can only be traced by an extra trait that refers to it. In the first chapter, we have seen that Heidegger claims that the Greeks kept the essence of concealment in what they experienced as unconcealment, namely *muthos* or *Sage*. In this way, he seems to claim that the essence of withdrawal and concealment can be brought into unconcealment in and by saying (*Sage*). According to Derrida, as we also saw in the second chapter, this is a bit too much. What is withdrawn, whether it concerns the essence of being, of language, or of thought, never simply comes into presence. The best we can do is trace it by an extra trait or treatment. At this point, we could locate the difference between Heidegger's saying and Derrida's account of language. Both are concerned with addressing what is concealed and withdrawn. Heidegger approaches this problem under the aspect of language as saying. Concealment is what withholds truth and keeps its proper essence ready in advance. In this sense, the word *Ereignis* is a word full of expectation and *suspense;* it is a term that announces in Heidegger's language what is to come: the event of disclosure in which concealment gives the proper essence that it withholds. Therefore, thinking entreats the unbroken essence of concealment into the open region and thus into its own truth.[81] Derrida argues that such a hopeful thinking of language that longs for the appropriate word, remains metaphysical in nature since it still aims at arriving at a proper name of being. In the end, the privileging of disclosure over displacement implies the affirmation of the traditional metaphysical quest for the proper name of being.[82] Therefore, Derrida approaches this problem by thinking language from the perspective of writing, translation, or the transference of metaphor, that is to say, the words we use to address concealment are not simply the words of a disclosing saying, but they are a supplement as well. Words always present a double, or simply put, words always represent something else. They introduce an extra trait thanks to which they *refer* to what withdraws itself; without these traces and traits we would not be related to concealment at all. At the same time, as supplement, they postpone and *suspend* the disclosure of the essence of this concealment. Moreover, because every word is at best a double of the essence of saying, the essence of saying is said with multiple words and in multiple languages. Derrida traces this problem of the multiplicity of languages in his discussion of Heidegger's comments on the proximity of thought and poetry: the essence of language appears in multiple ways in multiple languages.

In his approach to language, Derrida shows the difficulty of the question of (the meaning of) being. Due to its supplementary nature, language never simply shows what is. In his reading of Heidegger in "*Le retrait de la métaphore,*" we can discern this concern with respect to Heidegger's efforts to think being, to think the essence of thought and poetry, and to think the essence of language.

The Quasi-Metaphor of Metaphysics

The first line of thought of "*Le retrait de la métaphore*" discusses Heidegger's critique of metaphor. Derrida argues that this critique aims at a withdrawal (*retrait*) of the *concept* of metaphor; later in his essay, he relates this withdrawal as *retrait* to Heidegger's concept of *Entziehung*. According to Derrida, Heidegger's attempt to overcome the concept of metaphor opens up another form of metaphoricity, which Derrida calls "*quasi-metaphoricity.*" This quasi-metaphoricity is a form of metaphoricity that *opens up metaphysics and would be effaced by metaphysics* in its concept of metaphor. In this way, Derrida relates his own understanding of metaphoricity in "*La mythologie blanche*" to (his reading of) Heidegger's critique of metaphor, arguing that in Heidegger's analysis of metaphysics we can find other traces of metaphor than can be found in the concept of metaphor. According to Heidegger, the withdrawal and the concealment of being in metaphysics is due to the determination of being *as* a being. Metaphysics approaches being under the aspect of that being that is most present and that is taken for the measure of the beingness of other beings. Derrida proposes to interpret this "as" (being *as* a being) at the heart of metaphysics as a "*metaphorico-metonymical*" displacement. Metaphysics can only name being metaphorico-metonymically, that is, metaphysics never names the essence of being, but it names being *as if* it is a being. It uses (the name of) a being, such as subject, substance, Idea, and will to power, to name being. Hence, Derrida argues that Heidegger's discovery of the onto-theo-logical constitution of metaphysics implies that metaphysics names being metaphorico-metonymically and is thus always "in a tropical relation" to being.[83] Moreover, this metaphysical displacement of being is a form of concealment as disguise (*Verdeckung, Verstellung*) in Heidegger's thought. Thus, metaphysics is not only marked by approaching being as a being, but it is also marked by an effacement of this "as." This is the forgetfulness of metaphysics.

In this way, Derrida argues that the withdrawal of being in Heidegger's thought corresponds to the effacement of an originary metaphoricity in metaphysics. To overcome this withdrawal, Heidegger does not simply propose another being as the proper meaning of being, but he approaches the question of the meaning of being from the perspective of this withdrawal. As such, to overcome the forgetfulness of metaphysics, Heidegger needs to think this withdrawal as withdrawal. According to Derrida, to address the withdrawal of being, Heidegger withdraws the concept of metaphor in order to open up a new form of metaphoricity that allows him to approach the withdrawal of being. Therefore, the withdrawal of the concept of metaphor in Heidegger's thought is accompanied by a supplementary trait that would open up the perspective of metaphysics' quasi-metaphoricity with respect to being.

It is not entirely clear why Derrida invokes metaphor and quasi-metaphoricity here to understand the withdrawal of being and the forgetfulness of being. Heidegger himself does not use this terminology. Everything depends upon Derrida's interpretation that the metaphysical "as"—that is, being interpreted as a being—is somehow related to a metaphorical "as." However, as I have shown before in my discussion of Ricoeur's metaphorical "as," it is not very likely that Heidegger's use of "as" should be interpreted as a metaphorical "as." His "as" concerns the "as" of interpretation that speaks out of a whole to which it belongs. Even though this whole withdraws itself and is never present as such, we belong to it. In fact, the whole of disclosure forms our essence. Therefore, in order to address it as our essence, Heidegger takes great care to avoid any reference to metaphor, allegory, or metonym and rather speaks of this whole in terms of what is proper to us. Hence, to call Heidegger's way of speaking about this whole quasi-metaphorical, as Derrida does, is to go into the opposite direction as Heidegger does.

I propose to understand Derrida's *coup de force* in his reading of Heidegger as follows. What is essential in the concept of metaphor is the distinction between the proper and the metaphorical. To explain why Derrida calls Heidegger's qualification of metaphysics a "quasi-metaphorics," we need to consider the role of this distinction in Heidegger's qualification. The claim that metaphysics always interprets being as a being and therefore veils being means that metaphysics does not address being properly. Moreover, opposed to this metaphysical treatment of being, the proper essence of being is still withdrawn in concealment. In this sense, the language of metaphysics is a concealed (quasi-)metaphorical language, whereas Heidegger's attention to language as saying promises a more proper, disclosing saying of the essence of being.

If we follow Derrida in his proposal to see in Heidegger's thought a shift from a metaphysical concept of metaphor to the quasi-metaphoricity of metaphysics, we also see that Heidegger's language on being and truth is opened up by the logic of retrait/re-trait. In order to open up a new language, Heidegger needs to reappropriate metaphor—in particular the distinction between proper and nonproper. Thus, the withdrawal accompanied by a new trait or treatment of metaphor can be seen as the condition of possibility of Heidegger's language on being and truth. Moreover, in Derrida's logic of supplementarity, this displacement of metaphor is neither ever simply in the service of truth and disclosure, nor is the conception of truth and being the *telos* of this displacement. For Derrida, displacement itself opens up the possibility of approaching the unthought of metaphysics—

for instance, to think the unthought metaphoricity of the metaphysi-cal concept of metaphor. What is to be presented in the wake of this displacement is uncertain, but it is clear that the disclosure of the unthought is enabled by this displacement.

At this point, we see a clear difference between Heidegger's *Destruktion* and Derrida's *déconstruction*. Heidegger's *Destruktion* concerns the dismantling of the disguises and the displacement by metaphysics in the service of the disclosure of the essence of being. Derrida's *déconstruction,* on the other hand, dismantles the displace-ments by metaphysics by another displacement and is not in the serv-ice of truth as disclosure.[84] To understand this difference, we must be attuned to the distinction between language as saying and language as transference. Language as saying is simply disclosure. It presupposes the possibility of the disclosure of the essence of withdrawal and con-cealment. Even the essence of *lēthē* is unconcealed in *muthos,* accord-ing to Heidegger. Language as metaphoricity, on the other hand, implies that every articulation is itself in a metaphorical displacement. This means that every articulation is always overloaded (*surcharge*) with the possibility of a supplementary characteristic (*re-trait*) that displaces this articulation. We can only address or trace what with-draws itself, and we trace this by adding a supplementary trait.

Heidegger's Language

The second line of thought of "*Le retrait de la métaphore*" addresses the alleged metaphoricity of Heidegger's own language given his rejection of metaphor. To approach this question, Derrida examines the quasi-metaphoricity of Heidegger's (non)metaphor "the house of being." This expression should not be understood as a transference of the image of a house to language. Instead, Heidegger claims that being will one day say more about the home and about dwelling than the other way around. In a more general sense, this example indicates that Heidegger rejects the idea that his own language is metaphorical.

Derrida both agrees and disagrees with this latter remark. Indeed, Heidegger's language is not metaphorical if we understand "meta-phorical" from the perspective of a concept of metaphor; his language is a rupture with metaphysical language. Yet, his language also seems to introduce another characteristic of metaphoricity, and this characteristic can be traced in Heidegger's explanation of the expression "the house of being." By rejecting the idea that the image of a house is transferred to being, Heidegger rejects the common metaphysical concept of metaphor.[85] Yet, his alternative to the interpretation of this expression as metaphor is, strictly speaking, not a proper expression. Heidegger does not claim that being *already* says more about the home or dwelling, but "the house of being" expresses a promise. In this expression, being promises, one day, to say more about the home and dwelling.[86] Derrida remarks that in this way the home and dwelling become *unheimlich,* uncanny. Heidegger's expression indicates a resemblance that does not bring closer what is distant, but instead distances what *seems* close. What does this mean for the form of language Heidegger employs in his works? Apparently, this language cannot be called metaphorical in the classical sense of the word since in this classical sense a metaphor brings that which is unfamiliar closer on the basis of a resemblance. Derrida discerns a similarity between Heidegger's language and figures that employ similarities but do so in a different way than metaphor, namely, figures that use similarities to demonstrate a difference and to effectuate a distanciation. Think, for instance, of a parody or of the well-known double motive in nineteenth century novels. A parody as well as a double "resemble" the original so much that they are hardly distinguishable from it. Yet, they have the opposite effect of a metaphor. Instead of making familiar what is unfamiliar, they alienate us from the well-known and familiar original on the basis of a minute difference. A similar movement is brought about in the promising expression "the house of being" that defers its actual gift. As in *Mémoires pour Paul de Man,* Derrida suggests that the promise of a quasi-metaphor can never present what it promises—a proper name for being. Consequently, unlike a common metaphor that brings close what is distant, the quasi-metaphor of being suspends and defers the arrival of being.

Derrida next turns to Heidegger's discussion of the nearness between thought and poetry. Also in this context, the essence of thought is what is promised (*zusagen*), and thinking reaches the supposition (*gelangt in die Vermutung*) of the essence of thought. This promise addresses the disclosure of being as a disclosure *to come*. In Heidegger's expression, this disclosure has not yet arrived, but is only drawing near. In this sense, Heidegger's expression is ahead of itself and anticipates an arrival that has not yet taken place. Hence, the promised disclosure is still withdrawn, but also held ready in withdrawal. Derrida's discussion of *retrait/re-trait* proposes that expressions such as "the house of being" are traces or a signs that point to this withdrawal. They are supplementary traits that take the place of this disclosure just as this disclosure is still drawing near without arriving. Yet, the arrival itself, for which Heidegger has suggested the word *Ereignis,* seems to imply a genuine propriation (*eignen*). Opposed to this propriation, his current expressions are merely quasi-metaphorical.[87]

In the form of a promise, Heidegger anticipates what has not yet been fulfilled or disclosed. Heidegger's quasi-metaphorical language is thus full of the suspense of what is to come. Derrida discusses the notion of this metaphorical promise from the perspective of the logic of *retrait/re-trait:* the promise only addresses what is to come by displacing and deferring it. As a consequence, Heidegger's *suspense* of the "to come" (*à-venir*) changes into the *suspension* of the "to come" in Derrida's reading. In Derrida's reading, no appropriate or proper word exists that may be given by language to say the essence of language. As Heidegger puts it at the beginning of the first lecture of "*Das Wesen der Sprache,*" if we need to bring to language what has not yet been spoken, "then everything depends on whether language gives or withholds the appropriate word."[88] If this *suspense* is taken to be a *suspension,* then the question of language changes accordingly: by characterizing Heidegger's language as quasi-metaphorical, Derrida inscribes this differential structure of transference into the heart of Heidegger's language of the promise. Language can never get beyond its quasi-metaphorical position with respect to being.

Concealment of Essence and Essence of Concealment

Derrida's third line of inquiry in "*Le retrait de la métaphore*" is framed by the following question: if multiple languages exist, what does Heidegger mean by *the essence* of language? Derrida begins with the thesis that language is fundamentally multiple.[89] Therefore, the question of the essence of language always begins with the question of the *relation* between languages. In this third line of thought, Derrida examines Heidegger's use of the German verbs *ziehen* and *reissen* because they describe this very relation. To understand this complicated and very dense line of thought, I propose to interpret Derrida's analysis from the perspective of two theses.

First, if a language is a realm of disclosure, then the relation between (two) languages cannot be disclosed in either language. We can only trace this withdrawn relation by bringing it into play once more. One of Derrida's basic questions is how to address a "relation" that is always already effaced, withdrawn, and presented by a displacing supplement. Secondly, this relation between languages is prior to the essences of these languages.

Derrida traces this particular problem in Heidegger's work in his analysis of thought and poetry. Thought and poetry are two distinct discourses that receive their essences from their relation, which Heidegger determines as their "nearness." This "nearness" between thought and poetry is withdrawn: it has not yet been thought and therefore the essence of thought is "to come." Moreover, Heidegger determines this nearness as the nearness of saying. This implies that he addresses the question of the essence of language from the perspective of multiple discourses, but also places these multiple languages in light of that which gathers them. This and the above two theses guide Derrida's attention to Heidegger's discussion of the relation between thought and poetry.

Derrida notes that Heidegger determines this nearness in two ways: as *Beziehung* and as *Aufriß*. This means that he approaches this nearness along the lines of the attraction and bringing closer (*ziehen*) of thought and poetry and from the perspective of their tearing apart (*reissen*). Only by drawing near to poetry and thinking its *Beziehung* to poetry, can thinking hope to think its essence. However, the unity of this essence itself concerns the *Aufriß*, the tearing apart of thought and poetry that is the opening cut (*entame*) of both discourses.[90] Derrida stresses that neither this nearness nor this opening cut ever appear; only their withdrawal can be traced.[91]

Derrida's conclusions from this reading are twofold. First, both *Aufriß* and *Beziehung* are not proper phenomena. They do not belong to either language. Hence, they are excluded from both realms of disclosure. Therefore, they only appear in their inscription in thought and poetry as their effacement.[92] This indicates that thought can only relate to its relation with poetry—from which it receives its essence—by means of a word that supplements the effacement of this relation in thought itself. Once more we see that Derrida argues that we can only relate to what withdraws itself—this time, nearness and opening cut—by means of another trait. The words that Heidegger chooses are therefore not appropriate or proper words; they are quasi-metaphorical. Secondly, the multiplicity of thought and poetry and the withdrawal of their unifying essence can also be found in Heidegger's vocabulary. He is unable to discuss this essence by only *one* appropriate word, but he needs two. And when we need two words and describe two "essences," the question of *the* essence of language becomes "infinitely complicated."[93] The question of the essence of language and its appropriation in *Ereignis* continually moves between an attraction on the way to a unification and a setting apart on the way to a separation.

Along this line of thought, Derrida demonstrates that Heidegger's discussion of the essence of language always proceeds according to the logic of *retrait/re-trait*. He can only address the withdrawn unity of the essence of language by a multiplicity of supplementary traits. These traits always efface and displace this withdrawal. The traits of this withdrawal never lead to the disclosure of the essence of language or to the presence of the gift of this essence, because they are always discussed quasi-metaphorically by the supplement of another trait.

This complicated and cunning reading of Heidegger should not hide the fact that Derrida's deconstructive reading of Heidegger's conception of withdrawal displaces this conception in an important way. By combining *retrait* and *re-trait,* Derrida tries to inscribe the notion of displacement into Heidegger's notion of withdrawal. To show to what extent this inscription displaces Heidegger's own conception of withdrawal, I want to compare it to the analysis of Heidegger's conception of concealment. By combining the displacement of *re-trait* to the primary concealment of *retrait,* Derrida inscribes the displacement of *Verstellen* into concealment as *Versagen.* He inscribes *pseudos* into *lēthē.* Although I would not claim that such a reading of Heidegger is impossible, it is definitely not an innocent paraphrase of Heidegger's thought. It inscribes the supplementary displacement of *pseudos* in between the chiasmatic relation between *lēthē* and *alētheia.* Every word that says *lēthē,* and therefore in particular the Greek saying of *lēthē* in *muthos,* is a supplement and a sign that displaces *lēthē* and disrupts its concealment.

This inscription should not be taken lightly. It implies that the essence of concealment—if it still makes sense to talk about essence here—is always discussed in multiple and dispersed ways according to different supplementary traits. Such a broken essence of concealment completely disrupts the task of thinking as Heidegger articulates it in *Vom Wesen der Wahrheit:* "Philosophical thinking is the gentle releasement that does not renounce itself the concealment of being as a whole. Philosophical thinking is especially the stern and resolute openness that does not disrupt the concealing but entreats its *unbroken* essence into the open region of understanding and thus into its own truth."[94] According to Heidegger, one should not refuse oneself the unthought and the untruth of being. This nonrefusal is the opposite of disrupting or displacing this concealment. Only if we invite it *unbroken* into its own truth do we admit the essence of concealment. Not to refuse ourselves concealment is to open ourselves to the richest gift of thought: its unthought. From this perspective, the intricate relation between *retrait* and *re-trait* can only be read as a disruption of the unbroken essence of concealment, as a failure of the task of thinking and as a missing of the richest gift of thought.

Derrida would probably not disagree with this latter conclusion. In the logic of supplementarity, the unthought can only be thought by missing it. The latter formulation already indicates that this missing is not simply a negative aspect of language or a lack. Derrida's translation of *Entziehung* as *retrait* is in this sense exemplary. By missing and displacing the German *Entziehung* in its translation as *retrait*, he discloses the possibility of thinking the unthought of Heidegger's thought. Only by bringing into play an additional trait of withdrawal, the Heideggerian text on withdrawal gives itself to be read in a new way.

This example of a displacement shows perhaps most clearly that Derrida's complex argument of "*Le retrait de la métaphore*" proposes a similar perspective on metaphor as the one he unfolds in "*La mythologie blanche.*" Metaphor is in the first place a displacement. It is not a borrowing of meaning to be understood under the aspect of the disclosed, metaphorical meaning; metaphor is in the first place the "wandering of the semantic." This "wandering" is a dissemination of meaning(s). This means that it cannot be understood as a displacement within the horizon of a regulative idea of meaning or within the particular epochal realm of a disclosure. The displacement at stake in this wandering from one context to another is not guided by an encompassing meaning. Rather, it is itself the principle of a semantic transformation and innovation that both closes off and opens up the possibility of meaning in the first place.

Derrida's examination of metaphoricity has important consequences for the question of being as well. As he argues in his discussion of Aristotle in "*La mythologie blanche,*" metaphor as semantic wandering is also the suspension of the reference of language. Moreover, this wandering presupposes a fundamental multiplicity of languages, and hence a fundamental multiplicity of domains of disclosure. This means that the question of being becomes a highly complicated one: Derrida maintains that the question of being is always related to the question of the *whole* of being. That is to say, in the question of being, the multiplicity involved in language is brought back to an encompassing unity—even though this unity cannot be thematized as identity and is at best an horizon or a regulative idea. This presupposition of the *whole* of being not only plays an important role in Heidegger's thought on language, but it also plays implicitly a fundamental role in Ricoeur's understanding of the metaphorical reference. Without the presupposition of the whole of being, metaphorical reference would merely reach the world at *another* level and not at a *deeper* level, as Ricoeur maintains. Derrida, on the other hand, emphasizes the displacement and the wandering of metaphoricity. The principle he finds in this way is not the whole or the gathering of being, but the multiplication of traits preceding the disclosure of the essence of being.

Derrida concludes his famous essay "*La différance*" with a critique of Heidegger concerning the quest for a proper word in Heidegger's thought on the relation between language and being in "*Der Spruch des Anaximander.*" As in *Unterwegs zur Sprache,* everything depends on the gift or the refusal of the appropriate word (*das geeignete Wort*) that allows the essence of language to arrive in language. In his reading, Derrida insists that this proper word is a unique and a final word in Heidegger's thought. Against the background of this "finally proper name," *différance* appears as a correction. Derrida concludes "*La différance*" by quoting Heidegger as follows: "'Being / speaks / always and everywhere / throughout / language.'"[95] By marking the spaces with a solidus, Derrida suggests that if being indeed speaks always and everywhere throughout language, then it speaks at different places between different words. Consequently, it speaks differently and is said in different ways: every word traces this speaking of being differently. It is this multiplicity in language and of languages that Derrida stresses in each of his readings of Heidegger.

Let me conclude by pointing to a difficulty in Derrida's reading of Heidegger in "*La différance.*" The contrast Derrida creates between *différance* and Heidegger's allegedly metaphysical quest for an appropriate and a unique word is built upon the claim that Heidegger's "*hope*" and his expectant language aims at a *final* word.[96] However, it is rather doubtful whether we fully capture Heidegger's thought on promise, hope, and anticipation if we read this thought as aiming at this kind of finality. Of course, Heidegger insists on the moment of disclosure (*Ereignis*) and the quest for the appropriate word. Yet, this moment is also always a moment that is still *to come*. Therefore, it is indeed always attached to a hope and an anticipation, but this hope and anticipation cannot be simply classified as a metaphysical remainder, as Derrida argues in "*La différance.*" Heidegger's antici-pation, promise, and hope are always marked by a *provisionality* that is characteristic of thinking as thinking. The anticipation of thought never claims to speak the final word because it thinks being in an essentially provisional way.[97] In later texts such as "*Le retrait de la métaphore*" as well as *Mémoires pour Paul de Man*, Derrida is more aware of this aspect of Heidegger's thought: rather than relating the promise to a final word, he insists on an analysis of the promise as a deferral in Heidegger's work. Nevertheless, he still insists on the primacy of the proper in Heidegger's work, which would still refer to an affinity between Heidegger's thought of *alētheia* and metaphys-ics. By relating the appropriate word to its metaphysical inheritance, Derrida never explores another option. Against the background of his intriguing and often very convincing reading, one might still won-der whether it is not possible to reappropriate these notions in light of a thought that affirms the primacy of the promise, as Heidegger does, without immediately understanding it as supplementarity trait. Derrida's inscription of quasi-metaphoricity in Heidegger's thought allows him to address a number of fundamental questions with respect to Heidegger. Yet, he can only do this by sidestepping Heidegger's own continual refusal to use the notion of metaphor as a means to describe his own language. In this respect, it remains unclear and enigmatic in which sense Heidegger's text is the pivotal reference to understand how a new understanding of metaphor could arise.[98]

FOUR

Mimesis in Myth and Translation

> The concealing but also revealing character of every mirror — in-
> cluding that mirror which is the theater, art, the story and philoso-
> phy — exists in the first place such that reality appears where it in fact
> is not, namely in the mirror, on the stage, in the work of art, in the
> story or in the philosophical system. The appearance of reality there
> where it is not probably belongs to the very structure of the appear-
> ance of all that is called reality. This is what a radical reflection on
> mimesis teaches us.
>
> —Sam IJsseling, *Mimesis*

The above quote from IJsseling beautifully shows that mimesis, like metaphor, fundamentally involves both disclosure and displacement. All mimesis concerns the disclosure of reality at another place or another level than where it originally occurred — in a story, on a stage, and so on. The reinterpretation of this notion in hermeneutics and deconstruction is concerned with the question of the nature of the particular displacement at the heart of "the appearance of all that is called reality." Ricoeur, for instance, thinks that poetic mimesis does not produce something imaginary in the pejorative sense of the word, but rather discloses a dimension of reality that can only be disclosed by means of fiction, although this also presupposes an elevating displacement of reality to the level of the story. According to Ricoeur, "All *mimēsis*, even creative — nay, especially creative — *mimēsis*, takes place within the horizons of a being-in-the-world which it makes present to the precise extent that the *mimēsis* raises it to the level of *muthos*. The truth of imagination, poetry's power to make

181

contact with being as such—this is what I personally see in Aristotle's *mimēsis*."[1] In this chapter, I shall discuss the status of mimesis in the work of Heidegger, Ricoeur, and Derrida. Moreover, I shall illustrate this problem of mimesis by addressing one particular case of linguistic mimesis on which all three authors have written: translation. A translation is a mimesis of an original text; it transfers a text from its original language to a target language. As such, it discloses the text in a language to which it does not belong originally. This particular phenomenon allows me to address another theme that goes beyond the relation of mimesis and *muthos*, but which nevertheless plays between Heidegger, Ricoeur, and Derrida, namely, the themes of otherness and foreignness. Clearly, in all their vastness these themes go far beyond the scope of this study on truth and language: they involve discussions on ethics, politics, hermeneutic self-understanding, and so on. Yet, by limiting myself to the phenomenon of translation, I will be able to show to what extent the problem of truth and language concerns these themes too.

DISCLOSURE WITHOUT MIMESIS

Heidegger's comments on mimesis are as sparse as his comments on metaphor: *Nietzsche I* provides us with one of the few places in his work where a genuine reinterpretation of mimesis can be found. Nevertheless, according to authors such as Sallis, IJsseling, and Lacoue-Labarthe, Heidegger's work is implicitly marked by a "mimetology" (Lacoue-Labarthe). This hidden thought on mimesis would conceal the remnants of a form of Platonism in Heidegger's work. Due to these remnants, Heidegger considers mimesis to be a derivative notion that belongs to a Platonic dualism. Consequently, he would not have been able to develop an account of mimesis as primary, even though some of his analyses seem to require such an account.[2]

Mimēsis between Truth and Fiction I

In contrast to this unthought, however, Heidegger's explicit statements on mimesis are rather critical. His critique of mimesis runs along two lines of thought. The first line is perhaps not even a line of thought: when Heidegger mentions mimesis, he often does so by placing this notion in a list of Greek concepts that would be indebted to metaphysical thinking. In particular, he relates it to the concept of truth as *homoiōsis* (or correspondence) since also mimesis is guided by *homoiōsis* (or resemblance). In one typical example, he writes, "The truth of *physis, alētheia* as the unconcealment that is the essence of the emerging power, now becomes *homoiōsis* and *mimēsis,* assimilation and accommodation, orientation by...it becomes a correctness of vision, of apprehension as representation....The basic concepts *idea, paradeigma, homoiōsis,* and *mimēsis* foreshadow the metaphysics of classicism."[3] In this quote, Heidegger criticizes the metaphysics of presence and a conception of mimesis in its wake. Mimesis is primarily understood as an imitation of a more unconcealed and fully present Idea. This type of critique of mimesis coincides with Heidegger's critique of metaphor in *Der Satz vom Grund* and in *Hölderlins Hymne "Der Ister,"* where metaphor is discussed under the aspect of its belonging to the metaphysical opposition between the sensible and intelligible.

However, a second, more interesting line of thought can also be found. In this line, Heidegger actually rethinks and reinterprets the notion of mimesis in a reading of Plato (and not Aristotle), and in particular of book 10 of the *Republic.*[4] It has been claimed that this reading is classical, and that it marks Heidegger's inability to set aside this Platonic conception of mimesis and retrieve the notion of mimesis in light of truth as *alētheia* and in light of a more Aristotelian conception of mimesis.[5] Although this claim is not simply wrong—it remains to be seen what Heidegger's reading of Aristotle's conception of mimesis would have to say—yet his reading of Plato *is* concerned with truth as unconcealment. However, mimesis is not understood as a locus of unconcealment, but rather of concealment.

The title of Heidegger's reading immediately shows how according to him Plato's conception of mimesis drives a wedge between truth and poetry: the interpretation of poetry as mimesis implies that truth is denied to poetry. In line with a classical reading, he first addresses mimesis as imitation of the Idea. However, rather than simply claiming that mimesis remains with the Platonic dualistic conception of reality, he starts reading the problem of *alētheia* as unconcealment into the text of Plato. Although the Idea is the measure of truth in Plato's conception of mimesis as imitation, this Idea presupposes truth as disclosure. Heidegger writes, "The interpretation of Being as eidos, presencing in outward appearance, presupposes the interpretation of truth as *alētheia,* nondistortion [*Unverstelltheit*]."[6] To some extent, this reading does not surprise us: it refers the notion of *eidos* back to a more primordial conception of truth.[7] However, rather than thinking mimesis in light of this derived role of *eidos,* he interprets it in light of this original truth. Hence, mimesis is not simply the imitation of an Idea: in light of his own conception of truth and untruth, he interprets mimesis as *Verstellen,* that is, as a concealing displacement.

In at least three remarks, he develops this interpretation. Mimesis is described as the opposite of *Nichtverstelltsein,* that is, nondisplacedness. This latter notion only applies to the appearance of the Idea as such in Plato's thought. To explain this opposition, Heidegger refers to the mimesis of a mirror. A mirror lets a being exist as showing itself, but *in a displaced way* and not in sheer unconcealment.[8] As we have seen before, *Verstellen* is a form of appearing that covers up and hides. This concealing/unconcealing of *Verstellen* is the framework from which Heidegger understands Plato's concept of mimesis. Next, Heidegger understands Plato's description of the mimesis of a craftsman as a form of "obfuscation and displacement" (*Verdunkelung und Verstellung*): the wood of a bedstead and the stone used to build a house let the Idea of a bedstead and a house appear, but they do not let it appear as bright and splendid as the Idea itself.[9] Hence, mimesis is an appearance that dims the splendor of the Idea. Finally, Heidegger notes that for Plato mimesis is a form of *nachgeordnetes Her-stellen* (an inferior or subordinate creating). This subordinate creating is a decrease in the manner of producing (*Verringerung der Weise des Her-stellen*) and therefore an obfuscation and displacement.[10]

Along these lines, Heidegger shows how mimesis is related to *Verstellen* in Plato's thought. What is experienced in Plato's thought as most unconcealed is the Idea. The arts are merely mimetic: they conceal and displace the clarity of the appearance of the Idea. Hence, mimesis as displacement drives a wedge between truth as the unconcealedness of the Idea and the way this Idea is tarnished in the arts. Heidegger thus emphasizes, much like a classical reading, the *secondary* character of mimesis. However, unlike a merely classical reading, mimesis is approached under the aspect of Heidegger's conception of untruth as *Verstellen: mimesis is a form of displacement that does not show a being out of itself.* In fact, in light of Heidegger's reinterpretation of imitation (*Nachmachen*), we see how close this account of mimesis as *Verstellen* is to the definition of one of the forms of untruth in "*Der Ursprung des Kunstwerkes.*" In the latter text he describes displacement as a movement that moves one being in front of another and thus disguises it. In *Nietzsche I*, he interprets mimesis both as presenting (*dar-stellen*) a being *as another being* and as bringing a being to showing itself (*her-stellen*) *as another being.* The displacement of mimesis is thus also concerned with showing a being as a being that it is not.[11]

A Myth without Mimesis

This interpretation of mimesis has important consequences for Heidegger's account of art and of poetry in particular. Since mimesis is a form of *Verstellen*, it will never allow for an account of art that stresses art's essential disclosive power. In particular, it will never arrive at the essence of art for which poeticizing (*Dichten*) provides the model: like poetry, art allows the arrival of truth to occur, and therefore, "*All art,* as the letting happen of the advent of the truth of beings, is, *in essence, poetry*" (*Dichtung*).[12] This form of disclosure is without distortion and hence without mimesis. Moreover, to articulate the essence of poetry, Heidegger introduces the German *Sage*, which is a translation of the Greek *muthos*, as Lacoue-Labarthe points out.[13] Apparently, Heidegger argues that the myth created by the poet should be and can be without mimetic distortion, and in this light Plato's interpretation of art as mimesis can only be conceived as a concealment of the disclosive essence of poetry.

Heidegger's conception of a *Sage* without mimesis implies that poetic saying is in no sense a displacement of reality: it does not move something out of its proper or original place to let it appear elsewhere or on another level—this is what mimesis both in its Platonic and Aristotelian sense does. Hence, to claim that poetic saying does not involve mimesis is a claim on the original nature of poetic language in relation to the being of beings the poem discloses: poetic saying does not derive this being from another place where these beings would be originally; saying rather grants beings their being in the first place and is as such the locus of their being and of their presence. Mimesis can only be understood as the (distorting) repetition of this original disclosure.

Interpreters such as Derrida and Lacoue-Labarthe tend to understand this relation between myth and mimesis as a repetition of the Platonic distinction between original Idea and sensible derivative. Especially Lacoue-Labarthe emphasizes in his account of Heidegger's alleged onto-typology that Heidegger interprets the work of art (and that includes myth) from time to time as a *Gestalt*, as a standing and fixed model of truth. Despite the fact that myth is understood as poetic saying, that is, the *movement* from concealment to unconcealment, the work of art would result in a *fixed* model that resembles the Platonic Idea as a fixed truth and a complete presence. Even though Lacoue-Labarthe rightly points to the difficult notion of the *Gestalt* in Heidegger's account of the work of art, this interpretation shows that the parallel between Heidegger's account of art and a certain Platonism can only be demonstrated by focusing on the odd notion of the *Gestalt* alone and by effacing the importance of myth as poetic saying. Yet it is exactly the poetic saying that remains of crucial importance to Heidegger in his later works—unlike the figure of the *Gestalt*. The relation between *Sage* and mimesis is determined from the viewpoint of the relation between *Unverborgenheit* and *Verstellen*, between disclosure and displacement. Mimesis, in this conception, is not the reproduction of a pre-given fixed model of truth, as Lacoue-Labarthe claims, but the distortion of the poetic moment of disclosure.[14]

Instead of thinking of the disclosive dimension of art in relation to a mimetic displacement, Heidegger insists on the primordial gathering activity in the work of art. This gathering is related to Heidegger's account of *legein,* which we discussed in chapter 1. Moreover, since the essence of the work of art is related back to poetic saying and *muthos,* it is important to note that Heidegger also repeats an Aristotelian gesture: Aristotle explains *muthos* in his account of tragedy as that which gathers different characters, actions, situations, and so on, in the unity of a plot, the gathering of poetic saying. Clearly, in Aristotle's account, this gathering is the effect of mimesis: tragedy does not disclose the world as such, but discloses the world in elevated ways. (This will return in Ricoeur's explanation of *muthos* and mimesis.) By removing the notion of mimesis from this form of gathering, Heidegger tries to show how the work of art gathers beings together in a world. The world that is thus disclosed by the work of art is not a mimesis of a preceding world; it is simply the world in which people live.

This is most clearly demonstrated in Heidegger's analysis of the Greek temple. The Greek temple discloses the realm of the holy primordially: without this temple, the realm of the holy does not exist. As such, the temple lets beings be present in this realm.[15] In particular, this means that the temple lets the gods appear in their *presence.* These gods are not represented by the temple or by some object in the temple, as if this temple (or the objects it contains) is a placeholder of these gods and as if the gods were actually somewhere else. The gods do not exist at another place; they are only present in the shining splendor of the realm opened up by the temple.[16] As such, the gathering of gods and human beings in the realm of the holy is in no sense related to a *mimetic* activity in the work of art; it is the proper and original place in which human beings and gods are gathered together. Apparently, the gathering and joining of the work of art should not be mixed with forms of mimesis. Mimesis as *Verstellung* has the tendency to conceal the whole of the world that accounts for the possibility of its appearing. The temple as a work of art, however, discloses the whole of the world as a world in which human beings and gods co-belong. As being fundamentally a form of *Sage* and myth, the work of art is a myth without mimesis, that is, a myth that opens up by joining together.

In light of this explication, it is not at all obvious that Heidegger's account of poetics leaves room for an original mimesis, as is claimed by Sallis, Lacoue-Labarthe, and IJsseling.[17] However, to show how difficult Heidegger's work is with respect to the question of mimesis, let me recall another aspect of this work that might be more in line with the idea of an original mimesis. In the first chapter, I discussed Heidegger's interpretation of the relation between the divine *ho Logos* and the *homologein* of mortal human beings. Apparently, language has two appearances here: the *legein* of *Logos* and the *homologein* of mortal human beings. The latter *legein* is approached as a form of listening and as a form of agreeing (*Entsprechen*) to the former. Therefore, as a linguistic variant of *homoiōsis,* human speech is a form of *homologein.* This implies a hierarchy, and this hierarchy leads to a relation between *Logos* and human *legein* that clearly resembles a mimetic relation. If this is the case, it is different from an imitation (*Nachbildung*); rather, it should be understood as a form of complying, corresponding, and harmonizing.[18] To see how Heidegger introduces these forms of complying, corresponding, and harmonizing in his account of the relation between human language and the language of *Logos,* consider the following difficult passage from *Was ist das—die Philosophie?* Here, Heidegger writes,

> An *anēr philosophos* is *hos philei to sophon,* he who loves the *sophon; philein,* to love, signifies here, in the Heraclitean sense, *homologein,* to speak in the way in which the *Logos* speaks, in correspondence [*Entsprechen*] with the *Logos.* This correspondence is in accord with the *sophon.* Accordance is *harmonia.* That one being reciprocally unites itself with another, that both are originally united to each other because they are at each other's disposal—this *harmonia* is the distinctive feature of *philein,* of "loving" in the Heraclitean sense.[19]

The mimetic relation between *Logos* and human speech is described here as a form of co-belonging for which Heidegger uses the notions of love, harmony, correspondence, and accordance. In relation to this mimetic relation between the divine *Logos* and human *legein,* it is important to note that Heidegger does not only acknowledge a certain hierarchy, but that he also insists that these two forms of *legein* are not simply original: they find their provenance in "the simple middle" between them. Thus, this middle is originary.[20] Might this middle, which is obviously the movement of corresponding, harmonizing, and according itself, not refer to a form of original mimesis in Heidegger's account of language as *logos* and *legein?* If this is the case, the movement itself of joining and complying as harmonizing and according would count as an original mimesis. However, even if this is the case, it is clear that for Heidegger the simple middle as the provenance of both forms of speech is an original movement that gathers rather than displaces. If displacement is no longer relevant to think this original movement, does it make sense to call it mimesis at all? Perhaps, to clarify these issues and questions, it might be helpful to consider a less complicated situation: rather than addressing the relation between a divine and a human language, which always involves (the suggestion of) hierarchy, the issue of translation, which includes or at least seems to include two different languages on an equal level, might provide more clarity.

The Question of Translation

Heidegger's explication and application of translation has provoked much attention. For example, his assessment of the difference between German and Latin translations of Greek words introduces a strange asymmetry between German and Latin in relation to Greek, which has struck many interpreters as an odd Romantic remnant in his thought that he never truly explains.[21] In this section, I shall show the implications of Heidegger's account of translation for the notions of disclosure and displacement.

Original Translation

Heidegger makes in his *Parmenides* lectures a distinction between an original and a secondary form of translation. Secondary forms of translation are a paraphrase (*Umschreibung*), the substitution of one word by another and even the transference (*Übertragung*) of one language to another.[22] These forms are secondary since they are only possible in the wake of an original translation. This original translation is an occurrence in which our whole essence is taken over into the realm of an altered truth.[23] This definition of translation is, of course, highly intriguing since it relates the problem of the transition of the essence of truth, which I discussed in chapter 1, to the problem of translation.

Heidegger provides this definition in the beginning of his *Parmenides* lectures. In these lectures, he tries to provide a new entrance to the Greek experience of truth in the German language. However, the usual German translation of *Wahrheit* for *alētheia* does not suffice. Therefore, he suggests another translation: *Unverborgenheit*. This simple substitution of words—*Warheit* by *Unverborgenheit*[24]—as such, however, is powerless. It needs to be carried by a more profound transition, namely, a transition of experiences of truth. The word *Wahrheit* belongs to a specific experience of truth—a Latin one since it derives from *veritas*—and this experience of truth needs to be left behind in order to enter the realm of a Greek experience of truth. The word *Unverborgenheit* should speak out of this new, Greek realm of truth if it is to broach another experience of truth. Original translation is this more profound transition underlying the mere substitution of words. Hence, the substitution of *Unverborgenheit* for *Wahrheit* is only a *trace* of the original translation that enables it. As such, Heidegger's conception of an original translation is a beautiful example of an original displacement and an original mimesis: it closes one realm of truth and moves to another, and only on the basis of this original translation does a mimetic appropriation of the Greek experience of truth in the German language become possible.

I used the word "trace" in order to emphasize the hierarchy between the original translation and the secondary forms of translation such as a substitution. In the opening pages of the *Parmenides* lectures, Heidegger relates this original translation—that is, the one from Greek to German—to the saying of the poet: like the poetic word, which invites us to listen to a word as if we heard it for the first time, the original translation opens up an entirely new domain of experience. In the case of poetic saying, which reaches into the essence of language, Heidegger develops the idea of the nonessence (*Unwesen*) of language which would consist in the deterioration of this original saying: especially the becoming-common of poetic words marks this decay of language. In relation to translation, he also discerns such a form of decay, namely the translations proposed by a dictionary.[25] The dictionary may suggest that translation consists in the substitutions of words—however, this substitution as such is a latter, secondary form of translation that conceals the original one. Thus, substitution indeed possesses all the traits of a trace in Heidegger's sense of the word: it refers back to a more original translation and also tends to conceal.

It is important to emphasize that the resemblance between original translation and the disclosive saying of the poem is addressed in the opening pages of the *Parmenides*. Here, the closure of the experience of truth as *Wahrheit* is not deplored as a loss. Rather, the transition from one domain of truth to another is a pure gain in this situation: it gains the Greek experience of truth. That is, it is the disclosure of the very experience of disclosure. In §3 of these lectures, however, we come across another original translation: from Greek to Latin, from *alētheia* to *veritas* and from *pseudos* to *falsum*. These translations are not just substitutions of words, but are grounded in a transition from the Greek experience of truth to the Roman-Christian experience of truth.[26] In relation to his account of the translation from Greek to German—from *alētheia* to *Unverborgenheit*—Heidegger insisted on the disclosive quality of an original translation. Yet, in the case of the translation from Greek to Latin, Heidegger never mentions its disclosive capacity or its resemblance to a poetic saying. Rather, he interprets this change as a mere loss: the original experience of philosophy is lost in this transition from Greece to Rome. As he puts it in "*Der*

Ursprung des Kunstwerkes," this transition robs Western metaphysics from its ground: it becomes groundless.[27] *This* original translation, in contrast to the previous one, is described *as if* it is a secondary translation: it is only a decay of the original Greek experience.

We see what happens here in Heidegger's rhetoric: the notion of an original translation which seems to give rise to an idea of an original displacement in his work is divided. The first example, from Greek to German, is understood as a sheer disclosure. The second example, from Greek to Latin, is understood as a decay. This decay indicates that the original translation is not as original as it is said to be: Heidegger's interpretation of the disclosive and displacing character of this translation is not guided by the phenomenon of an original displacement itself, but it is (also and mainly) guided by a reference to a particular domain of truth, namely the original Greek one. The strange asymmetry between the two examples of an original translation indicates that the assessment of the meaning of the original translations is oriented by a particular realm of disclosure rather than by the original displacement at work in original translation itself. In particular, this implies that the role of the original translation is not to give the foreign language its own place, but to account for the decay in the history of metaphysics and to account for the possibility to return to its origin. Hence, a particular hierarchy installs itself in the phenomenon of original translation: the Greek experience is that to which the German thinker should listen, and he should regain the as yet unsaid possibilities of the Greek language.

Appropriating the Essence of the German Language

The account of translation in the *Parmenides* lectures is not completely determined by the orientation to the Greek language. Besides reviving the possibilities of Greek thought and speech, Heidegger is also guided by another motive: to let the German language arrive at its proper essence.[28] Although this second orientation only plays a marginal role in the *Parmenides* lectures, it becomes the central focus of his comments on translation in *Hölderlins Hymne "Der Ister."*

As is well known, Heidegger argues that the main concern of the poet Hölderlin is "the becoming-homely in that which is one's own." In this formulation "what is one's own" (*das Eigene*) is the essence of the German language.[29] However, to appropriate this essence, a detour along "that which is foreign" (*das Fremde*) is necessary. This indispensable foreign language is not just any other country or language, but it is a foreign language that is the provenance of the home-coming. As such, as Heidegger notes, that which is foreign is *one* with that which is one's own: it is the beginning of that which is one's own.[30] In Hölderlin's case, the appropriation of the German language requires a dialogue (*Zwiesprache*) with the ancient Greek poets Sophocles and Pindar.

The way Heidegger elaborates this specific relation between the Greek and the German language is quite interesting. On the one hand, the German language arrives at that which is proper to it only by means of a detour along the Greek language. The Greek language of the Greek poets is even called the provenance of the home-coming. In this sense, the foreignness of the foreign language makes an appropriation of the essence of one's own language possible in the first place. Since that which is one's own is not given prior to this journey through the foreign land, one might have the impression that this journey is a wandering in the sense of Derrida's *errance:* a dissemination that does not know where it is going since it is not guided by a preceding entity as its goal. However, on the other hand, this journey is always also a journey on its way to the essence of the German language: even though this essence is clearly affected by the Greek language — this foreign language is the provenance of its essence — it is at the same time never contaminated by it. How can we understand an affecting that does not contaminate?[31] Heidegger emphasizes, at least twice, that gathering what is one's own and what is foreign together in a dialogue produces a unification (*die Einigung*) in which each language receives its proper place as a setting apart (*Auseinandersetzung*) — thus, this unification is never a contamination.[32] Translation is this typical dialogue between two languages: it is "the encounter (*Auseinandersetzung*) with a foreign language for the sake of appropriating one's own language."[33]

To further explain this affecting without contamination, let me suggest that Heidegger distinguishes between what we could call archeological and teleological moments of translation. The archeological moment implies that the appropriation of the German language is referred back to its provenance in a foreign language. Hence, that which is foreign fundamentally affects that which is one's own. The foreign language gets mixed up with one's own language since the former is the provenance of the latter. The teleological moment, however, describes that this contamination does not affect the ultimate goal of translation: the appropriation of one's own language. This moment indicates that the foreign language and one's own language are not mixed up but remain distinct. How does Heidegger combine these two moments? Although the idea of contamination and dissemination seems to be present in the archeological account, Heidegger proposes an alternative figure to describe how the foreign and one's own language can be gathered together and, at the same time, remain distinct. As opposed to contamination as *wirre Vermischung,* Heidegger describes the dialogue of translation as a *fügende Unterscheidung,* a distinction in which the elements that are being set apart comply with each other; a complying distinction, as we could translate it. This means that the foreign language as well as one's own language is only itself in its compliance with the other. This is how Heidegger combines the idea that the appropriation of one's own language needs the other language with the idea that this does not imply a contamination: the gathering together of the two languages in a dialogue reconciles these two ideas. This example of translation shows us once more how Heidegger provides a fruitful combination of the disclosure of the essence of language with a fundamental gathering. Also, in the case of translation, the multiplicity of languages can only be dealt with from the perspective of the essence of language as saying, that is, showing and gathering. In this case, it is language as dialogue that gathers and thus shows each of the languages in its proper place.

This account of a complying distinction gives rise to two questions. The first question is whether this complying can be universalized to a general conception of translation as a relation between any two languages. This does not seem to be the case: the relation described here is the relation between Greek and German. It is not clear at all that this would apply to, for example, German and Latin as well. In fact, one might expect that it does not since the Latin language contaminated the German language with non-German words such as *Falsch*, as Heidegger suggests in the *Parmenides* lectures. The turn to Greek, on the other hand, seems to open up the possibility of a purification rather than a contamination. The second question is more relevant and inspires Levinas's critique of Heidegger. One might wonder whether the complying distinction as the basic characteristic of the dialogue between the Greek and the German can do justice to the alterity of the foreign language: The mutual complying of that which is foreign and that which is one's own, does it not rob the foreign language from its alterity, that is, from its interruption of any order? This Levinasian question inspires Derrida in some of his later reflections on Heidegger's work as we shall see in a later section.

The Proper Possibilities of the German Language

One might wonder whether the course of the previous discussion does not leave room for a third account of the multiplicity of languages: (1) The *Parmenides* lectures describe how the German language serves the disclosure of the original Greek possibilities of thought. (2) The *Ister* lectures describe how the German language can come into its own thanks to the journey along the Greek language; here, the appropriation of the German language is the real goal of this second exercise. (3) In line with this increasing importance of the German language, one might wonder whether it is not possible to find in Heidegger's work an emphasis on linguistic possibilities that belong to the German language alone. In *De l'esprit*, Derrida notes that Heidegger's interpretation of the word *Geist* (spirit) depends on possibilities that are proper to the German language alone: the relation between *Geist* and flame can only be thought in German and not in Greek.³⁴ In fact, Derrida discerns a number of such examples: words from Trakl's poetry that Heidegger can only interpret by going to their foundation in the German idiom.

To see how this latter option is related to the question of translation, let me refer once more to the *Parmenides* lectures in which Heidegger notes that *translation*—the setting over in another domain of truth—does not require the alteration of a linguistic expression.³⁵ We do not even need to change language in order to be set over in another domain of disclosure. In particular, he gives the example of poetry: "the poetry of a poet…stands within its own proper unique word."³⁶ Therefore, the interpretation of this poetry requires a typical displacement, exemplary for original translation: a displacement that does not disperse language, but one that guides the interpreter/translator in a unique direction, namely, toward the unique disclosive power that corresponds to the singular idiom of the poet. Hence, in this context, original translation coincides with *Erörterung*: it displaces in order to reach into the place of the poet's proper idiom and corresponding *Gedicht*.

In the specific example of Heidegger's reading of Trakl, the multiplicity of languages is approached from the perspective of the primacy of the German language. Even the multiplicity of poetic idioms is related back to the primacy of this language: Heidegger's interpretation of Trakl's words indicate that finding the place of Trakl's idiom coincides with placing this idiom in the realm of an original German language. In the context of the question of what a foreign language can still mean here, one example is of special interest: Heidegger's translation of *fremd* or "foreign" in Trakl's poetry. This word is related to the old German *fram*, which would mean "to be on the way to." More specifically, Heidegger claims that "the strange goes forth, ahead."³⁷ However, this wandering is not an erring; it is no *errance*. It knows where it is going: "foreign" denotes to be on the way to its own, proper place (*Ort*). Hence, like before, that which is foreign (*das Fremde*) is never simply foreign because, in the context of an original translation as *Erörterung*, it is more than ever a variant of the ultimate goal of Heidegger's thought: the displacing movement of original translation is a movement guided by the promise of arriving at the proper place of the poet's unique idiom, his hearth and home—which is ultimately a name for being.[38]

EMPLOTMENT AND THE INVENTION OF COMPARABLES

The concept of mimesis plays a central role in Ricoeur's poetics of narrative developed in *Temps et récit* and *Soi-même comme un autre*. In contrast to Heidegger, who proposes a *muthos* without *mimesis*, Ricoeur insists that the disclosive quality of a *muthos* depends on the mimetic activity in poetics. To understand the difference with Heidegger, it is important to see the inspiration of Aristotle. For Ricoeur, *muthos* is not another word for saying, but he explicates it as a variant of plot, which is the meaning Aristotle gives to *muthos* in the *Poetics*. For Aristotle, mimesis is first and foremost the representation of human action in a plot: "Now the action is represented in the play by the plot. The plot, in our present sense of the term, is simply this, the combination of incidents, or things done in the story."[39] Ricoeur tightens the Aristotelian bond between mimesis and plot. For him, the poetic act *par excellence* is the mimetic act of gathering together events, situations, characters, and actions in one plot. Thanks to this "emplotment" (*mise en intrigue*), the multiplicity of events, situations, characters, and actions are understandable in light of the invented plot. Ricoeur, like Heidegger, affirms the importance of both disclosure and gathering to account for the possibility of understanding (human) existence. The story, since it can be followed by a listener or reader, accounts for human action in an understandable way. However, by emphasizing the mimetic moment in both this disclosure and this gathering of emplotment, neither of the two notions are primordial: they occur as the representative act of emplotment. The truth of fiction is the positive counterpart of the displacement of existence by mimesis.

In *Temps et récit,* the major task of emplotment is to solve the paradox of temporality: how to combine the succession of events with the temporal unity of a story? Ricoeur writes, "By mediating between the two poles of event and story, emplotment brings to the paradox [of temporality] a solution that is the poetic act itself. This act, which I just said extracts a figure from a succession, reveals itself to the listener or the reader in the story's capacity to be followed."[40] Ricoeur's thorough account of mimesis deepens his idea that the realm of poetics is a necessary medium to understand that which Heidegger tried to do immediately in his fundamental ontology of *Sein und Zeit*. In *Temps et récit*, Ricoeur adds the three moments of mimesis to the account of Dasein's immediate self-understanding to arrive at a more convincing account of how human beings understand themselves and their actions mediated by the stories they tell and read. These three moments are mimesis as prefiguration, configuration, and refiguration.

Prefiguration describes the fore-understanding involved in any poetic act. Emplotment is not purely spontaneous, but it presupposes a familiarity with the conceptual network of action, with the laws of the genres of narrative developed in a tradition, with the symbolic meaning of certain actions or gestures, and so on. These ingredients of fore-understanding are intersubjective or rather they stem from a belonging to a tradition: they are needed for both readers and writers. For instance, even a writer who deviates from a genre of narrative presupposes that the reader is familiar with this genre in order to perceive how he or she plays with this genre.

Prefiguration is thus the poetic form of fore-understanding. The notion of *configuration* already deviates from Heidegger's account in *Sein und Zeit*. For Heidegger, understanding and fore-understanding are more or less the same: the project (*Entwurf*) of understanding provides the interpretation with a fore-structure. The fore-dimension of understanding comes into play at the moment of interpretation. Configuration, however, is the poetic moment of project. This poetic project introduces a moment of distanciation or deviation with respect to the moment of prefiguration. Rather than simply imitating the examples of the tradition, the poetic project consists in the configuration of a new plot. Thus, it transforms the tradition and transforms practical understanding. The configuration of a story gathers and rearranges these notions in the temporal whole of a story.[41] In this sense, the mimesis of action in configuration is not simply an imitation of the conceptual network of action, but presents and *actualizes* these notions in the coherence of an intelligible story, rendering them meaningful on a different, narrative level.

The play between prefiguration and configuration marks Ricoeur's account of tradition as a dialectic between *sedimentation* and *innovation*. Sedimentation concerns the forms, genres, and types that provide the narrator with particular examples and rules of composition in configuration. Simply put, we tell stories because we are told stories. As such, the sedimentation of tradition is the process by which certain forms of narrative, which one day were novel, are grasped and *explained* in terms of rules of composition. This does not mean that the greatness of the individual work is reducible to a genre, but it does mean that every literary invention obeys certain rules of composition.

Although we tell stories because we are told stories, we do not tell the same stories. In fact, we even do not tell them in the same way. The other pole of the dynamics of tradition is innovation. Although guided by particular examples of composition, the imagination is capable of configuring an unheard-of plot. This novelty not only concerns the novelty of another plot according to the same old rules. The imagination is capable of inventing new rules of composition and new forms of narrative. Of course, even though these stories can be understood, their rules are not immediately known. It is first experienced as a shock to the audience since it deviates from the forms it knows. Yet, these innovations are "rule-governed deviation."[42] *Deviation* means only deviation with respect to the sedimented forms of narrative, not with respect to forms and genres as such. *Rule-governed* refers to the fact that despite this shock and despite the audience's incapacity to grasp the novel rules immediately, this deviation nevertheless has an intelligible composition. The new rules of composition can and will be explained—in the sense of *Erklären*—in due time. In this way they will become part of the sedimentation of tradition for future generations of readers and writers. The shock of the deviation does not remain a shock, but the deviated configuration is ultimately rec-ognized as a repeatable rule itself.

Clearly, the novelty of this structural innovation of the forms of composition is not the ultimate interest for hermeneutics. The nov-elty implied in configuration also has an ontological and temporal dimension: a plot opens up the imaginary world of a story. As we saw before, the distanciation of configuration is a distanciation with respect to the world we actually inhabit. It does not reach immedi-ately into being and into our ownmost possibilities. The configura-tion discloses a new, understandable, fictional world. This opening up of a fictional world deserves to be called "disclosure" in the ontological sense of the word since it is a mimesis of the world we inhabit. Thus, showing something entirely new, the new configura-tion can be used to reinterpret the world we inhabit. *Refiguration* is the poetic form of this reinterpretation: the story provides us with a new figure to understand the temporality of our action. The term "refiguration" is the narrative equivalent of the term redescription developed in his *La métaphore vive.* Like redescription, refiguration carries the weight of the ontological postulate of poetics. However, unlike redescription, refiguration does not concern the redescription of this or that being; it refigures the temporality of our existence. In this sense, since it reaches the temporality of our being, refiguration comes closer to the ontological stakes of Heidegger than redescrip-tion ever could.[43]

Mimesis between Truth and Fiction II

In one of the quotes above, Ricoeur noted that emplotment provides a solution to a temporal paradox: the different events are gathered together in the temporal unity of a story. Underneath this temporal paradox, two important, related metaphysical paradoxes or dichoto-mies hide: the dichotomy of identity and difference and the dichot-omy of the same and the other. To some extent, Ricoeur's work has a definite Hegelian inspiration: identity and difference as well as the same and the other cannot be left as antitheses; they need to be rec-onciled dialectically. However, Ricoeur tries to avoid the Hegelian solution.[44] In his famous formula, Hegel tries to solve the tension between identity and difference by dialectically relating them in a new identity: the identity of identity and difference. In this solution, it is the identity of the philosophical concept that solves the paradox. It is common practice in contemporary thought to disagree with Hegel and, in order to overcome his solution, mediate the terms of the paradox by something that is vaguely characterized as being neither identity nor difference. However, does such a "neither identity nor difference" provide a genuine solution? What can we say positively about this "neither identity nor difference"? With respect to these questions, Ricoeur's poetics provides different and perhaps more substantial alternatives to the Hegelian identity of identity and difference. In fact, his analyses of resemblance, mimesis, emplotment, and analogue all propose poetic mediations of identity and difference or of the same and the other, which are all "neither identity nor difference" and "neither same nor other", respectively, but which at the same time receive a more positive determination. Let me indicate two typical examples.

As we saw in the previous chapter, a resemblance gathers heterogeneous elements by showing their homogeneity. The act of emplotment does something similar in a temporal setting: it gathers a heterogeneous series of events in the temporal unity of a plot. Emplotment is confronted with the tension between the chronology of events without unity—temporal difference—and the identity of a plot, which often can be paraphrased in one or two sentences. Emplotment aims to mediate these two poles of time.[45] In this way, the solution to the paradox of temporal identity versus temporal difference in human life does not receive a *conceptual* solution, but receives a *poetic* solution by means of emplotment: in the same way as resemblance expresses in a metaphor the identity of two beings while not erasing their difference, the temporal unity of a series of dispersed events is expressed in a narrative by emplotment. According to Ricoeur, such a poetic solution of the problem of human temporality is the best option we have: we can only hope to understand the temporality of our action if we approach it from the perspective of mimesis, since mimesis is a way to reconcile the identity and the difference in time. This also means that the identity and the difference of the time of human action are relative—at least from the point of view of understanding: we only understand this identity and difference in light of the emplotment that reconciles them.

Another example concerns the question of the relation of a historical narrative to the past it narrates. The underlying metaphysical question is here whether this relation should be accounted for in terms of sameness or rather in terms of otherness. Ricoeur insists that both accounts fail. The idea that the past is identical to its "reeffectuation" in the historians thought fails to account for the alterity at stake in the (mimetic) repetition of the historian.[46] However, the idea that the past is radically different from the historian's account of it is also untenable since such a radical difference cannot do justice to the positive fact that something of the past persists in the present.[47] To integrate both the sameness and the otherness in the relation of the historian to the past, Ricoeur proposes the genre of the analogue. The relation between a historical narrative and its past is not a form of reproduction or equivalence, but rather a metaphorical relation: "things must have occurred *as* they are told in a narrative...the *being-as* of the past event is brought to language."[48] Consequently, in our understanding of the past we never encounter the same of the past as such or the other of the past as such, but we always encounter an analogue of the past, which reconciles sameness and otherness. To anticipate Ricoeur's account of translation, historical narrative creates a *comparable* of the past. From the points of view of understanding and epistemology, mimesis is primordial: our access to the past is always mediated by a mimesis and thus by the genre of the analogue. Consequently, the sameness as well as the otherness of the past are relative: they are only understood in light of an analogue. Both sameness and otherness are relative with respect to an analogue by which we gain access.

These two examples demonstrate that the mimetic mediation between identity and difference and the analogical mediation between sameness and otherness have an ontological meaning. The notion of being-as is the poetic solution of the paradox of being and being-not, which does not favor either of the poles of this paradox. Being-as plays the same role as before. On the one hand, it is the only form of being accessible to the understanding. In this sense, hermeneutic understanding of existence is not built upon a direct access of a particular being (*in casu,* Dasein) to its being, but it presupposes the mediating role of the poetic language of metaphors, fictional narratives, and historical narratives. In terms of the two metaphysical distinctions discussed above, mimesis is presupposed in the understanding of the sameness and the otherness of the life world and the historical past with regard to the fictional world and the historical narrative. Hence, Ricoeur's mimesis is an original mimesis, but in a particular sense: *the understanding originates in mimesis.* On the other hand, the mediation of being-as has existence or the reality of the historical past as its vanishing points: our actual being-in-the-world is *as* the being-in-the-world depicted in literature, and the past is *as* it is narrated in the story. Both forms of "as" imply a being-not in the being they disclose. Hence, although understanding originates in mimesis, mimesis remains secondary in relation to being. To be more precise, the "is not" at the heart of mimesis implies a certain deficiency or finitude on the part of human understanding. As Ricoeur already noted in his essay "*Existence et herméutique*" from the 1960s, ontology is the promised land for a philosophy that begins with language: it is a land which hermeneutics will never actually enter. Although hermeneutics is moved in every step it takes by this promise, the fulfillment of this promise is postponed indefinitely.[49] The "is not" in the poetic truth of mimesis implies a similar delay: the invention of mimesis never attains its ultimate referent but by its as-structure defers the arrival of the ultimate goal that inspires the hermeneutic understanding and is promised to it. In the context of Ricoeur's discussion of narrative, this delay has three theoretical consequences.

Multiple Stories

The first consequence is rather obvious. Since no narrative actually reaches the level of the life world or the past as such, every narrative only tells us part of the story. Or, more precisely, since the mimetic structure of a story never arrives at reality as such, an encompassing story does not exist: every narrative only provides us with a comparable of reality. Consequently, narrative understanding never arrives at the whole of being. This implies a definite difference with Heidegger's thought. The attention to the configurative activity of emplotment indicates that Ricoeur is interested in a similar dimension of language as the one Heidegger discussed in his interpretation of *legein* as gathering. Yet, Ricoeur insists on the finitude of every configuration and its distanciation to being. Therefore, Ricoeur insists on the multiplicity of narratives, since, as he writes in the case of historical narrative, the distanciation intrinsic to historical narrative implies the requirement of a "*rectification* without end."[50] This means, in other words, a continuing effort to tell new stories that aim to create an equivalent of the past. In the case of fictional narrative, Ricoeur argues that the richness of the schematizing quality of the imagination itself allows it to narrate the same occurrence in multiple ways and disclose it each time differently. Extrapolating this multiplicity, Ricoeur even introduces the notion of untold stories.[51] That is, there are always stories to be told, which disclose yet another meaning of the same occurrence. In either case, it is clear that the mimetic character of narrative implies that every story configures being only *partially* and *imperfectly.*

Mimesis as Disfiguration

The question of the truth of narrative is affected by the same tension between the original character of mimesis in relation to understanding and its secondary character in relation to being. As we noted in the previous chapter on metaphor, Ricoeur brings into play both the notion of truth as correspondence and truth as disclosure. The latter truth is the truth of poetics. Although it is the only truth available for us to reach being, it is a partial and imperfect truth. Clearly, the claim that the disclosure of narrative is partial and imperfect can only be maintained in light of the secondary character of mimesis in relation to being: at the background a conception of the unity of being and a conception of truth as the correspondence to this unity plays an important role.

More importantly, going beyond Ricoeur's explicit comments, this regulative idea of the unity of being is crucial to understand why he singles out the notion of emplotment as the most important characteristic of mimesis. Occurrences, actions, and agents are intelligible thanks to this emplotment. However, this intelligibility is more than a kind of self-deception of human beings. Ricoeur insists that emplotment is more than a mere fiction. It is a form of disclosure. Would this not imply that emplotment itself, as a configurative act, is an imitation or mimesis of the gathering of being and of truth as the whole of being? That is to say, does the truth value of emplotment not *presuppose* the unity of being as its regulative idea?

These latter two questions arise as soon as one notices that Ricoeur's claim that configuration is the distinctive mark of literature is not as common as one might think. For some forms of literature, the claim that configuration is its distinctive mark might even lead us wrongly astray. In a brief remark on James Joyce's novel *Ulysses*, Ricoeur seems to allow another kind of literature that could be called a form of disfiguring literature: he describes Joyce's work as a form of *disfiguration*.[52] He makes this remark in his discussion of the *antinovel*, which concerns a type of literature that tries to parody different paradigms of narrative in order to refrain from developing a plot itself. Nevertheless, Ricoeur still claims that this kind of novel is mimetic in nature.[53] Although he is right in this respect, it is not clear how the antinovel can be understood from the framework of mimesis as configuration. Yet, this is what Ricoeur does. He argues that Joyce's work is an example of a writing that requires that the reader repeats and completes the configuration of the work. The *Ulysses* is a perfect example in this respect: it challenges "the reader's capacity to configure what the author seems to take malign delight in disfiguring."[54] In this extreme case, the reader carries the burden of emplotment because emplotment is abandoned by the work itself. This remark introduces a rather strange consequence of the emphasis on emplotment as the central notion for reading literature: even though Joyce's book does not provide a plot, the plot is still essential to the work as literature. Therefore, the emplotment should be brought about by the reader! It is difficult to understand what Ricoeur exactly means by this. In fact, he seems to overdo his emphasis on configuration as the main characteristic of *all* literature.

To arrive at a different understanding of Joyce's work, Derrida follows another trace. He argues that Joyce "repeats and mobilizes and babelizes the (asymptotic) totality of the equivocal."[55] He explains that Joyce brings into play at once a multiplicity of stories, myths, religion, science, philosophy, psychoanalysis, literature, and so on. This shows that the antinovel is indeed concerned with mimesis; it is a form of repetition and strives to bring into play the whole reservoir of the literary tradition. However, it does not repeat this reservoir *by means of emplotment.* It does not add yet another (paradigm of) configuration to the immense body of literature developed in the occidental tradition. Instead, by incorporating a multiplicity of stories, myths, religion, and so on, into one work, Joyce is involved with a mimesis of the *multiplicity* of stories. That is, he tries to express in literature the experience, essential to Ricoeur's thought as well, that our understanding of the world is marked by an equivocal tradition. To bring the multiple voices of this tradition into play at once is not to configure, but to *disfigure:* dismantling the different configurations is essential to grasp the fundamental multiplicity at stake in our literary tradition. Read in this way, Joyce's fiction is neither a form of emplotment nor a work that requires an emplotment on the part of the reader. What speaks from Joyce's work is the primacy of cross-fertilization and hybridization of different stories in a new work of literature. The repetition of tradition by means of this hybridization shows another aspect of the transformative quality of mimesis that operates on the basis of a dismantling of given configurations.

In contrast to this more Derridean reading, Ricoeur's tendency to overemphasize configuration seems to imply an incapacity in his poetics of narrative to appreciate a form of literature that tries to articulate one of the basic experiences of Ricoeur's own hermeneutics, namely, the fundamental multiplicity of stories through which we understand the world. In terms of mimesis, Ricoeur seems to miss one form of mimesis. He distinguishes prefiguration, configuration, and refiguration, but he neglects disfiguration as a separate moment of mimesis. Lacoue-Labarthe uses this term to indicate the weakness of myth (*la défaillance du mythe*).[56] The weakness of myth is exactly the weakness of a configuration to disclose its own imperfectness, to address its difference with other stories, and to open up the dissemination of cross-fertilization. In literature, the antinovel develops this form of mimesis. Coming back to the questions that opened up this discussion of Joyce, we could say that the difference between a thought that emphasizes configuration and a thought that emphasizes disfiguration is a difference concerning the question of truth. The former thought lets itself be guided by the promise of a unity of reality: narrative configuration is not only a displacement, but a displacement that discloses by bringing together. The latter thought insists on the primacy of displacement in mimesis.

The Regulative Idea of Truth

To understand the above remarks fully, we need to discuss a third element of Ricoeur's account of the secondary character of mimesis with respect to reality: Truth as a regulative idea. As I noted above, the central role of mimesis for the understanding mirrors the problem of human finitude in Ricoeur's thought. Such a finitude always runs the risk of referring back to a form of infinity that precedes and founds it; in this case, the infinity of truth and being itself. Even though Ricoeur denies the possibility of an encompassing story, since storytelling is a finite human activity, this regulative idea indicates that ultimately, these stories co-belong and concern the same reality.

The notion of a regulative idea always runs the risk of a Hegelian critique, as Derrida notes in "*Violence et métaphysique.*" Like Husserl, Ricoeur affirms the *irreducibility* of a bad infinity or an endlessness of the understanding. In relation to Husserl's emphasis on endlessness, Derrida asks rather pointedly,

> Can this *be said*, can one think the "false infinity" as such (time, in a word), can one pause alongside it as alongside the truth of experience, without *already* (an already which permits us to think time!) having let the *true* infinity, which then must be recognized as such, be indicated, presented, thought and stated? What we call philosophy, which perhaps is not the entirety of thought, cannot think the false, nor even choose the false, without paying homage to the anteriority and the

> superiority of the true (same relationship between the other and the same).[57]

Hence, in a more or less Hegelian fashion, Derrida argues that the affirmation of the irreducibility of the bad infinity pays homage to the superiority of the true infinity.[58] Between brackets Derrida repeats the Hegelian formula of the identity between identity and difference in the (Levinasian) vocabulary of the same and the other. As we have seen in the previous discussion, Ricoeur emphasizes the originality of another mediation between identity and difference. Applied to these forms of mediation, Derrida's comments imply that they, despite Ricoeur's explicit denial of it, would presuppose the superiority of identity and sameness. If we follow Derrida on this point, we see a paradox unfolding in Ricoeur's thought. On the one hand, he develops a rich conception of narrative and metaphor that allows him to articulate poetic, mediating terms between identity and difference in order to account for the fundamental multiplicity of human understanding. On the other hand, he embeds this conception in a metaphysics invoking a regulative idea of truth that is vulnerable to a Hegelian critique.

How to respond to such an objection, and to what extent can it be raised as a genuine objection against Ricoeur's thought? To answer this question, it is important to see the thoroughly Kantian background of Ricoeur's position in this respect. Derrida's Hegelian response to Husserl's affirmation of an irreducible bad infinity is based upon the claim that the endlessness thought in a regulative idea presupposes a concept of the true infinity. For Kant, however, this is highly problematic. The notion of the regulative principle is introduced in a discussion of the metaphysical status of the principle of totality.[59] In the realm of the senses, beings are given to us as appearances, and every appearance (*Erscheinung*) or empirical representation is always conditioned (*bedingt*) by the forms of time and space. Consequently, if we try to determine the conditions of some appearance in the realm of experience, we find a condition which itself is not absolute but again conditioned. Hence, in the experience the totality of conditions is never actually given (*gegeben*), but only given as a task (*aufgegeben*) in the regress.[60] This regress as a task means that when presented with an appearance, which is always conditioned, we are assigned the task to look for its conditions. In this sense, the principle of totality guides and regulates our understanding. As such, this principle is a regulative one. Moreover, since we never reach the absolute, unconditioned totality of conditions, this principle is not a constitutive one. As Kant writes, reason only postulates this principle; it does not anticipate an object corresponding to it. Such an anticipation is simply impossible since it would imply that an unconditioned object could be given, but as we noted, an object is always given in the realm of the senses and is therefore always conditioned. This regulative status of the regress also implies that we cannot determine whether this regress is infinite or finite: does it give rise to an infinite or a finite sequence of conditions? Kant mentions the example of determining the ancestors of a particular living human being.[61] We have no empirical ground that allows us to state that this sequence of ancestors is indeed infinite, let alone the possibility to go back to this infinite sequence. The only thing we may conclude is that we have not found any empirical ground that founds the claim that this sequence of ancestors is finite. Hence, rather than being concerned with an infinite (*infinitum*) sequence, the regress is concerned with an indeterminate (*indefinitum*) sequence. This indeterminacy is crucial since it allows Kant to think how reason broadens and widens the scope of human understanding beyond the realm of what is presently empirically given, without claiming any objective knowledge of something transcending the realm of appearance.

This determination of Kant's regulative principle forms the background of Ricoeur's explication of the relation between the whole of being and human understanding. Although the whole of being is never given as such, it is the regulative principle of hermeneutic understanding. Already in "*Existence et herméneutique,*" Ricoeur notes that in opposition to Heidegger, his hermeneutics derives from the idea that an actual ontology of human existence is not given (*donnée*), but only aimed at (*visée*).[62] Rather than using the term "regulative principle," Ricoeur uses the term "horizon" to describe the status of an ontology in relation to hermeneutic understanding. When we consider his description of this term in his book on Freud from 1965, it is clear how much it derives from Kant. "Horizon is the metaphor for what approaches without ever becoming a possessed object."[63] Like the regulative idea, a horizon does not correspond to a particular object, and like the regulative idea, a horizon broadens and widens the scope of understanding beyond that which is presently given to the experience. In particular, in relation to the question of mimesis, it broadens and widens the scope of particular stories, thus inviting us to create and write other, as yet untold stories.

In distinction to Heidegger, this Kantian heritage allows Ricoeur to integrate a critical moment into his hermeneutics on multiple levels.[64] In distinction to Derrida's Hegelian critique, Ricoeur would probably maintain that contrary to Hegel's claims, infinity is not given as an object. In fact, it is not even clear that the regress concerns an actual infinity rather than a sequence of indeterminate length. As such, the whole of the world and the whole of being remains a vanishing point. Nevertheless, perhaps in distinction to Kant, Ricoeur does not only describe this idea of the whole of being and of an ontology of human existence as a regulative idea. He also calls it a promise, as I noted above. What exactly is the status of this promise that cannot be fulfilled in philosophy? Does it reinstall a transcendental illusion? Does it indeed anticipate a transcendental signified to which, according to Derrida, hermeneutics would be indebted? In one of Ricoeur's conversations with Richard Kearney, the latter asks whether "the conflict of interpretations of human discourse could be...reconciled" in a "unifying center." Ricoeur responds that the task of philosophy is "to keep open the irreducible plurality of discourse" and "to abandon...our tendency to reduce all other discourse to our own totalizing schemata of thought." This is a very cautious response that says the hope for the reconciliation of different discourses and multiple narratives has to be distinguished sharply from a reduction to our own way of thinking. He continues, "If there is an ultimate unity, it resides elsewhere, in a sort of eschatological hope," and he concludes, "But this is my 'secret,' if you wish, my personal wager, and not something that can be translated into a centralizing philosophical discourse."[65] The truth, then, of this ultimate unity and this promised land of ontology resides elsewhere, beyond the scope of a philosophical hermeneutics in a personal conviction and wager. In light of this response, the question must be raised to what extent these two domains can be separated and demarcated and to what extent such a personal wager leaves its imprint on a philosophical thought. If the latter is the case, the truth or at least part of the truth of emplotment lies elsewhere.

The Dialogical Gathering of the Same and the Other

Ricoeur's effort to mediate the ancient metaphysical oppositions of identity and difference as well as of sameness and otherness without falling into the trap of privileging one of the poles of these oppositions, remains an important theme in the setting of his more anthropological and practical enterprise of *Soi-même comme un autre*. In this work, he raises the question of how a hermeneutics of the self always conceives of the self and its identity in relation to multiple forms of otherness.[66] To see how Ricoeur approaches the relation between self and other, it is instructive to consider how he conceives of the difference between his and Levinas's discussion of the relation between sameness (*le même*) and otherness (*l'autre*).

For Levinas, the identity of *le même* is always linked to an ontology of totality.[67] In this context, the other is that which is exterior to this totality and upsets this totality. For Levinas, this particular attention to the same or the self as the whole of being in contrast to that which escapes this whole and which may disrupt this whole is understood as a critique of Heidegger's thought on being. In particular, he notes that the relation to the other is a relation to an absence that is radically subtracted from the process of disclosure and concealment altogether.[68] The other is only present in the world in the form of a trace. Leaving a trace is its being: the other is absolutely and always already passed by.[69] As such a trace, it upsets and deranges the order of the world as an order of appearing and hiding, and as an order in which everything has a proper place. I recall these basic insights of Levinas since Derrida's discussion of alterity in relation to Heidegger's account of *logos* as gathering is clearly indebted to them.

In contrast to Levinas and Derrida, Ricoeur approaches the notion of the self differently. Consequently, also the notion of otherness has a different place and function. Ricoeur does not approach the notion of the self in light of the question of the whole of being. Rather, by focusing on the self as a human self, he is able to show how the self is characterized by three fundamental passivities, that is to say, it finds in itself and in its relation to the world three elements that do not find its origin in itself. Thus, it is characterized by three forms of alterity: the self is confronted with the alterity of its body, with the alterity of the other person, and with the alterity of the injunction that appeals to its conscience.[70] The practical import of these issues is beyond the scope of this study. Nevertheless, these forms of alterity beautifully show how Ricoeur understands the relation between the same and the other in his hermeneutics of the self. First, they show how the self does not coincide with one of the poles of the opposition—it is neither the same nor the other. Rather, self-understanding presupposes a certain primordial relatedness between the same and the other. Only in and as this relatedness, the sameness and the otherness involved in the self are accessible to the hermeneutic understanding. Secondly, in relation to the second form of alterity and in response to Levinas, Ricoeur interprets this relatedness as a form of *dialogical* reciprocity between the same and the other. He asks, "Finally, to mediate the opening of the Same onto the Other and the internalization of the voice of the Other in the Same, must not language contribute to its resources of communication, hence of reciprocity, as is attested by the exchange of... question and answer in which the roles are continuously reversed? In short, is it not necessary that a dialogue superpose a relation on the supposedly absolute distance between the separate I and the teaching Other?"[71] In this quote, Ricoeur points to dialogue as the locus in which the other and the self are not simply absolutely distanced, but gathered together in a dialogical speech. Since dialogue is the superposition of the relation between self and other, these latter two refer back to this gathering, which precedes the distance between myself and the other. It is only by this superposition that the relation between the other and myself can be understood as a reciprocal one: dialogue as the play of question and answer gives both the self and the other the chance to speak. However, with Levinas (and Derrida for that matter) one may fear that such a superposition might be a violent act that effaces the alterity of the other. Let me point out only one problem.

The gathering of dialogue presupposes that the conversation partners have something in common. As Gadamer points out in *Wahrheit und Methode,* a dialogue presupposes that the two conversation partners speak the *same* language. Only then, the possibility of understanding each other is possible.[72] However, if this presupposition of speaking the *same* language is required to understand how the voice of the other can be internalized and how the relation with the other should be understood, does this not imply that the relation between the other and myself is once again placed under the auspices of the category of sameness? At this point we see that Ricoeur proposes a completely different perspective than the one Derrida develops, for instance, in *Mémoires pour Paul de Man* and which I briefly pointed to in chapter 2. For Derrida, the "internalization of the voice of the Other" does not presuppose the sharing of a language since this process cannot be fully understood from the perspective of understanding. Rather, speaking for the other should result "in speech always saying something other than what it says."[73] Thus, rather than sharing the same language with the other, internalizing the voice of the other only has a chance when one speaks in a double tongue, so to speak, when one speaks more than one language at the same time.

Translation as the Creation of Comparables

The above discussion suggests that the relation between the other and the same is founded in dialogue. Hence, this relation is subsumed under the requirement of speaking the same language. This raises the question of how Ricoeur would account for a relation between that which is foreign and that which is one's own that necessarily transgresses the situation of a shared language: translation. Does the problem of translation give rise to a different account of the relation between the same and the other?

Although Ricoeur's reflections on translation are not as fully developed as many of the other themes I consider in this study, he nevertheless discusses this topic on at least three occasions in the second half of the 1990s.[74] In relation to the previous discussion, his account of translation is highly interesting since he acknowledges from the outset of his discussion that a translation needs to deal with two irreducible languages: they cannot be reduced to each other or to a third, metalanguage. Due to this irreducible linguistic difference, a complete transference of the original text to the object language is impossible. Does this imply that the mimesis of translation is merely a form of decay?

Ricoeur's entrance to the question of translation is different from Heidegger's. For Heidegger, as we discussed, translation is in the first place that which sets us over into a changed domain of disclosure. Secondly, in his reading of Hölderlin, he is interested in the foreign language as a means of appropriating that which is proper to us. Ricoeur, on the other hand, writes, "Have we not been set in motion by the fact of human plurality and by the double enigma of incommunicability between idioms and of translation in spite of everything?"[75] The question of human plurality, rather than the appropriation of that which is one's own, guides him. Moreover, confronted with the untranslatability of idioms and the empirical fact of the existence of translation, he decides not to give a theoretical explanation of the (im)possibility of a perfect translation. Instead, he tries to characterize the work of the translator given these difficulties. To do so he approaches the "work of translation" as a parallel of both the Freudian work of memory and of mourning.[76] In this way, he shows how a translation may cope with the irreducible difference between languages.

As a work of memory, the work of translation has to deal with two resistances, which come from the side of the original language and the object language, respectively. On the one hand, to transfer a foreign text into one's own language requires that the work of translation confronts "the sacralisation of the language called mother tongue." It should overcome "the pretense of self-sufficiency" of this language by showing that the foreign text may enrich this mother tongue with new forms of expression. On the other hand, it has to deal with "the presumption of non-translatability" of the idiom of the original language.[77] Even though it cannot copy the idiomatic elements perfectly, it needs to find an equivalent in the object language. Ricoeur refers especially to the example of poetry in which the relation between the signifier and the signified is often extremely tight. A similar problem occurs when we try to translate the fundamental words of a philosophical oeuvre—Heidegger's for instance—which often also depend on a certain idiomatic dimension of the language in which it was written. Hence, in both cases, the work of translation consists in not succumbing to the seduction to approach either of the two languages as a closed and purely singular or even sacred language: the act of translation shows that the foreign idiom can be related to the mother tongue, thus problematizing the self-sufficiency of the latter and the unapproachability of the former.

As a work of mourning, a translation has to deal with the impossibility, as Rosenzweig wrote, "to serve two masters": a translation serves the original text as well as the object language.[78] The work of mourning consists in the recognition that these two masters indeed have different and incompatible demands: the impossibility cannot be overcome. Therefore, a translation has to renounce the ideal of a perfect translation. Every translation testifies always also of a difference with the original text. In line with this resignation, the work of translation has to renounce the project of a universal language. Human language is and remains a plurality of irreducible languages. Within such a language, translation assumes the risky game of faithfulness to and betrayal of the original text as well as the object language.[79]

These two dimensions of the work of translation indicate that a translation will never simply reduce the difference between the original text and its translation. This impossibility of reduction coincides with the lack of a standard that would allow us to call a translation a good translation. Such a standard, as Ricoeur indicates following Quine, would be a variant of the argument of the third man of which

Plato speaks in the *Parmenides*.[80] In fact, such a standard would be a third text distinct from the two available texts—the original and the translation—such that this third text would carry the identical meaning of these two texts and such that they would be rewordings of this third text. However, since such a third text does not exist, a criterion for a good translation cannot be given. The lack of such a measure implies that "a good translation can aim only at a supposed equivalence that is not founded on a demonstrable identity of meaning. An equivalence without identity."[81] Hence, Ricoeur describes the phenomenon of translation along similar lines of thoughts as he describes metaphor and mimesis. A translation cannot hope for an identity, but it derives from one presupposition or one hope, namely that an equivalence can be construed. Like historical narrative, which provides an analogue of the past, the work of translation consists of the "construction of the comparable" (*construction du comparable*) text.[82] Hence, the linguistic act of translation, like the act of meta-phorizing and emplotment, concerns the invention of an equivalence without identity and a correspondence without adequation.[83] Clearly, as in the case of narrative, the equivalence of translation is always marked by an "is-not." In this case, the play of equivalence between identity and difference and between sameness and otherness becomes a play of fidelity and betrayal. As Ricoeur writes, "Grandeur of trans-lation, risk of translation: creative betrayal of the original, equally creative appropriation by the reception language."[84]

To some extent, the invention of a correspondence without adequation provides a Ricoeurian version of Heidegger's attention to corresponding and harmonizing, which we encountered in his description of human *homologein;* also this corresponding is without adequation. However, for Heidegger the guiding question in this quest for corresponding and attunement is always the quest for that which is one's own and the essence of one's own language. Thus, appropriating a foreign text or poem is only interesting when it is in service of the appropriation of what is proper to one's own language. Ricoeur, on the other hand, starts with the experience of the plurality of human languages. He enters the problem of translation through the foreign rather than through the appropriation of that which is one's own. Since language is the plurality of languages, translation as the disclosure of a foreign text in one's own language is not a means to find the proper dimensions of one's own language, but a form of "linguistic hospitality," as Ricoeur calls it.[85]

Two questions remain. In the first place, to account for the fact that translation is an invention of an equivalent without adequation, one needs to affirm a relation between two languages without reducing their difference. Ricoeur describes this as "the impassable status of the dialogicality of the act of translating."[86] Apparently, dialogicality is used here as a word to describe how a translation brings together two languages or two ways of speaking without losing their difference. In this way, translation is a dialogue: it brings together and keeps apart. Yet, this is a very general and unspecified characterization of dialogue. In fact, in light of the discussion of the previous section, one might wonder what "dialogicality" exactly means. It cannot be a play of question and answer since such a play presupposes the sharing of a language. Rather than presupposing a shared language, a translation aims at creating a linguistic locus in language that allows for such a play despite the difference: a translation is not preceded by the play of question and answer, but rather makes it possible between two people who speak a different language. In this sense, translation is not a form of dialogue, but rather precedes and enables dialogue.[87]

In the second place, it is not entirely clear how to combine translation described as a work of memory and a work of mourning with translation described as the construction of a comparable. The latter description points to the result of a translation: once a translation is given, our language is enriched with the comparable of a foreign text. One could argue that our understanding of a translation as a comparable provides us with a sense of the difference between the original text and its translation. In this sense, our understanding of this difference derives from the comparable nature of the translation. On the other hand, however, as work of mourning and memory, translation as work presupposes a more primordial experience of the foreignness of the foreign text: while one translates, that is, while a comparable is not yet available, one is already coping with this foreignness and with its inescapable effacement in the ultimate resulting translation. One might wonder whether, rather than merely presenting a comparable, a translation should not also aim at a result in which this preceding experience of foreignness and interruption can still be traced. This brings us to a more Derridean account of translation, as we shall see below.

HETEROGENEITY IN MIMESIS

Derrida radicalizes the idea we already encountered in the opening quote of this chapter: mimesis conditions every appearance. No appearance simply shows what is where it is. Rather, it shows what is by means of what it is not—by means of a supplement or a trace—and shows it elsewhere, at a place where it does not properly belong. Along this line of thought, Derrida examines how mimetic displacement can be found in the very heart of disclosure. As in his descriptions of the *originary* trace and the *arch*-writing, in which he grants an original place to notions that are classically considered to be secondary, his account of mimesis points to, what we could call with Lacoue-Labarthe, the notion of an original mimesis.

Mimesis between Truth and Fiction III

The idea of an original mimesis can already be traced in Derrida's early essay "*La double séance*," which opens with the question of what happens between truth and literature.[88] In line with Heidegger's considerations on the relation between art and truth in Plato's *Republic,* Derrida notes that the in-between of literature and truth has always been articulated as mimesis in the history of philosophy. In fact, it is organized by a particular philosophical interpretation of mimesis.[89] The main characteristic of this interpretation is that mimesis is thought to be secondary to truth: mimesis is always understood as being in *service* to truth. Unlike Heidegger, Derrida does not limit himself to a discussion of the Platonic interpretation of mimesis, but he also includes an Aristotelian one.[90] In fact, these two interpretations are the mainstream philosophical interpretations of mimesis, as he writes, "Now, mimesis, all through the history of its interpretation, is always commanded by the process of truth: 1. either,…*mimēsis* signifies the presentation of the thing itself…2. or else *mimēsis* sets up a relation of *homoiōsis* or *adequatio* between two (terms)."[91] In his description of the Platonic approach, Derrida emphasizes the importance of the concept of *homoiōsis*. In this perspective, what is imitated is more real, essential, and true than the imitation.[92] Mimesis is a double and a representation of what is first given on its own.[93] Hence, the imitated is the truth of the imitation, and the imitation should correspond to the imitated. As an imitation, such a mimesis might be helpful to arrive at the truth—for instance, in education, mimesis can be helpful in this way. However, if it does not refer back to the original, the imitation transforms from something that serves the truth into something that distorts it.

Derrida adds to this characterization that even those conceptions of art and poetics that seem to challenge this Platonic hierarchy between the natural and the artistic, by claiming that art liberates human beings from nature and discloses something more than it imitates, *still* remain within the *same* determination of mimesis.[94] Hence, also the Aristotelian account would remain within this determination. From a Heideggerian and Ricoeurian point of view, this sameness might be difficult to capture. In his explanation of this sameness, Derrida moves without hesitation from one concept—truth as *homoiōsis* or correspondence—to another one—truth as *alētheia* or presentation and disclosure. In this latter conception of mimesis, art discloses something more than nature discloses out of itself. Thus, it enriches the self-disclosure of nature. Ricoeur's conception of mimesis is clearly indebted to this Aristotelian heritage.

Nevertheless, despite this difference, Derrida insists that also this latter form of mimesis is interpreted as being in the service of truth, albeit truth as presentation. In its Aristotelian conception, nature doubles itself by means of mimesis in order to appear and "to shine in its *alētheia*."[95] Thus, the appearance of nature requires its own doubling in art and poetry; it requires the detour of mimesis to come to presence. Nevertheless, this means that mimesis is considered as a detour that is completely in the service of its ultimate goal: the manifestation of nature. Although as a detour, mimesis is an alienation of nature, it does not threaten, displace, or conceal the disclosure of *phusis*, ultimately. This Aristotelian line of thought implies that mimesis has nature as its point of departure and has the presentation of nature as its goal. This line of thought is an important source of inspiration for Hegel. The doubling of spirit in nature is a self-alienating, mimetic detour that is necessary to return to an enriched, self-understanding of spirit. Unfortunately, Derrida does not explicate how he connects Heidegger to this second understanding of the relation between truth and mimesis. By invoking Heidegger in his explanation of truth as *alētheia*, Derrida seems to suggest that Heidegger takes up this conception of the relation between truth and mimesis. However, we have seen that although Heidegger clearly speaks about a relation between nature, appearing, and art in his understanding of *poiesis* and *technē*, he does not understand this form of appearing of nature and of art as a form of mimesis. In light of the previous section, we do see how close Ricoeur's analysis of mimesis and narrative is to this description: the distanciation intrinsic to emplotment is ultimately not a form of alienation but rather a necessary detour such that human existence can be presented in an elevated way to the understanding.

Commenting on these two interpretations of mimesis, Derrida writes, "In each case, *mimēsis* has to follow the process of truth. The presence of the present is its norm, its order, its law."[96] Hence, it is the presence of the present that relates the two notions of truth involved in the two interpretations of mimesis. In a Platonic approach, this presence concerns an eternal presence: an origin that shines somewhere, but is concealed in mimesis. Mimesis as a supplement of this origin adds absence. In an Aristotelian approach, the presence is that of a final cause and of a future presence. Mimesis thus helps nature to come to its presence. In this perspective, mimesis is also determined by a lack of presence itself: the self-presentation of nature is the goal of the movement of mimesis. However, the moment of mimesis itself is merely an intermediate moment in which pure presence is still lacking, and thus needs to be surpassed.

Derrida's alternative approach to mimesis proceeds from the fact that in both cases, mimesis is indispensable. Thus, presence is enabled only by a certain absence. The Platonic origin only appears to us in and thanks to mimesis. Mimesis is simply added to this origin as something that subsequently can be subtracted from its appearance, but it is an addition that is required for this origin to appear in the first place. Rendering something in words is one of the examples of this medial character of mimesis: for Socrates in the *Phaedo,* the true beings themselves are blinding; they only appear to us in language. This appearance in language, however, also always implies that only a double appears; the origin is never given in its pure presence.[97]

Similarly, the Aristotelian attention to mimesis as a helpful medium to let nature come to full presentation should be understood from a certain primacy of mimesis, according to Derrida. In the Aristotelian-Hegelian account, it is clear that mimesis is a necessary detour to come to the presentation of nature. However, in this Aristotelian-Hegelian account, the mimetic movement is understood under the aspect of a final cause or "an eschatology of the identical," as Lacoue-Labarthe calls it.[98] In line with what Ricoeur argues, Lacoue-Labarthe notes that Hegel's identity of identity and difference subsumes mimesis under an original gift of identity, which in turn determines the movement of mimesis. Mimesis without identity is the alternative, poetic solution to the dialectic of identity and difference.[99] In such an Aristotelian perspective, mimesis is a movement determined by a lack of presence and attracted by a full presence. For Derrida, however, to come to presence is to come to presence *in a medium.* It is the transformation of this mimetic movement itself that accounts for any differentiation, either as enrichment or as impoverishment of meaning. For Derrida, this principle of mimetic difference, which allows beings to come to presence in another way and elsewhere, is also the very principle that defers and suspends any full presence. To some extent, this is very close to Ricoeur's position: for a philosophy that starts with language, such as his hermeneutics, a full presence of being is out of the question. For Ricoeur, only a partial understanding by means of different configurations is possible. Ontology remains the promised land that hermeneutics will never enter. However, in contrast to Ricoeur, Derrida argues that this very structure of a promise that cannot be fulfilled does not stem from a source exterior to language, that is, from a promised presence. Rather, this latter promised presence is an effect of the very promising structure of mimesis itself. Hence, mimesis is not simply a form of emplotment and of gathering together, but in and as this gathering it is a form of *Versprechen:* it promises a presence that is given nowhere in the present but is given only in the form of a promising supplement, mimesis.

Mimesis in the Self-Relation

In contrast to the Aristotelian conception of mimesis, the concept of an original mimesis develops an alternative to a metaphysics that is marked by a teleology. Mimesis represents the moment of the *not-yet* of the full disclosure of the *telos.* The claim that this mimesis is original means that the not-yet is primary—even in relation to its ultimate end. This structure of a not yet in relation to an end recalls Heidegger's analysis of death and of the wholeness of Dasein's existence in *Sein und Zeit.* In fact, the question of how the human being can relate to the wholeness of its existence is a question that beautifully illustrates how Heidegger, Ricoeur, and Derrida conceive of the notion of mimesis in relation to an end.

In the well-known §48 of *Sein und Zeit,* Heidegger argues that the relation of Dasein to its death is marked by "a not-yet" (*ein Noch-Nicht*).[100] This not-yet, however, is to be distinguished from the not-yet at work in a teleology: An unripe piece of fruit attains its goal and completion by the process of ripening in the ripe fruit. In this sense, the unripeness of the piece of fruit can only be understood as a privation, that is, as a lack of the actuality of the full-grown, ripe version of it. Death, however, cannot be understood in this way. Death is not the completion of Dasein's existence. Dasein can never experience the actuality of its death since death terminates its existence. Hence, the relation of Dasein to its end cannot be understood from the metaphysical framework of potentiality and actuality. Rather, Dasein relates to death only as to its ownmost and ultimate possibility: Dasein is *"always already its not-yet."*[101]

This, of course, has important implications for the wholeness of Dasein's existence. Namely, this wholeness can never be understood from the point of view of actuality or presence. Although Dasein *is* always between birth and death, it is neither present at the moment of its birth nor at the moment of its death. Consequently, the temporality that is needed to describe this wholeness of Dasein's existence can never be understood from the Husserlian perspective of time-experience since this time conception understands both past and future as modifications of the present as the lived now of consciousness. If the whole of Dasein's existence is only given as this in-between between birth and death, one could wonder how this whole can ever be meaningful to and be appropriated by Dasein. Although death is considered to be Dasein's most *proper* possibility, its indeterminacy as well as its impossibility might tempt one to think that it is more appropriate to say that death *expropriates* Dasein's existence. At this point, Heidegger would disagree: the possibility to relate to its death as its ultimate possibility is Dasein's only entrance to the wholeness of its existence as a proper or authentic potentiality-for-being. This relation of Dasein to its proper potentiality-for-being transgresses phenomenology in a strict sense, as Derrida points out: not an experience but an attestation (*Bezeugung*) provides this potentiality for being to Dasein's understanding.[102] This attestation attests to Dasein's "potentiality-for-Being-one's-Self."[103]

It is intriguing to see that Heidegger's description of the self-attestation of Dasein does not involve mimesis at all. Against the background of what we have seen so far, we can understand why: mimesis would only conceal Dasein's proper potentiality for being. At this point we see a particular difference between Heidegger and Ricoeur. The latter pays a lot of attention to the role of attestation in *Sein und Zeit* (especially in relation to conscience), and he would probably agree that this potentiality-for-Being-one's-Self is the ultimate concern of a hermeneutics of the self.[104] Nevertheless, such a self-understanding can only arrive through narrative. Without the mimetic operation of emplotment, no attestation can occur since it lacks any content. Consequently, we relate to the whole of our existence by means of the stories we tell and are being told about (our own) birth and death. Only by means of these stories we get a sense of what our potentiality-for-being-one's-self involves. Ricoeur thus places us in a mimetic relation to the whole of our existence. Clearly, Heidegger would protest against this conception. The simple fact of the plurality of stories that are being told can illustrate why Heidegger would protest: this plurality as such can never give rise to an account of the *wholeness* of our existence. Hence, although these stories may provide content to our self-understanding, they cannot answer the question of what it is that makes this whole a whole rather than a dispersed multiplicity. Perhaps Ricoeur, in turn, would protest by claiming that this wholeness can only be a regulative principle for the understanding: every factual self-understanding is marked by multiplicity. A direct attestation of the wholeness of existence is not possible. Yet, the question remains of whether this wholeness should be granted an ontological primacy, as Heidegger does, or should rather be limited to a practical one, as Ricoeur's theory of narrative suggests in accordance with Kant's thought.

In addition, another issue is at stake in this discussion on attestation. Ricoeur does not only emphasize the mediating role of narrative in self-understanding, he also stresses that the phenomenon of attestation cannot be understood as something that originates in Dasein alone, as Heidegger suggests when he writes that Dasein calls itself in conscience. The call of conscience is not only attestation, as Ricoeur notes, but it is also injunction.[105] As an injunction, the call of conscience is a call that comes from the other and commands us. Thus, the phenomenon of conscience is a phenomenon that includes both the self and the other: it refers back to self-attestation as well as to an injunction by the other. Clearly, these issues concern the ethical status of the call of conscience. For Heidegger, the foreignness of the voice of the one who calls is only a foreignness of proper existence with respect to everyday existing in the they.[106] For Ricoeur, the call does not simply call from one's authentic existence, but is an ethical injunction that comes from the other.

In relation to these issues, Derrida adopts a third position. In opposition to the conception of the primacy of wholeness, he stresses the originality of the other. In Heidegger's conception of death, it is death that provides Dasein with its individuality or mineness (*Jemeinigkeit*). Derrida, on the other hand, follows a more Levinasian account: the notion of the self is constituted by an original mourning and thus presupposes the other inside oneself as different from the self.[107] To some extent, this brings Derrida close to Ricoeur. They both claim that a self-relation presupposes a relation to alterities. However, an important difference arises here. The alterities intrinsic to Ricoeur's conception of the self are not of the order of mourning. For instance, the reciprocal relation to the other presupposes that the other is still alive and can speak for itself. Moreover, it presupposes that the other shares my language: only thanks to such a linguistic togetherness in a lively conversation in one language, the voice of the other can be received. It is only in Ricoeur's analysis of translation that an equivalent of the work of mourning appears, which is first and foremost a renouncing of a perfect translation, that is, a translation without remainder. For Derrida, on the other hand, such a work of mourning constitutes the self and its self-relation: the relation to the other in the self is a relation of mourning and remembrance, that is, it is a work that remembers the voice of the deceased other while at the same time being mindful of the irrecoverable loss of this voice.

In his beautiful but difficult essay *Béliers,* Derrida problematizes the presupposition of the reciprocal relation between the self and the other. Even a dialogue between two living conversation partners should be understood in light of the future time in which one of the two will have died. He writes, "From the first encounter, interruption anticipates death, precedes death. Interruption casts over each the pall of an implacable future anterior. One of us two will have had to remain alone. Both of us knew this in advance. And right from the start. One of the two will have been doomed, from the beginning, to carry alone, in himself, both the dialogue, which he must pursue beyond the interruption, and the memory of the first interruption."[108]

Hence, the living dialogue should not be understood in light of a *reciprocal* relationship between the self and the other, but rather in light of the nonreciprocal, future relationship that already determines the current dialogue as an anticipation on the work of mourning and remembrance. This work continues the dialogue while remembering "the first interruption." Why is it necessary to consider the dialogue in light of this "pall" of the future, and what does this first interruption tell us about dialogue? Derrida insists on the singularity of *each* of the voices that speak. In light of this interruption it turns out that each of the conversation partners speaks a different language and with a different tone of voice. This problematizes every reciprocity from the outset. Hence, the wholeness itself loses its primacy by the specific nature of the mimetic structure in our relation to the other's death in the work of mourning and remembrance.

Alterity as Being Out of Joint

The previous discussion places the priority of displacement over disclosure in a specific light. As we noted before, Derrida is critical about Heidegger's emphasis on gathering in the notion of *logos*. To give one additional proof of this, let me quote Derrida's use of the term logocentrism in his reading of Heidegger in "*L'oreille de Heidegger.*" Usually, Derrida interprets logocentrism as the primacy of presence over absence, such as the presence of the father to his sons, his *logoi*. In relation to Heidegger, he explains logocentrism as follows: "And whether it is a matter of *Versammlung* or of *Sein*, this always passes through the *logos* and concenters itself around *logos*. At bottom logocentrism is perhaps not so much the gesture that consists in placing the *logos* at the center as the interpretation of *logos* as *Versammlung*, that is, the gathering that precisely concenters what it configures."[109] Derrida characterizes Heidegger's emphasis on gathering as a form of logocentrism. This means that the effectuated configuration becomes the center from which the movement of language is to be understood. Hence, logocentrism is characterized by the interpretation of a preceding movement of language as configuring or gathering. This interpretation, however, implies a reversal of the relation between configuring or gathering and the movement of language preceding it. As opposed to Heidegger's emphasis on togetherness and gathering, Derrida points to the primacy of otherness. As a consequence, also the movement of displacement, up to now discussed as the basic model of passage and transference, is placed in this light of alterity.

To show what this notion of alterity does to configuration and gathering, let me recall that Ricoeur's account of emplotment focuses on a new configuration of time in order to render it intelligible. For Ricoeur, time is only intelligible if it is rendered into a whole. Also Heidegger, though in a different way, turns to the question of time and temporality in order to think the wholeness of Dasein's being.[110] Derrida's emphasis on otherness, however, approaches the question of time from a completely different experience: not the wholeness of Dasein or the integrality of human action intrigues him, but rather the Shakespearian experience that "time is out of joint."[111] In *Spectres de Marx,* Derrida contrasts this experience of time explicitly to Heidegger's analysis of joining (*Fügen*) and gathering (*Versammlung*). In particular, he discusses Heidegger's interpretation in "*Der Spruch des Anaximander*" of *dikē* (justice) as *Fug* and *Fuge,* that is, as joint and accord.[112] Under the guidance of the question of justice, Derrida examines the difference between, on the one hand, his own and Levinas's emphasis on heterogeneity and alterity in justice and, on the other hand, Heidegger's insistence on thinking justice as *dikē* from the perspective of harmony and accord.[113] In particular, he asks about the meaning of giving and giving justice, and he points out that Heidegger describes "to give" not as "to give away," but as to let and to admit (*zugeben*) the other what belongs to him or her. This letting and admitting is possible *because* both the other and I belong together in the same accord.[114] Hence, the possibility of letting the other that which is proper to him or her—which is usually understood as justice—depends upon the accord in which the other and I are joined together. In this way, we can see why Heidegger skips a more common analysis of justice of giving the other what belongs to him or her, and moves immediately forward to that which precedes and enables such a common justice, namely *dikē* as joining and according.

Derrida criticizes this Heideggerian emphasis on accord and joint since he fears that this attention to the primacy of accord and harmony runs the risk of treating the question of justice within an "inevitable totalizing horizon."[115] His questions circle around a metaphysical question: *how to characterize what precedes the presence of a present being*. What is earlier than every present being? Heidegger responds to this question by pointing out the primacy of harmony, of joining, and of the whole to which we belong and with which we should comply in order to let all the beings be as they are. Derrida understands this attention to an accord(ing) with the whole and to giving everything and everyone its due within the boundaries of this accord as a movement that is on its way to a totality, and thus also to an encompassing grasp of the whole as totality. It is important to note that this Derridean interpretation of Heidegger's attention to harmony (*Einklang*), accord, corresponding (*Entsprechen*), and so on, contradicts Heidegger's understanding of these issues. As I noted in the first chapter, the latter's retrieval of the question of the whole is born from a critique of the metaphysical tendency to treat the question of the whole as a totality. Hence, Derrida's claim that Heidegger's analysis of complying with, joining, and wholeness leads to an "inevitable totalizing horizon" goes against the grain of Heidegger's focus and seems to be guided by Levinas's account of Heidegger's thought of being as belonging completely to the realm of sameness (*le même*). In fact, one might wonder whether Derrida's defense of Heidegger against this Levinasian critique in "*Violence et métaphysique*" does not apply to his own comments in *Spectres de Marx*. In "*Violence et métaphysique*," he argues that Levinas necessarily affirms the ontological violence he discerns in Heidegger's thought. Moreover, in this text Derrida defends Heidegger (as well as Husserl) against the claim that they would try to think a totality. For Heidegger, the whole is the element to which we always already belong. It is the element that precedes every appearance and in which every being is given to us as this or that being. No effort to accord

with the whole can be completed; it can never be an encompassing movement since such a movement would imply that we would
uproot ourselves from this whole. Every effort to comply with this
whole is a form of anticipation and a being ahead of oneself. To use
Derrida's own reading from *Mémoires pour Paul de Man,* the movement of complying and gathering is rather an unfulfilled promise than
a presence. Also for Heidegger, as Vedder shows convincingly, the
anticipation of the whole is marked by an inescapable provisionality,
hence the horizon of Heideggerian thought can never simply be seen
as "inevitable totalizing," as Derrida claims.[116]

Nevertheless, Derrida's question with respect to the phenomenon
of letting the other that which belongs to him or her is pertinent. To
be precise, it does not concern the phenomenon of letting as such,
but rather the primacy of gathering with respect to this phenomenon.
In *Mémoires pour Paul de Man,* when he describes how to let someone speak who passed away, Derrida notes that to let the other speak,
it is necessary to make the other speak.[117] This indicates that letting
requires an activity on the part of the one who lets the other speak
and who, by this very activity, risks contaminating and displacing the
voice of the other: the one who lets the other speak always takes the
risk of distorting the other's voice. He or she has to take this risk in
order to let the other speak in the first place. At this point, we come
across a variant of the idea we have seen a number of times now: a
displacement is found at the heart of the disclosure of a letting that
allows the other to appear. However, this displacement does not yet
show us why the one actually lets the other speak. Why does the one
feel obliged and has "no choice to let the other speak," and thus to
risk this displacement? To answer this question, Derrida adds that
the other has "*already* spoken."[118] Hence, the one who lets the other
speak does not do something out of him or herself, but responds to
"the other who speaks 'before' and 'outside' it," that is, he or she
responds to something that precedes this speech.[119]

This theme of an otherness that precedes the movement of letting
something to the other, is also present in *Spectres de Marx.* The question of how to do justice to the other (and to the other's voice) leads

us to a "pre-" that precedes the movement of gathering. The movement of gathering does not only go back to a displacement, but this
displacement has a provenance. This provenance also *precedes* gathering and, therefore, it cannot be thought in terms of gathering alone.
It rather involves something other than or heterogeneous to the realm
of gathering, as Derrida writes, "The heterogeneity of a *pre-*, which,
to be sure, means what comes before me, before any present, thus
before any past present, but also what, for that very reason, comes
from the future or as future: as the very coming of the event. The
necessary disjointure, the de-totalizing condition of justice, is indeed
here that of the present—and by the same token the very condition
of the present and of the presence of the present."[120] To some extent,
and it is important to emphasize this, this quote repeats Heideggerian
themes, such as the critique of a metaphysics of presence: it indicates
that the past and the future cannot be understood as modifications
of the presence of the present. Yet, it also differs from Heidegger. It
describes a fore-structure and a future that are heterogeneous: both
are *other than* presence. Derrida's insistence on heterogeneity and
otherness indicates that a critique of presence is not exhausted by
an account that proceeds from the uncanniness (*Unheimlichkeit*) of
that which is one's own, as Heidegger does. In Heidegger's case, the
confrontation with that which is foreign or different only shows that
we have not yet appropriated our own essence. As such, its only focus
is the appropriation of the essence of one's own language and one's
own realm of disclosure. Derrida, however, argues that the question
of justice cannot be thought in these terms. If justice as giving to the
other depends upon the movement of according and complying with
one's own realm of disclosure, it can only give to others that already
belong to this realm of one's own. If this were the case, the alterity of
the other would derive from this realm of disclosure. Derrida, however, argues that the otherness of the other, whether it concerns the
other language or the other individual, always belongs to a different
realm, which cannot be presented as such in the clearing in which we
dwell.

Caressing the Other's Idiom

This latter emphasis on an alterity that cannot be disclosed as such in our realm of presence, guides us to the problem of translation. To some extent, the question of translation is concerned with the same issue as the one we encountered in the passage from *Mémoires pour Paul de Man:* a translator aims at letting a foreign text speak in our own language. Moreover, as in the case of speaking for the other, this letting runs the risk of distorting and displacing the original. Finally, as in the case of speaking for the other, the appeal to translate refers back to something beyond and outside the translation: the original text, which has never been present and will never be present as such in the target language.

The issue of translation plays an important role throughout Derrida's work.[121] To some extent, translation plays a similar role as metaphor. As in the case of metaphor, Derrida problematizes the concept of translation that is typical for philosophy, namely a Platonic concept of translation that claims that all univocal meanings are univocally translatable since the meaning of a text or an expression can be distinguished from its carrier, the specific language in which it is written or said.[122] The thesis that univocal meanings are translatable is a variant of the sole thesis of philosophy.[123] Parallel to his treatment of the concept of metaphor, Derrida dismisses this metaphysical concept of translation in order to bring a more primordial form of *translatability* to light. This translatability does not presuppose a nonincarnated language, but is rather a figure of thought to approach the question of how one idiom is transferred to and transformed in another one by translation. Clearly, in these terms—transference and transformation—the issue of translation is merely a variant of the displacement in repetition, which occupies Derrida from the outset of his work on iterability and supplementarity.[124] As such, as Crépon demonstrates, translation, like writing, is involved in the typical "survival" of a work in a tradition.[125]

At the same time, beyond its intrinsic displacement, translation is also a work of language concerned with the singularity of the other's idiom as such. Translation is the (impossible) effort to touch the singularity of an idiom while leaving it untouched. Derrida describes this beautifully in his essay "*Qu'est-ce qu'une traduction 'relevante'?*":

> If I love the word, it is only in the body of its idiomatic singularity, that is, where a passion for translation comes to lick it as a flame or an amorous tongue might: approaching it as closely as possible while refusing at the last moment to threaten or to reduce, to consume or to consummate, leaving the other body intact but not without causing the other to appear—on the very brink of this refusal or withdrawal—and after having aroused or excited a desire for the idiom, for the unique body of the other, in the flame's flicker or through a tongue's caress.[126]

This quote describes the chance of the work of translation: to approach and to touch an idiom in its singularity while leaving it untouched. At the same time, taken in isolation, this quote might leave a somewhat unbalanced impression, and one might wonder what Derrida could mean with a caressing that leaves the caressed object untouched. In other texts, in particular in some of his texts on Celan, Derrida insists that the above chance of translation does not exist without an intrinsic risk of violence. In an interview with Évelyne Grossman, in a discussion of the singularity of (the body of) a poem of Celan, Derrida notes that "to translate is to lose the body. The most faithful translation is violent: one loses the body of the poem, which exists only in the German and once only." Yet, as in the case of letting the other speak, this unavoidable violence is placed under an imperative, as Derrida argues in *Béliers:* "*I must* translate, transfer, transport (*übertragen*) the untranslatable in another turn even where, translated, it remains untranslatable. This is the violent sacrifice of the passage beyond— *Übertragen: übersetzen.*"[127]

In "*Des tours de Babel,*" Derrida relates this ambiguity of chance and risk to the promising structure of translation.[128] From Benjamin's essay "*Die Aufgabe des Übersetzers,*" Derrida borrows the messianic theme of an ultimate reconciliation of languages that would be anticipated by translation. Although Benjamin points to the particular survival of a text beyond the means of its author, the goal of translation is not communication, but rather an intralinear version of the sacred text.[129] Such a version touches not so much on the singularity of its original idiom but rather on a reconciliation of languages: the goal of translation is "to re-mark the affinity between the languages," as Derrida notes.[130] Ricoeur considers this Benjaminian messianic affinity of languages to be an example of a form of perfect translation, which translation as a work of mourning has to learn to renounce.[131] How does Derrida interpret this affinity? When Benjamin describes the goal of translation as the *Ausdruck*—the expression—of the affinity of languages in translation, Derrida explicates this word as re-mark rather than as simple presentation since no translation actually presents this affinity.[132] Rather, translation is a promise. He continues, "But a promise is not nothing, it is not simply marked by what it lacks to be fulfilled. As promise, the translation is already an event, and the decisive signature of a contract."[133]

Given the structure of the promise as risk and chance and the fact that a translation can never present what it promises, it is safe to conclude that Derrida would subscribe to Ricoeur's comment that a translation has to renounce the ideal of a perfect translation. However, unlike Ricoeur, he also notes a definite affinity between his and Benjamin's conception of translation. In Benjamin's essay, Derrida discerns the motive that he embraces in "*Qu'est-ce qu'un traduction 'relevante,'*" namely the motive of translation "to touch the untouchable, that which remains of the text when one has extracted from it the communicable meaning." Nevertheless, this affinity does not concern the harmony of language as such.[134] If we reread *Des tours de Babel* in light of Derrida's remarks on translation in "*Qu'est-ce qu'un traduction 'relevante'*" or in his readings of Celan, we have to conclude that the untouchable to which a Derridean translation strives is not so much the Benjaminian "harmony of languages."[135] In fact, such a harmony remains too close to the gathering movement Heidegger discerns in language and which Derrida problematizes throughout his work. His other, later texts on the topic of translation indicate that, if it is meaningful to speak about an affinity of languages, this affinity consists in the fact that every language is marked by a singular, idiomatic structure. This is why Derrida refers to the "translator-poets." He writes, "It is their task to explain, to teach, that one can cultivate and invent an idiom, because it is not a matter of cultivating a given idiom, but of producing the idiom."[136] To touch the untouchable idiom of a foreign poem or a foreign thinker, the translator has to let the poem speak in another language by inventing a new idiom in this language. This invention re-marks the original idiom: it touches the poem's original idiom and makes the poem speak in another language without presenting the poem as such.

The issue of translation thus beautifully shows how Heidegger, Ricoeur, and Derrida deal with the question of mimesis and the relation to the foreign intrinsic to it. For Heidegger, mimesis is not an issue. Even though a translation discloses a foreign text elsewhere than in its original language, he avoids the problem of mimesis by emphasizing that translation is not so much concerned with the disclosure of the particular aspects of the foreign text and its idiomaticity. The encounter with a foreign text, poem, or thought is first and foremost a necessary moment in the relation to our own language. This is due to the fact that the encounter with foreignness and alterity is preceded by the gathering and according movement of language. As such, translation testifies of the difference of languages by pointing to their co-belonging. Even the hospitality of a "hospitable dialogue" with a foreign language is carried by this primordial co-belonging that keeps the languages strictly apart, in order to avoid any form of confusion and contamination.[137]

Ricoeur, in contrast, argues that translation, as the hospitality of language, is grounded in the experience of the irreducible multiplicity of human language. Therefore, the mimetic moment of translation is crucial to allow another language to appear in one's own language. He describes this mimetic operation as the construction of comparables, which enrich our language. This construction of comparables does not leave room for any purity; the question of the essence of one's own language disappears and makes room for a conception of the mutual, reciprocal influence of languages. His insistence on the work of translation as a work of memory and mourning demonstrates that both the unification and the purification of languages are impossible.

Derrida also points out that the issue of translation guides us to the primacy of the multiplicity of languages as well as to the impurity of the boundaries between languages: "At the word go we are within the multiplicity of languages and the impurity of the limit." Moreover, like Ricoeur, Derrida calls the work of translation a work of mourning and memory.[138] In this sense, he agrees with Ricoeur that the invention of new idioms in one's own language is necessary, while renouncing the ideal of a perfect translation. However, Ricoeur's insistence on the construction of a comparable cannot be found in Derrida. This need not surprise us since the invention of a comparable establishes a relation between two languages: from now on they are comparable, and this means that only from now on we may hope to understand the idiomatic differences. Once more, we see that mimesis is original for Ricoeur in relation to the constitution of meaning and the possibility of understanding. One might wonder, however, as I noted above, whether this account of translation as the construction of a comparable can be reconciled with the account of the work of translation. The latter, as I indicated above, proceeds from another experience of the foreignness of a foreign idiom as well as from the experience of translation as a form of interruption. This latter dimension of translation marks Derrida's focus on translation as a promise and a work of mourning and remembrance: it mourns the loss of the original idiom by remembering the interruption, and it caresses the original idiom by inventing the other's idiom anew, at another place and in another language.

Disclosure and Displacement in Hermeneutics

Heidegger, Ricoeur, and Derrida are all three, though in different ways, concerned with the questions and problems that arise in the wake of a thinking that begins with language, to paraphrase Ricoeur's statement at the end of "*Existence et herméneutique.*" In the previous chapters we have seen how the pair of concepts disclosure and displacement sheds a light on the different interpretations that are given to such a thinking that has language as its point of departure. By means of an examination of the issues of writing, metaphor, mimesis, and translation I described how the relation between truth, untruth, and language guides Heidegger's, Ricoeur's, and Derrida's reflection on these issues. Rather than repeating these analyses, I would like to show in this concluding chapter how these three perspectives on disclosure and displacement inform their account of hermeneutics, interpretation, and the practice of reading.

DISCLOSURE AND DISPLACEMENT IN HERMENEUTICS AS ANNOUNCEMENT

Heidegger's work, as I noted in the first chapter, is marked by a continual effort to rethink truth as *alētheia* or unconcealment. His account of the essence of language emphasizes the primacy of the disclosive dimension of language. This disclosive movement from concealment to unconcealment is the fundamental focus in his reflections on (poetic) language and truth. As this movement, disclosure

236

depends on the primacy of a certain concealment. In particular, in his quest for the essence of language, he emphasizes that words disclosing this essence are still lacking. Therefore, "everything depends on whether language gives or withholds the appropriate word." This typical formulation also characterizes what Heidegger means by being "on the way": not yet to have arrived at this appropriate word, but to be guided by the promise of an event that will provide it. In this sense, as Derrida emphasizes again and again, Heidegger's wandering expressed in this "on the way" is not the same as his wandering understood as *errance*. To approach this difference, I suggested to consider more carefully how Heidegger understands truth as a struggle with a twofold untruth. The simple concealment of *lēthē*, which precedes every presence and presencing, is different from the complex concealment of *pseudos*, which always involves both appearance and disguise and which is characterized first and foremost by the disguise of the realm of disclosure to which we always already belong and which the thinker tries to bring to the fore.

I suggested to interpret the latter form of concealment as Heidegger's version of displacement since he often renders *pseudos* in the German as *Verstellen*. My analysis of Heidegger's critical comments of writing, metaphor, and mimesis, which are all linguistic phenomena involving displacement, corroborates the idea that Heidegger understands displacement as a secondary phenomenon and remains, at least in the eyes of Ricoeur and Derrida, too Platonic in this respect. For Heidegger, however, this characterization is not intended as an adoption of a Platonic theme. The stakes are different: if one wants to understand how language can disclose being as such and how it can disclose beings as they are, neither writing as the flight from thinking and as the displacement of the disclosive power of saying, nor mimesis and metaphor, which tend to present beings by means of a being they are not, can be considered as valid candidates to think this disclosive dimension of language. In particular, an account of art and poetry should avoid these latter two phenomena since they drive a wedge between truth and language. A thinker can only be a genuine *philomuthos* if he or she knows how to overcome this Platonic wedge and its derivatives in Western thought. In fact, his interpretation of Heraclitus's notion of *philein* as complying with and harmonizing affirms the idea discussed at the end of chapter 1 that only a thought that seeks the proximity of and the co-belonging with poetic saying can hope to find this disclosive dimension of language. Hence, the Heideggerian thinker cannot be but a *philomuthos*.

If we ask what a disclosive saying actually is, one of the answers might be announcement (*Kundgabe*). With this word, we enter the realm of Heidegger's determination of hermeneutics. Even though he drops the term hermeneutics in his later work, he does not do this because he wants to get rid of the meaning of announcement. Rather, in contrast to his earlier work, he tries to distinguish interpretation from announcement.[1] In *Unterwegs zur Sprache*, Heidegger emphasizes that announcement as the genuinely disclosive dimension of hermeneutics precedes interpretation,

> I[nquirer]: The expression "hermeneutic" derives from the Greek verb *hermēneuein*. That verb is related to the noun *hermēneus,* which is referable to the name of the God *Hermēs* by a playful thinking that is more compelling than the rigor of science. Hermes is the divine messenger. He brings the message of destiny; *hermēneuein* is that exposition which brings tidings because it can listen to a message. Such exposition becomes an interpretation of what has been said earlier by the poets who, according to Socrates in Plato's *Ion* (534e) *hermēnēs eisin tōn theōn*—"are interpreters of the gods."
> J[apanese]: I am very fond of this short Platonic dialogue. In the passage you have in mind, Socrates carries the affinities even further by surmising that the rhapsodes are those who bear the tidings of the poets' word.
> I[nquirer]: All this makes clear that hermeneutics means not just the interpretation, but, even before it, the bearing of message and tidings[2]

Hermēneuein as *Kundgeben* means "to make known" or "to disclose."[3] This is quite as we expect it to be. Yet, with Nancy we may wonder whether one should not also emphasize that the announcement of hermeneutics is always already also a displacement. Especially in the dialogue to which Heidegger refers in the above quote, this is the case. According to Plato's *Ion,* announcement occurs through the poets and, subsequently, through the rhapsodes. As such, we never hear the words of the gods themselves, but we only hear them in a derived way and with a voice that is not theirs, that is, we hear them by means of a displacement. In fact, Heidegger is aware of this. In his lectures on Hölderlin's poems *Germanien* and *Der Rhein,* he first emphasizes (as we expect him to do) that the poet says in a show-ing, revealing way. However, he also notes that the poet transfers and hands down the hints (*Winke*) of the gods to us.[4] The language of the gods consists of these hints, and the words of the poets draw the rest of the people in the vicinity of these hints. Here, at the heart of the question of what hermeneutics and announcement is, Hei-degger cannot withdraw from using a figure of thought that employs an unmistakable displacement.

DISCLOSURE BY MEANS OF DISPLACEMENT

In the previous chapters we have seen to what extent Ricoeur's herme-neutics is indebted to Heidegger's work. The primacy of disclosure can also be traced in Ricoeur's work. Yet, he corrects Heidegger's work in an important way by adding the notion of distanciation. This notion is very important since it allows him to rethink the relation between the understanding of being, which is the ultimate goal of hermeneutics, and the explanation of the different human sciences. More importantly, however, distanciation allows him to show the extent to which the products of the poetic imagination are involved in our self-understanding.

In chapter 2 we noted how Ricoeur places displacement and dis-tanciation under the aspect of the primacy of meaning. In fact, since he considers the repeatability of meaning to be an essential charac-teristic of discourse, he can argue that the materiality of writing does not threaten the event of language, but that it makes language more spiritual. In this way, it seems that the displacement of language loses its threatening, distorting character, which Heidegger rediscovered in Plato's conception of *pseudos.* More importantly, along these lines of thought, meaning becomes the vanishing point of every interpretation for Ricoeur: meaning as a regulative idea attracts interpretations and guides the process of interpretation. From a Heideggerian point of view, this might imply that Ricoeur subsumes the ideas of "announcement" and "making known"—that is, the original meaning of hermeneutics—under the interpretation of meaning, as Nancy in fact argues.[5] However, this reading is perhaps a bit too quick. Without a doubt, Ricoeur subscribes to the primacy of the manifestation of language. His concern is, however, that this manifestation involves both concealment and unconcealment. This concern can already be traced in his work on the symbol: the symbolic manifestation of reality is a manifestation that consists of a contamination of disclosure and disguise. In the first, naive listening to the symbol, we are unable to defend ourselves against the distortions at work in symbolic manifestation. By means of distanciation and interpretation, Ricoeur strives to make both the distorting and the disclosing dimensions of the symbol visible. Hence, the detour along interpretation is necessary to clarify the symbolic manifestation and to distinguish the distorting and disclosive elements of symbolic manifestation. The goal, however, of this detour is to return to listening to the symbol and to place ourselves once again in the realm of the symbolic manifestation.[6] As such, the disclosure of language is both the beginning and the end of interpretation.

In his poetics from the 1970s onward, the importance of this motive of distanciation only increases. Hermeneutics is no longer restricted to the field of linguistic expressions with multiple meanings (symbols), but as he writes in *Interpretation Theory*, "I think today, however, that metaphoric and symbolic language is not paradigmatic for a general theory of hermeneutics. This theory must cover the whole problem of discourse, including writing and literary composition."[7] Why is it necessary to extend the field of hermeneutics in this way? In the previous chapters, I have suggested that this is necessary since the disclosure that arises in the wake of distanciation is not only the consequence of a critical attitude. In his later work, Ricoeur adopts the Aristotelian insight that nature needs the mimesis of art to be brought to presence. Hence, distanciation is not only a way of purifying an already given manifestation, but in the wake of distanciation a particular form of disclosure, namely poetic disclosure, is opened up. This poetic disclosure is original for the human understanding: this understanding requires the mimetical configurations of the imagination to come to self-understanding and to understanding the world it inhabits.

With this expansion of the field of hermeneutics, the problem of multiplicity becomes more and more important for Ricoeur: multiple stories present us with multiple possibilities of living; multiple historical narratives present us with multiple equivalents of the past; multiple translations present us with multiple comparables of a foreign text. None of these stories, narratives or translations is sufficient. Each one requires an additional one in order to supplement it and to take into account features that the others could not account for. This is the way in which a thinking that begins with language is confronted with the fact that being is said in many ways, even though its unity and its wholeness is presupposed as a regulative idea guiding our understanding of the relation between these multiple stories, historical narratives, and translations.

DERRIDA ON DISCLOSURE AND DISPLACEMENT

More than a century before Derrida's reflections on the status of the preface in Hegel's thought, Kierkegaard published a small book consisting only of prefaces.[8] From a Hegelian perspective, "when one begins the book with the subject and the system with nothing, there apparently is nothing left over to say in a prologue."[9] Within this perspective, the prologue is superfluous and seems to be something entirely different than the main part of the book. Opposed to this perspective, Kierkegaard describes the foreword as a mood and as the tuning of a guitar.[10] By means of a beautiful metaphor, he describes how the preface, as something accidental and sudden, can breach and broach the main text of a book in an entirely unexpected way: "It is a frequently corroborated experience that a triviality, a little thing, a careless utterance, an unguarded exclamation, a casual glance, an involuntarily gesture have provided the opportunity to slip into a person and discover something that had escaped more careful observation."[11] The preface, however accidental and trivial we may think it is, precedes and thus attunes our reading of the actual body of a book. This example of a fore-word as the fore-structure guiding our practice of reading and understanding a text is important to all three thinkers: Heidegger, Ricoeur, as well as Derrida. In the latter's perspective, however, the example of the preface is exemplary. First, the preface, preceding the main body of a book, is *another* text, often thought to be completely external to the actual body. On the other hand, the preface has a definite surplus-value for our reading of a text. It traces and marks, breaches and broaches the themes discussed in the main body of a text. Thus, the main text is never simply approached as such; it is always already displaced by the inscription of the preface into it. Paraphrasing Heidegger's description of *Verstellen* in "*Der Ursprung des Kunstwerkes,*" we could say that one text, the preface, displaces another, that one text puts itself in front of another. This displacement, however, does not occur within an already given realm of disclosure, which it would distort, but precedes and enables the chance of a disclosure of (the meaning) of the text.

At the end of "*La structure, le signe et le jeu,*" Derrida comments on interpretation as follows:[12]

> There are thus two interpretations of interpretation, of structure, of sign, of play. The one seeks to decipher, dreams of deciphering a truth or an origin which escapes play and the order of the sign, and which lives the necessity of interpretation as an exile. The other, which is no longer turned towards the origin, affirms play.... For my part, although these two interpretations must acknowledge and accentuate their difference and define their irreducibility, I do not believe that today there is any question of *choosing*—in the first place because here we are in a region (let us say, provisionally, a region of historicity) where the category of choice seems particularly trivial; and in the second, because we must first try to conceive of the common ground, and the *différance* of this irreducible difference.... I employ these words, I

admit, with a glance towards the operations of childbearing—but also with a glance toward those who...turn their eyes away when faced by the as yet unnamable which is proclaiming itself and which can do so, as is necessary whenever a birth is in the offing, only under the species of the nonspecies, in the formless, mute, infant, and terrifying form of monstrosity.[13]

These comments can be read as a critique of Ricoeur's attention to the conflict of interpretations in the 1960s. It is not a matter of choosing between different conflicting interpretations, according to Derrida. It is a matter of thinking their difference. The task of thinking this *différance* is the task of thinking the birth of other words and other articulations. The disclosure of something unheard-of—namely the common ground of these two interpretations of interpretation—requires the distortion and the displacement of the apparent opposition of the two types of interpretation. In particular, this means that we cannot approach the unheard-of if we simply repeat the metaphysical gesture and refer to a transcendental signified to account for this opening.[14] Lacking any given form or species, Derrida describes this unheard-of as a monstrosity, as something that announces itself but has not yet arrived or taken shape. This reference to the monstrous in this account of interpretation is also a reference to disclosure and to language as showing (*montrer*), as Derrida explains elsewhere.[15]

Derrida approaches the problem of opening the unthought as the problem of the "as yet unnamable" that announces itself. The verb *annoncer* (translated here as "to proclaim") relates Derrida's comments on the preceding dimension of interpretation(s) to Heidegger's explication of *hermēneuein* as *Kundgeben*. His insistence on the "as yet unnamable" relates these comments to Heidegger's problem of being on the way to language and of thinking the unthought, which always means that words are as yet still lacking and that we are awaiting the gift of a word. Derrida adds to Heidegger's proposed understanding of *hermēneuein* that this disclosure is always only a promise and a wandering as *errance*: it never actually, in the present, provides what it promises. Thus, this early quotation already anticipates

Mémoires pour Paul de Man, in which the difference with Heidegger's thought is understood as the difference between *sprechen* and *(sich) versprechen*.

Where do these reflections on disclosure and displacement in relation to these different understandings of hermeneutics leave us? Heidegger's, Ricoeur's, and Derrida's reflections on language are all concerned for the unthought, which announces itself and draws near but is never captured. Within the realm of this issue of the unthought, the poetic dimension of language plays a privileged role because it is the dimension of language *par excellence* where this announcement and this drawing near occur. The unthought is the ultimate provocation of thought, in the double sense of the word: it questions and disrupts the results of philosophy. But by questioning these results it also challenges thought to think more and to respond to the appeal of the unthought that announces itself. In fact, at stake in these analyses of the unthought is the question of how (philosophical) thought itself belongs to this unthought as the realm of its very possibility. Without a doubt, Heidegger's attention to the unthought, the to come, and disclosive saying; Ricoeur's attention to the innovative dimension of the (poetic) imagination that creates and discovers the world; and, Derrida's displacing *différance* that traces the as-yet-unheard-of monstrosity of a promised future are all concerned with this very possibility of philosophical thinking.

Inspired by this attention to the unthought, this study has tried to show how the works of Heidegger, Ricoeur, and Derrida on language and truth are guided by the question: "How to attest to the unthought of language in thinking?" Whether language provides thought with the appropriate word(s) to think its unthought or not, depends on one's understanding of the proper. Yet, we have at least some words at our disposal and two words in particular, "disclosure" and "displacement," to respond to the ways in which these three major writers announce the unthought of language in their thinking.

NOTES

Throughout this book, I cite the original version of the work unless a direct quote of the English translation appears in the text; in that case, the English translation is cited.

Notes to Introduction

1. Husserl, *Krisis,* 372.
2. Derrida, *De la grammatologie,* 203.
3. Ricoeur, *Le conflit des interprétations,* 28.
4. Heidegger, *Sein und Wahrheit,* 131–32; Heidegger, *Parmenides,* §7.
5. Gadamer, *Wahrheit und Methode,* 392.
6. Aristotle, *Rhetoric,* 1411b24–12a5; All Aristotle quotations are from Barnes, *The Complete Works of Aristotle.*
7. Ricoeur, *La métaphore vive,* 392.
8. Taylor, *Human Agency and Language,* 222–23, and Gadamer, *Wahrheit und Methode,* 422–31.
9. Cf. Plato, *Republic,* book 10, 595a–97e.
10. Ibid., book 3, 386b.
11. Plato calls the poet not a maker (*demiourgos*) as the god who creates the bed (as it is, its *Idea*) or the craftsman who creates a bed (he presents the *Idea* in a particular medium), but he calls the poet an imitator, concluding, "Then imitation is far removed from the truth, for it touches only a small part of each thing and a part that is itself only an image" (*Republic,* 598b; cf. Cooper, *Plato: Complete Works,* 1202). This leads to the ironic consequence that one of the thinkers who has extensively used myths in his dialogues approaches the language of the poets by measuring its *distance* to truth, and argues that it is not creative, but a mere imitation.
12. Steiner, *After Babel,* 84–85; Taylor, "Language and Human Nature," and "Theories of Meaning," *Human Agency and Language,* 215–92.
13. Steiner, *After Babel,* 85.

14. Cf. Berman, *L'épreuve de l'étranger.*
15. Aristotle, *Metaphysics,* 982b18–19.

Notes to Chapter 1

1. Heidegger, *Feldweg-Gespräche,* 99.
2. Heidegger, *Wegmarken,* 180.
3. As Heidegger puts it: "Die veritas als adaequatio rei (creandae) ad intellectum (divinum) gibt die Gewähr für die veritas als adaequatio intellectus (humani) ad rem (creatam)" (ibid., 181).
4. Ibid., 378–79.
5. "In solcher Weise stellt der Metaphysik überall das Seiende als solches im Ganzen, die Seiendheit des Seienden vor (die *ousia* des *on*)" (ibid., 378). See also "Die onto-theo-logische Verfassung der Metaphysik," in Heidegger, *Identität und Differenz,* 51–83.
6. Heidegger, *Pathmarks,* 278. Cf. Heidegger, "Die Metaphysik als Geschichte des Seins," in *Nietzsche II,* 363–416. Note that the translation writes the English translation of *Sein* as "Being," with a capital B. I will not do this in my text.
7. Already in *Sein und Zeit,* Heidegger determines the *Destruktion* of the history of philosophy as a critique that aims at the current way of treating the history of ontology; cf. Heidegger, *Sein und Zeit,* 30–31. He still uses the word *Destruktion* in this way in Heidegger, *Zur Sache des Denkens,* 13. The dismantling of philosophy serves to provide us a provisional insight in the sending of being.
8. The German *im Ganzen* can mean both "in general" and "as a whole."
9. In his work on being-in-common (*être-en-commun*), Nancy furthers this line of Heidegger's thought in a more politically ontological context; cf. Nancy, *La communauté désoeuvré,* and *Le sens du monde.*
10. Heidegger, *Being and Time,* 59.
11. Ibid., 56–57.
12. Heidegger, *Sein und Zeit,* 198–99.
13. Ibid., 291–93.
14. Robinson's translation gives "state-of-mind"; cf. Heidegger, *Being and Time,* 172. I prefer to use the German term.
15. Heidegger, *Sein und Zeit,* 293.
16. "*Die Stimmung hat je schon das In-der-Welt-sein als Ganzes erschlossen und macht ein Sichrichten auf…erst möglich*" (ibid., 182).
17. Ibid., 191–92.
18. Cf. Derrida, *L'écriture et la différence,* 427.
19. Cf. Ricoeur, *La métaphore vive,* 387.
20. Heidegger, *Sein und Zeit,* 293.
21. "They" is the anonymous mass of people in which no one is authentically his or herself, but understands his or herself in terms of this mass alone.
22. For a number of such characterizations, see Heidegger, *Sein und Zeit,* §38.

23. Heidegger, *Being and Time*, 212. "Gossiping" and "passing the word along" are translations of *Nachreden* and *Weiterreden*, respectively; cf. Heidegger, *Sein und Zeit*, 224.

24. Heidegger, *Being and Time*, 265.

25. Heidegger, *Sein und Zeit*, 223–25.

26. Heidegger, *Being and Time*, 189.

27. Heidegger, *Sein und Zeit*, 199–200.

28. Ibid., 44.

29. Heidegger, *Being and Time*, 217. The German allows a more smooth articulation of this phrase: "*Sinn ist das durch Vorhabe, Vorsicht und Vorgriff strukturierte Woraufhin des Entwurfs, aus dem her etwas als etwas verständlich wird*" (*Sein und Zeit*, 201).

30. See also Heidegger, *Logik*, 129–30. In this passage, Heidegger refers to Aristotle's *On Interpretation*, 17a1–3. Aristotle's turn of phrase *logos apophantikos* is usually translated as "statement-making sentence," cf. Barnes, *Complete Works of Aristotle*, 1:26. Heidegger relates *apophantikos* to "pointing out" or "showing," and he translates the phrase from *On Interpretation* as " 'Jedes Reden weist zwar auf etwas hin (bedeutet überhaupt etwas) — aufweisend, sehenlassend dagegen ist nicht jedes Reden, sondern nur das, darin das Wahrsein under Falschsein vorkommt' (als die Weise des Reden)." The same sentence is usually translated as "Every sentence is significant...but not every sentence is a statement-making sentence, but only those in which there is truth or falsity.."

31. An assertion lets a being be seen from itself. Heidegger uses this phrase at least twice: "Die Rede 'läßt sehen' *apo*...von dem selbst her, wovon die Rede ist" (*Sein und Zeit*, 43); "Seiendes von ihm selbst her sehen lassen" (205).

32. Ibid., 213.

33. Heidegger, *Being and Time*, 208–09.

34. Cf. Heidegger, *Sein und Zeit*, 204–213, 295.

35. Heidegger, *Being and Time*, 199.

36. Ibid., 200.

37. Cf. Heidegger, *Sein und Wahrheit; Vom Wesen der Wahrheit;* and "*Platons Lehre der Wahrheit*," in *Wegmarken*, 201–236. For Plato's parable, see *Republic*, 514a–18c.

38. Heidegger, *Sein und Wahrheit*, 127.

39. Plato, *Republic*, 514a–18c (all Plato references are to Cooper, *Plato: Complete Works*); Heidegger, *Sein und Wahrheit*, 128.

40. Heidegger, *Sein und Wahrheit*, 131–32.

41. Ibid., 133.

42. Ibid., 137.

43. Ibid., 140; cf. also Heidegger, *Vom Wesen der Wahrheit*, 32–38.

44. Heidegger, *Sein und Wahrheit*, 138; cf. 140; *Vom Wesen der Wahrheit*, 34–35; and *Wegmarken*, 218–19, 228–29.

45. Heidegger, *Sein und Wahrheit*, 140; cf. *Vom Wesen der Wahrheit*, 32–38.

46. Heidegger, *Sein und Wahrheit*, §29; my translation of the title.

47. Ibid., 222.

48. Heidegger also makes this claim in *Parmenides,* 72–74.

49. Heidegger, *Sein und Wahrheit,* 165.

50. Heidegger writes about this battle: "zwar von Platon selbst nicht gewußt oder gewollt" (ibid., 165).

51. Heidegger, *On Time and Being,* 70. For the whole remark, see Heidegger, *Zur Sache des Denkens,* 85–88. On the question what this means for the change of the essence of truth, cf. Bernasconi, *Question of Language,* 17–23 and Peperzak, "Heidegger and Plato's Idea of the Good," 264–69.

52. Peperzak ironically remarks, "Heidegger seems to suggest that the word *alētheia* is wiser than the philosophers who pronounced it" (ibid., 266). The word *alētheia* indeed contains more to be thought than the Greek philosophers have thought in it. This unthought remainder is exactly its richness. However, whether this idea of an unthought wealth deserves the *irony* contained in Peperzak's remark remains to be seen: is it not the basic experience of every reading that a book contains more than its author intended—even if this author is a philosopher?

53. Cf. Heidegger, *Zur Sache des Denkens,* 85.

54. "Das Ungedachte ist sein höchstes Geschenk, das ein Denken zu vergeben hat" (Heidegger, *Was heißt Denken?,* 82).

55. Heidegger, *Sein und Wahrheit,* 184.

56. Ibid., 184. The German *Verstellen* has all these three meanings: to disguise, to distort, and to displace.

57. Ibid., 188.

58. Cf. ibid., 184–88.

59. Ibid., 226–29. Cf. Heidegger, *Parmenides,* 42–48.

60. Ibid., 44–45; *Sein und Wahrheit,* 227.

61. Heidegger, *Parmenides,* 44.

62. Heidegger, *Sein und Wahrheit,* 227.

63. Heidegger, *Parmenides,* 47.

64. Gadamer, *Neuere Philosophie I,* 248.

65. Heidegger, *Parmenides,* 47.

66. Ibid., §3.

67. Heidegger, *Early Greek Thinking,* 71; cf. 59–78. The original reads: "*Die A-lētheia ruht in der Lēthē,* schöpft aus dieser, legt vor, was durch diese hinterlegt bleibt.... Die Unverborgenheit braucht die Verborgenheit, die *Lēthē,* als ihre Rücklage, aus der das Entbergen gleichsam schöpft" (Vorträge und Aufsätze, 225–26).

68. Heidegger, *Pathmarks,* 148.

69. Heidegger, *Parmenides,* 33.

70. Ibid., 34.

71. "Das anfängliche Gegenwesen zur *a-lētheia* ist die *lēthē,* d.h. die als Vergessung sich entziehende zeichenlose Verbergung" (ibid., 140). "Was ist dann,

wenn die Seinsvergessenheit die Geschichte des geschichtlichen Menschentums ungesehen und zeichenlos umirrt?" (166).

72. Ibid., 105.

73. Plato, *Republic*, 614b–21d.

74. Heidegger, *Parmenides* (translation), 126.

75. Heidegger, *Parmenides*, 179.

76. Ibid., 183.

77. Ibid., 183.

78. Heidegger, *Parmenides* (translation), 127.

79. Heidegger, *Pathmarks*, 152.

80. Heidegger, *Sein und Wahrheit*, 125.

81. Heidegger, *Parmenides* (translation), 128. Note that this phrase still stands after Heidegger's remarks on the untenability of the claim of a change of the essence of truth. Heidegger says only that the myth provides thought with the domain in which Homer mentions (*nennt*) alētheia. Nevertheless, this claim is still important in his *Parmenides* lectures. The antropomorphic character of Plato's myth would imply the first signs of a change concerning the essence of *lēthē* into a forgetfulness by man; cf. Heidegger, *Parmenides*, 192.

82. Ibid., 183, 189.

83. "Dieses entziehende und die Verborgenheit 'vor-enthaltende' Gegen-wesen zur Entbergung enthält im voraus ihr Wesen" (ibid., 189). In the English translation, *im voraus* is rendered as "at the same time also." See Heidegger, *Parmenides* (translation), 127. "In advance" would be a better translation to indicate the relation with Heidegger's attention to being ahead of oneself.

84. Heidegger, *Parmenides* (translation), 127.

85. Ibid., 127.

86. Heidegger, *Sein und Zeit*, 223–25.

87. Heidegger, *Holzwege*, 1–74. Translations are taken from "The Origin of the Work of Art," in *Poetry, Language, Thought*, 15–87.

88. Cf. Heidegger, *Sein und Zeit*, §40.

89. Heidegger, *Poetry, Language, Thought*, 54, 53–54.

90. For lighting as the open place: "*Inmitten des Seienden im Ganzen west eine offene Stelle*," Heidegger, *Holzwege*, 39–40; for quoted passage, *Poetry, Language, Thought*, 53; for how beings appear, *Zur Sache des Denkens*, 87–88; and, for truth as "battle," *Holzwege*, 41–42.

91. Heidegger, *Poetry, Language, Thought*, 54.

92. Cf. Levinas, "*La trace de l'autre*." See Derrida's reference to this concept in *L'écriture et la différence*, 117; *De la grammatologie*, 102–03; and *Marges de la philosophie*, 22.

93. Heidegger, *Unterwegs zur Sprache*; "*Logos (Heraklit, Fragment 50)*," in *Vorträge und Aufsätze*, 211–34.

94. "Sie möchten uns vor eine Möglichkeit bringen, mit der Sprache eine Erfahrung zu machen.…machen heißt hier: durchmachen, erleiden, das uns

Treffende empfangen, insofern wir uns ihm fügen. Es macht sich etwas, es schickt sich, es fügt sich" (Heidegger, *Unterwegs zur Sprache*, 149).

95. Ibid., 150.

96. See also Heidegger, "*Der Satz vom Grund*," in *Der Satz vom Grund*, 171–89.

97. Heidegger, *Unterwegs zur Sprache*, 149.

98. Ibid., 174.

99. Heidegger, *On the Way to Language*, 59.

100. Heidegger, *Unterwegs zur Sprache*, 249–50.

101. Ibid., 247.

102. Ibid., 254.

103. For the gift of presencing, Heidegger, *Zur Sache des Denkens*, 12; for the withdrawal of *lēthē*, 50.

104. At this point, we can locate Badiou's critique of Heidegger in Badiou, *Manifeste pour la philosophie*, and *L'être et l'événement*, 141–49. According to Badiou, Heidegger binds or "sutures" philosophy to poetics. This is problematic because poetics is only one domain of truth besides three others: politics, love, and science. Because he sutures philosophy to poetics, Heidegger is unable to think nature and ontology as mathematics, as Badiou does in *L'être et l'événement*. Lacoue-Labarthe argues that what is at stake here in Badiou's critique is not so much poetry as such, but Heidegger's tendency to relate philosophy to myth (*Sage*), which Lacoue-Labarthe relates to the lack of a more positive retrieval of mimesis in Heidegger's thought. Cf. "*Poésie, philosophie, politique*," in Lacoue-Labarthe, *Heidegger*, 43–77. Whatever one may think of this, it is clear that a lot of Heidegger's later work is devoted to the reading of poetry. In this chapter, I only mention part of Heidegger's reading of George's poem "*Das Wort*," but this reading may be extended by other readings, of which probably Heidegger's readings of Hölderlin are the most famous.

105. Poem quoted in Heidegger, *Unterwegs zur Sprache*, 152–53; *On the Way to Language*, 60, 62.

106. For Heidegger's attention to making something shine, or *energeia*, see *Zur Sache des Denkens*, 81, and IJsseling, *Mimesis*, 53–57.

107. Ricoeur, *La métaphore vive*, 387.

108. Heidegger, *Unterwegs zur Sprache*, 159.

109. Heidegger, *On the Way to Language*, 66.

110. Ibid., 59.

111. See also Steiner's description of poetry from the second half of the nineteenth century (Rimbaud, Mallarmé, George, etc.), in Steiner, *After Babel*. "The concept of 'the lacking word' marks modern literature," according to Steiner (184). In modern poetry, "established language is the enemy. The poet finds it sordid with lies. Daily currency has made it stale" (186); "The poetry of modernism is a matter of structured débris: from it we are made to envision, to hear the poem that might have been, the poem that will be if, when, the word is made new" (190). In Heidegger's experience with language, guided by the works of

poets, we see that all of these elements recur: the distrust of everyday language, the problem of concealment and the lack of an appropriate word, as well as the expectation that the appropriate word is about to occur and may give itself so that truth may occur and beings may be given in unconcealment.

112. Heidegger, *Unterwegs zur Sprache*, 241.

113. Ibid., 241–42.

114. Ibid., 241.

115. For *Logos* as the name of being, Heidegger, *Vorträge und Aufsätze*, 233; for *Logos* as speech and as bringing to language, 214, 232; for the quoted passage, *Early Greek Thinking*, 77; and for Heidegger's Aristotelian interpretation, *Vorträge und Aufsätze*, 218.

116. Heidegger, *Vorträge und Aufsätze*, 222.

117. "*Das All des Anwesenden*" (ibid., 229).

118. Ibid., 228–29.

119. By relating the difference between these two interpretations of the *hen* to the difference between an onto-theo-logical and an non-onto-theo-logical conception of the whole, I propose a somewhat different interpretation of the *hen* than Schürmann does in his magnificent study on the anarchy principle; cf. Schürmann, *Heidegger on Being and Acting*, 177–79.

120. Heidegger, *Vorträge und Aufsätze*, 226.

121. Ibid., 221–22.

122. Ibid., 230.

Notes to Chapter 2

1. Heidegger, *Was heißt Denken?*, 20.

2. For a more extensive account of Heidegger's conception of writing, see IJsseling, "*Heidegger en het geschreven woord*"; IJsseling, "*Sprache und Schrift.*"

3. Ricoeur, *Interpretation Theory*, 39; Ricoeur refers to the examples of Bergson and Rousseau. The latter is also an important example to Derrida, cf. Derrida, *De la grammatologie*. The title of this section refers to Gadamer's "*Unterwegs zur Schrift?*" in *Griechische Philosophie III*, 258–69.

4. Plato, *Republic*, 518b–c; all Plato references are to Cooper, *Plato: Complete Works*.

5. Ibid., 518c–d.

6. Plato, *Seventh Letter*, 341c.

7. Ibid., 344b.

8. Plato, *Second Letter*, 314a–c. See also Plato's remarks on the long education of the philosopher in book 7 of the *Republic*, 539–40.

9. Plato, *Second Letter*, 314a–c.

10. Plato, *Seventh Letter*, 344c–d.

11. Plato, *Phaedrus*, 274c–75b.

12. Ibid., 275a; my italics.

13. Ibid., 275d–e.

14. Ibid., 275d.

15. Ibid., 275a.

16. Plato, *Phaedrus,* 276a.

17. Husserl, *Krisis,* 371–72.

18. Gadamer, *Truth and Method,* 392.

19. Ricoeur uses the same notion of "spiritual" in his comment on writing, see Ricoeur, *Interpretation Theory,* 31.

20. Gadamer, *Truth and Method,* 392.

21. "Now spoken sounds are symbols of affections in the soul, and written marks are symbols of spoken sounds. And just as written marks are not the same for all men, neither are spoken words. But what these are in the first place signs of—affections of the soul—are the same for all; and what these affections are likenesses of—actual things—are also the same" (Aristotle, *On Interpretation,* 16a1–10).

22. Note that Gadamer refers to another passage of Plato to show that we can also find the importance of language for understanding in his work: "After this, he said, when I had wearied of investigating things, I thought that I must be careful to avoid the experience of those who watch an eclipse of the sun, for some of them ruin their eyes unless they watch its reflection in water or some such material. A similar thought crossed my mind, and I feared that my soul would be altogether blinded if I looked at things with my eyes and tried to grasp them with each of my senses. So I thought I must take refuge in discussions and investigate the truth of things by means of words" (Plato, *Phaedo,* 99d–e).

23. Gadamer, *Truth and Method,* 390.

24. Derrida, *La voix et le phénomène.*

25. Gadamer, *Truth and Method,* 397.

26. Ibid., 387; translation modified. I have replaced "conversation" with "dialogue."

27. Gadamer plays with the affinity between *ins Spiel bringen* and *aufs Spiel setzen;* see Gadamer, *Wahrheit und Methode,* 392.

28. Ibid., 389.

29. Gadamer, *Truth and Method,* 370.

30. Gadamer, *Wahrheit und Methode,* 392.

31. Heidegger, *Unterwegs zur Sprache,* 151.

32. For the quote, Gadamer, *Truth and Method,* 394; for the horizon of the text, see *"Die hermeneutische Bedeutung der Zeitenabstandes,"* in *Wahrheit und Methode,* 296–305; for the horizon within a dialogue, 393.

33. Ibid., 395–96, 398.

34. For the quote, see Gadamer, *Truth and Method,* 394; Gadamer calls writing the *"abstrakte Idealität der Sprache"* (*Wahrheit und Methode,* 396); for the correction of meaning, 401.

35. Derrida, *L'écriture et la différence,* 411.

36. Gadamer, *Wahrheit und Methode,* 391, 397, 397–98.

37. Ricoeur, *From Text to Action,* 76; my italics.

38. Ricoeur, *Du texte à l'action,* 109–10.

39. Ricoeur, *The Conflict of Interpretations*, 66.

40. Ricoeur, *Interpretation Theory*, 78; *"La fonction herméneutique de la distanciation,"* in Ricoeur, *Du texte à l'action*, 113–31. Other important references are *"Qu'est-ce qu'un texte?,"* 153–78; *"Herméneutique et critique des idéologies,"* 367–416; Ricoeur, *La métaphore vive*, 87–100.

41. Cf. Ricoeur, *Interpretation Theory*, 1–8; *La métaphore vive*, 88–100.

42. To some extent, discourse is comparable to *parole,* but in Ricoeur's and Benveniste's work, discourse opens up the realm of semantics. Cf. Benveniste, *Problèmes de linguistique générale.*

43. Agamben, *Language and Death*, 23–36.

44. Ricoeur, *From Text to Action*, 78.

45. Cf. the first part of Nancy, *Le partage des voix.*

46. Ricoeur, *Du texte à l'action*, 115–20; *Interpretation Theory*, 8–22.

47. Ricoeur, *Du texte à l'action*, 116–117, 119.

48. Heidegger, *Sein und Zeit*, 296; *Being and Time*, 266–67.

49. Ricoeur, *Interpretation Theory*, 26.

50. See Lawlor, "Dialectic and Iterability," and *Imagination and Chance.*

51. Ricoeur, *La métaphore vive*, 92–93.

52. Derrida, *Marges de la philosophie*, 375.

53. In a well-known discussion on ideality and iterability with the American philosopher John Searle, Derrida notes the following of Searle's exclusion of certain ways of speech in his determination of the concept of promising: "Tant qu'elle n'intègre pas la *possibilité* des cas limites, la possibilité *essentielle* des cas dits marginaux... *dans* le concept idéal d'une structure dite 'normale,' 'standard,' etc....on peut dire que la formation d'une théorie générale ou d'un concept idéal reste insuffisante, faible ou empirique. L'idéalisation pratiquée reste alors elle-même défectueuse, elle n'a pas pris en compte des prédicats essentiels. Elle échoue à rendre compte de cela même dont elle se propose le concept idéal" (Derrida, *Limited Inc.*, 215).

54. Ricoeur, *Du texte à l'action*, 53, 140, 404; *Interpretation Theory*, 27, 42. Ricoeur calls his conception of the text a furthering of Gadamer's account of *Schriftlichkeit* with certain adaptations; cf. Ricoeur, *Du texte à l'action*, 405.

55. Ricoeur, *Interpretation Theory*, 93; my italics.

56. Husserl, *Krisis*, 371.

57. Ricoeur, *Interpretation Theory*, 31.

58. Derrida also insists on the iterability at the heart of every ideality: "Il n'y a pas d'idéalisation sans itérabilité (identifiante), mais pour la même raison, en raison de l'itérabilité (altérante), il n'y a pas d'idéalisation pure, à l'abri de toute contamination. Le concept d'itérabilité est ce singulier concept qui rend possible la silhouette de l'idéalité, donc du concept, et donc de toute distinction, ou de toute opposition conceptuelle" (Derrida, *Limited Inc.*, 216).

59. This difference between hermeneutic and disseminal experience and its relation to the theme of writing in Plato's *Phaedrus* occupies Derrida until his final texts; cf. Derrida, *Béliers*, 39–40, 47.

60. Cf. Ricoeur, *Du texte à l'action*, 87–89, 120–24, 157, 163–69; Ricoeur, *Interpretation Theory*, 71–88.

61. Ricoeur, *Du texte à l'action*, 105, 109; see also "*Herméneutique et critique des idéologies.*"

62. In relation to Aristotle's account of being-true and being-false, Ricoeur introduces this concealing and unconcealing aspect of language also in his account of a hermeneutic of the self; see Ricoeur, *Soi-même comme un autre*, 347–51.

63. Ricoeur, *Interpretation Theory*, 75–79; *Du texte à l'action*, 174, 396.

64. Ricoeur, *Interpretation Theory*, 36–37.

65. In particular, Derrida points to the interruptions and undecidables Gadamer's hermeneutic reading of Celan takes into account; see Derrida, *Béliers*, 34–38.

66. The French *présentifier* is a translation of the German *Vergegenwärtigen*. The world of the text is an imaginary one created by literature, a literary imaginary; see Ricoeur, *Du texte à l'action*, 158.

67. Ricoeur, *La métaphore vive*, 51–61, 388; *Temps et récit 1.*

68. Ricoeur, *From Text to Action*, 86; "interpréter, c'est expliciter la sorte d'être-au-monde déployé devant le texte" (Ricoeur, *Du texte à l'action*, 128).

69. Ricoeur, *Du texte à l'action*, 128.

70. For the destination, see Ricoeur, *Interpretation Theory*, 37; for redescription, see *Du texte à l'action*, 129.

71. Ricoeur, *Interpretation Theory*, 43, 94.

72. "Hermeneutics of suspicion" is a term used by Ricoeur in *De l'interprétation* to refer to the thought of Nietzsche, Marx, and Freud.

73. Note that despite his attention to prejudices, Gadamer would not disagree with this description. His description of the interpretation of a text as a conversation in which a *fusion of horizons* can take place, shows that the text itself has something to say on its subject matter and is not simply reduced to the horizon of the interpreter. Instead, the interpretation of the text should lead to a fusion of horizons and should extend the horizon of the interpreter. See also Ricoeur's comment in Ricoeur, *Du texte à l'action*, 110, and *Interpretation Theory*, 94.

74. Ricoeur, *Interpretation Theory*, 93–95. Clearly, this theme is furthered in the development of a hermeneutic of the self in Ricoeur, *Soi-même comme un autre*.

75. Lacoue-Labarthe, *Heidegger*, 106.

76. Derrida, *Béliers*, 54.

77. "On dérive la présence-du-présent de la répétition et non l'inverse" (Derrida, *La voix et le phénomène*, 58); his intention is to "restaurer l'originalité et le caractère non dérivé du signe contre la métaphysique classique" (57).

78. Cf. "*Envoi,*" in Derrida, *Psyché*, 109–43. The second half of Marrati's beautiful study gives a very clear exposition of the difference between Heidegger and Derrida from the perspective of the notion of representation and sending (*envoi*). See Marrati-Guénoun, *La genèse et la trace.*

79. His reading of Husserl has been commented extensively, see for instance:

Lawlor, *Derrida and Husserl,* and Bernet, et al., *Derrida et la phénoménologie.* For a thorough account of the specific place of Derrida's reading of Husserl's *Der Ursprung der Geometrie* in relation to the development of his account of writing, see Kates, "Derrida, Husserl and the Commentators."

80. Derrida, *De la grammatologie,* 203ff.

81. *Der Ursprung der Geometrie* appeared as *"Beilage III,"* in Husserl, *Krisis,* 365–86.

82. Derrida, *The Origin of Geometry,* 164.

83. Derrida, *L'origine de la géométrie,* 84.

84. Husserl, *Krisis,* 371.

85. Ricoeur, *La métaphore vive,* 92. In this respect, Ricoeur seems to be quite close to Husserl.

86. Lawlor, *Imagination and Chance,* 72.

87. Derrida, *L'écriture et la différence,* 411.

88. Ibid., 427.

89. Derrida, *Béliers.*

90. Derrida, *Sovereignties in Question,* 144.

91. Derrida, *Positions,* 62.

92. Derrida, *Sovereignties in Question,* 146.

93. Ibid., 162.

94. Derrida, *Dissemination,* 71 / *La dissémination,* 80.

95. Plato, *Phaedrus,* 230d-e; Scully, *Plato's Phaedrus,* 7.

96. He also uses this wording in *"La mythologie blanche,"* Derrida, *Marges de la philosophie,* 253. I will return to this theme in chapter 4.

97. "Pharmaceia" is not only a name but is also the plural of *pharmakon.*

98. *Phaedrus,* 229e–30a.

99. Toward the end of the dialogue, Socrates wakes up from his slumber and loses his interest in both Phaedrus and writing.

100. Similarly, Gadamer claims: "Plato hat vielmehr stets anerkannt, daß es dieser Vermittlungen [vom logos] des Denkens bedarf, wenn sie auch als stets überholbare angesehen werden müssen. Die Idee, das wahre Sein der Sache, ist nicht anders erkennbar als im Durchgang durch diese Vermittlungen" (Gadamer, *Wahrheit und Methode,* 434).

101. For the illumination of *logos,* see Derrida, *La dissémination,* 93; for the disclosure of the origin, cf. the Idea of the Good in Plato, *Republic,* 508b–c, and Derrida, *La dissémination,* 92–93; for source and resource, see 94–95.

102. Derrida, *Dissemination,* 168.

103. See also Derrida, "On Reading Heidegger."

104. The main reference is *"Signature événement contexte,"* in Derrida, *Marges de la philosophie,* 365–93.

105. Derrida, *Margins of Philosophy,* 320–21.

106. Ricoeur brings this difference also to Derrida's work as is clearly visible in his round-table discussion with Derrida. For a transcript of this discussion, see Lawlor, *Imagination and Chance,* 131–63.

107. Derrida, *Memoires* (translation), 50–51; Derrida, *Mémoires,* 64.

108. Derrida, *Dissemination*, 63.

109. Heidegger writes, "Solches Geben läßt einem anderen das gehören, was als Gehöriges ihm eignet" (Heidegger, *Holzwege*, 356–57). I shall return to this passage in the fourth chapter.

110. Derrida, *Politiques de l'amitié*, 378.

111. Cf. Heidegger, *Sein und Zeit*, §17; Derrida, *Heidegger et la question*, 184.

112. Heidegger, *On the Way to Language*, 123.

113. Heidegger, *Unterwegs zur Sprache*, 233–34.

114. In his analysis of Derrida's claim that Heidegger's work is logocentristic, Gadamer points to this particular aspect of Heidegger's work. See "Hermeneutics and Logocentrism," in Michelfelder & Palmer, *Dialogue and Deconstruction*, 114–25. Yet, by focusing on a shared dismantling of metaphysics, Gadamer tends to miss the particular difference between Heidegger and Derrida in their approach to metaphysics, and in particular, to language.

115. Heidegger, *Parmenides*, 131–32.

116. Derrida considers this as an important proof of Heidegger's tendency to devaluate writing, see Derrida, *Heidegger et la question*, 202–03.

117. Heidegger, *Was heißt Denken?*, 20.

118. Heidegger, *What Is Called Thinking?*, 17.

119. Heidegger, *Was heißt Denken?*, 81–86.

120. Heidegger, *What Is Called Thinking?*, 76.

121. Ibid., 75.

122. Heidegger, *Parmenides*, §3.

123. Derrida, *Marges de la philosophie*, 151.

124. Heidegger, *Was heißt Denken?*, 25–29; Heidegger, *Parmenides*, 119–27.

125. Heidegger, *Parmenides* (translation), 84, 85.

126. Heidegger, *Parmenides*, 125–26.

127. Derrida, *Heidegger et la question*, 202–03. See also IJsseling, "*Sprache und Schrift*," 114.

128. Derrida, *Heidegger et la question*, 184–85.

129. Heidegger, *What Is Called Thinking?*, 18.

130. Derrida, *Heidegger et la question*, 184.

131. Heidegger, *Zur Sache des Denkens*, 50.

132. Derrida, *Mémoires*, 140–42.

133. Derrida, *Memoires* (translation), 140.

134. Ibid., 146–47.

135. Ibid., 96, 97.

136. Heidegger, *On the Way to Language*, 59.

137. Derrida, *Memoires* (translation), 98.

138. In this passage from *De l'esprit*, Derrida refers to his reading of de Man; cf. Derrida, *Heidegger et la question*, 112–18.

139. Also in the logic of autoimmunity developed in *Voyous*, this double bind is typical for Derrida's conception of the promise. He writes, "It is thus indeed

already a question of autoimmunity, of a double bind of threat and chance, not alternatively or by turns promise and/or threat but threat in the promise" (Derrida, *Rogues,* 82).

140. Derrida, *Of Spirit,* 105.

141. Derrida, *Heidegger et la question,* 194–95, 201–02.

142. Derrida, *Positions,* 62.

143. Derrida, *Psyche II* (translation), 57.

144. "*Die Sprache im Gedicht,*" in Heidegger, *Unterwegs zur Sprache,* 31–78; Derrida, *Heidegger et la question,* 209; cf. 207, 214. Derrida finds a similar motive in Heidegger's attention to Trakl's unique emphasis of the word *Ein* in the expression "Ein *Geschlecht,*" see 216–17; on *Geist,* cf. Derrida, *Heidegger et la question,* 82–83, 136. On the latter page, Derrida states it plainly, "*Or la* Versammlung, *ce rassemblement en l'Un, Heidegger l'appelle aussi* Geist."

145. "*Die Erörterung bedenkt den Ort,*" Heidegger, *Unterwegs zur Sprache,* 33; "Le lieu est toujours, pour Heidegger, lieu de rassemblement (*Versammlung*)" (Derrida, *Heidegger et la question,* 65).

146. Heidegger, *On the Way to Language,* 160.

147. My translation. The standard English translation reads: "The poet's statement remains unspoken" (ibid., 160). This translates the phrase "Das Gedicht eines Dichters bleibt ungesprochen" (Heidegger, *Unterwegs zur Sprache,* 33).

148. Derrida, *Heidegger et la question,* 217.

149. Heidegger, *Unterwegs zur Sprache,* 33.

150. Derrida, *Heidegger et la question,* 134.

151. "Elle recourt toujours en des moment décisifs à une ressource idiomatique, c'est-à-dire intraduisible si l'on se confie au concept courant de la traduction" (ibid., 217–18). For the numerous examples Derrida gives, see 16, 85–91, 95–96, 101, 218–21.

152. Ibid., 87.

153. Heidegger, *Reden und andere Zeugnisse eines Lebensweges,* 679. Derrida refers to this remark in *Heidegger et la question,* 87.

154. Derrida, *Marges de la philosophie,* 377.

155. Derrida, *Sovereignties in Question,* 102, 103, 162.

156. Derrida, *Psyche* (translation), 97.

157. Derrida, *Memoires* (translation), 15.

158. Ibid., 76.

159. Ibid., 140, 29, 80.

160. Ibid., 139; cf. his remark "Car je ne 'critique' jamais Heidegger sans rappeler qu'on peut le faire depuis d'autres lieux de son texte" (Derrida, *Heidegger et la question,* 216).

161. Derrida, *Memoires* (translation), 31, 38, 58, 66.

Notes to Chapter 3

1. See Greisch, "*Les mots et les roses*." See also §3 and §5 of the final study in Ricoeur, *La métaphore vive*.

2. Heidegger, *Wegmarken*, 313–64; see also *Unterwegs zur Sprache*, 255.

3. Heidegger, *Principle of Reason*, 48.

4. Used by Aristotle in *Rhetoric*, 1406b20–25.

5. Heidegger emphasizes the same intrinsic relationship between metaphor and the metaphysical dualism of the sensible and the intelligible in his lectures on Hölderlin's poem *Der Ister;* see *Hölderlins Hymne "der Ister,"* 17–19.

6. Hegel, *Vorlesungen über die Ästhetik*, 518.

7. Heidegger, *Der Satz vom Grund*, 72.

8. Aristotle, *Poetics*, 1459a8.

9. Heidegger, *Unterwegs zur Sprache*, 167–85.

10. Ibid., 176.

11. Ibid., 184–85.

12. Ibid., 185.

13. "Wenn jedoch die Nähe von Dichten und Denken eine solche des Sagens ist, dann gelangt unser Denken in die Vermutung, das Ereignis walte als jene Sage, in der die Sprache uns ihr Wesen zusagt" (ibid., 185).

14. Aristotle, *Poetics*, 1457a30–b10; *Rhetoric*, 1410b12.

15. Derrida, *Psyché*, 83–84; see Heidegger, *Wegmarken*, 313, and *Unterwegs zur Sprache*, 255.

16. Heidegger, *Wegmarken*, 358.

17. Jean Greisch also points to this distrust; cf. Greisch, "*Les mots et les roses*," 453. Greisch mentions that Heidegger's alleged metaphoricity differs from Gadamer's attention to the fundamental metaphoricity of language. To explicate Greisch's comment, we could point exactly to this problem of the direction of transference. In Gadamer's account of the metaphoricity of language, language transfers known expressions to express resemblances with unknown things. This movement from familiar to unfamiliar guided by a resemblance is exactly how Gadamer describes the metaphoricity of language; see Gadamer, *Wahrheit und Methode*, 433.

18. Of course, this becomes most clear in Heidegger's analysis of anxiety (*Angst*) in §40 of *Sein und Zeit*. Being-in-the-world as such is only disclosed when every being has lost its familiar meaning and we are in a state of uncanniness.

19. Heidegger, *Unterwegs zur Sprache*, 151.

20. Derrida, *Psyché*, 79–81.

21. Heidegger, *Unterwegs zur Sprache*, 191–97.

22. Ibid., 192–93.

23. Ibid., 296.

24. Ibid., 195.

25. Heidegger quotes the following: "'Dies Wie ist immer ein Bruch in der Vision, es holt heran, es vergleicht, es ist keine primäre Setzung…,' 'ein

Nachlassen der sprachlichen Spannung, eine Schwäche der schöpferischen Transformation'" (ibid., 195–96).

26. Aristotle, *Rhetoric*, 1406b20.

27. Ibid., 1410b12.

28. Ricoeur, *La métaphore vive*, 37.

29. Aristotle, *Rhetoric*, 1410b18–20. See also Ricoeur, *La métaphore vive*, 34–40.

30. Aristotle, *Rhetoric*, 1411b26, 1411b31. See also Ricoeur, *La métaphore vive*, 388–92.

31. My translation; "The word of thinking is not picturesque; it is without charm. The word of thinking rests in the sobering quality of what it says. Just the same, thinking changes the world" (Heidegger, *Early Greek Thinking*, 78); "Das Wort des Denkens ist bildarm und ohne Reiz. Das Wort des Denkens ruht in der Ernüchterung zu dem was er sagt. Gleichwohl verändert das Denken die Welt" (Heidegger, *Vorträge und Aufsätze*, 234). To relate this sobriety to Hölderlin is in agreement with Lacoue-Labarthe's work on Hölderlin, see *"Hölderlin et les Grecs,"* in Lacoue-Labarthe, *L'imitation des modernes*, 71–84; and Lacoue-Labarthe, *Heidegger*.

32. Heidegger, *Unterwegs zur Sprache*, 196.

33. See Ricoeur, *Du texte à l'action*, 127–28, and *Interpretation Theory*, 37; for quote, *Du texte à l'action*, 148.

34. Ricoeur, *La métaphore vive*, 387.

35. Ricoeur, *From Text to Action*, 8; *The Rule of Metaphor*, 364n.91.

36. Aristotle, *Poetics*, 1457b6–9; cf. Ricoeur, *La métaphore vive*, 19–34.

37. Aristotle, *Poetics*, 1406b21; cf. Ricoeur, *La métaphore vive*, 87.

38. Vedder, *"On the Meaning of Metaphor,"* 199–201.

39. Ricoeur, *Du texte à l'action*, 22–23.

40. Ibid., 24–25.

41. Ibid., 25–26.

42. Ricoeur, *La métaphore vive*, 375–76.

43. Ibid., 388.

44. Aristotle, *Rhetoric*, 1411b27, 1411b32; see Ricoeur, *The Rule of Metaphor*, 308, and *La métaphore vive*, 390.

45. Ibid., 389.

46. For *l'éclosion de l'apparaître*, see ibid., 389; for the elevation of reality, see 61. Ricoeur calls such reality *"un déplacement vers le haut"* and *"surélévation"* (57).

47. On metaphorical language, see ibid., 357, 361, 392–93; on the concept of metaphor, 25; on the emergence of possibilites, 392.

48. Derrida, *Marges de la philosophie*, 284.

49. Aristotle, *Topics*, 139b32–35, 140a9–11. Derrida quotes the first passage in *Marges de la philosophie*, 300.

50. Ricoeur, *La métaphore vive*, 398.

51. Ibid., 375–76.

52. Ricoeur, *The Rule of Metaphor*, 297.

53. Ricoeur, *La métaphore vive*, 375.

54. Ibid., 375.

55. Ricoeur, *The Rule of Metaphor*, 261; Lawlor, *Imagination and Chance*, 63.

56. Ricoeur, *La métaphore vive*, 383.

57. Kant, *Kritik der Urteilskraft*, §49.

58. France, *Le jardin d'Epicure*, 195–223; Derrida, *Margins of Philosophy*, 213.

59. Ibid., 211, 215.

60. From Ricoeur's analysis we can deduce that he approaches the problem of the philosophical metaphor along two lines. (1) Most of them are dead metaphors such as *begreifen* and *Sinn*. These are no longer metaphorical. They have become words with (at least) two clearly distinct meanings in the lexicon—a physical, sensible one and a conceptual one. This polysemy does not lead to any confusion: the context determines which meaning is meant. (2) On the other, he also recognizes living metaphors in philosophy such as Heidegger's *a-lētheia* and Hegel's *Wahr-nehmung*. These metaphors create new meaning, but *in philosophy* this new meaning always gives rise to a regulated equivocality: Ricoeur compares them to the analogy of being in *La métaphore vive*, 370–71, 394.

61. Derrida, *Margins of Philosophy*, 219. Note that "metaphorics" means here the development of a concept of metaphor encompassing the entirety of metaphors at work in the texts of philosophy.

62. In the opening pages of "*La structure, le signe et le jeu*," Derrida develops similar thoughts on the center and the law of a structure: "C'est pourquoi, pour une pensée classique de la structure, le centre peut être dit, paradoxalement, *dans* la structure et *hors de* la structure. Il est au centre de la totalité et pourtant, puisque le centre ne lui appartient pas, la totalité *a son centre ailleurs*" (Derrida, *L'écriture et la différence*, 410).

63. Derrida, *Marges de la philosophie*, 272.

64. Derrida, *Margins of Philosophy*, 270.

65. See "*Tympan*," in Derrida, *Marges de la philosophie*, esp. i–iii.

66. Derrida, *Psyché*, 111–12.

67. Ricoeur, *La métaphore vive*, 362–74; see Derrida, *Psyché*, 69–74.

68. Ricoeur, *The Rule of Metaphor*, 285.

69. He writes that the opposition of effective and effaced metaphors is a constant in metaphysical discourse, see Derrida, *Marges de la philosophie*, 268–69; see *Psyché*, 73–74.

70. Derrida, *Memoires* (translation), 38.

71. Derrida, *Psyché*, 69–70.

72. Derrida, *Marges de la philosophie*, 273; Ricoeur, *La métaphore vive*, 372.

73. Derrida, *Limited Inc.*, 215.

74. Derrida, *Marges de la philosophie*, 320.

75. Ibid., 282.

76. Ibid., 283–84.

77. Ibid., 287.

78. Ibid., 288.

79. Ibid., 295–302.

80. "[La métaphore] peut manifester des propriétés, rapporter les une aux autres des propriétés prélevées sur l'essence de choses différentes, les donner à connaître à partir de leur ressemblance, sans toutefois énoncer directement, pleinement, proprement l'essence, sans donner à voir elle-même la vérité de la chose même" (ibid., 296–97).

81. I paraphrase Heidegger, *Pathmarks,* 152; see also Heidegger, *Wegmarken,* 199.

82. See Derrida, *Marges de la philosophie,* 29.

83. Derrida, *Psyché,* 79.

84. For a more thorough and very clear exposition of the relation between Heidegger's *Destruktion* and Derrida's *déconstruction,* cf. Bernasconi, "Seeing Double: *Destruktion* and Deconstruction," in Michelfelder & Palmer, *Dialogue and Deconstruction,* 233–50. See also Derrida, *Le toucher,* 74; "The 'World' of the Enlightenment to Come," 51–52n11.

85. Derrida, *Psyché,* 83.

86. Ibid., 83.

87. Ibid., 83–86. As Heidegger does with the notion of *eigen,* Derrida plays on all the notion of *propre*: property, propriety, appropriation, one's own, and so on. However, Derrida does so in order to show that the "proper" word (especially the words "*propre*" or "*eigen*" themselves) are always already improper due to their metaphorical and supplementary overload (*surcharge*) of every word. In particular, every appropriation of a word, and therefore, the occurrence of every appropriate word, requires this metaphorical and supplementary dimension of language. Note that Derrida has, in his later work, a definite sense of Heidegger's particular use of the "proper." "It is as if Heidegger said, following a now somewhat traditional motif, that the proper of man is this experience that consists in exceeding the proper, the proper in the sense of what is appropriated in the familiar. On this issue Heidegger will not go so far as to say 'there is no proper of man,' but rather that this proper has as its basic trait, if not a certain impropriety or ex-propriation, as [*comme*] uncanny, non-appropriated, even non-appropriable, stranger to *heimisch,* to the reassuring proximity of the identifiable and the similar, to the familiar, to the interiority of home" (Derrida, *Sovereignties in Question,* 128).

88. Heidegger, *On the Way to Language,* 59.

89. "*Car il y a toujours* plus d'une *langue dans* la *langue*" (Derrida, *Psyché,* 90).

90. Ibid., 88.

91. Note that the text to which Derrida refers in Heidegger to argue that *Aufriß* is and remains concealed does not exactly say that *Aufriß* remains concealed. The concealment to which Derrida refers in his essay is a disguise (Heidegger uses the verb *verhüllen*) that only lasts if we do not pay proper attention to *Aufriß;* see also Heidegger, *Unterwegs zur Sprache,* 240–41.

92. "Son inscription [de l'Aufriß], comme j'ai tenté de l'articuler de la trace ou de la différance, *n'arrive qu'à s'effacer*" (Derrida, *Psyché,* 89).

93. This paraphrases Derrida's remark on the death of metaphor: "(et quand il y a deux morts, le problème de la mort est infiniment compliqué)" (ibid., 73).

94. Heidegger, *Pathmarks,* 152; my italics.

95. "*La différance,*" in Derrida, *Marges de la philosophie,* 1–29; Derrida, *Margins of Philosophy,* 27.

96. Derrida, *Marges de la philosophie,* 29.

97. The relation between anticipation and provisionality can be traced quite clearly in Heidegger's thought in the German *vorlaufen* and *Vorläufigkeit;* see Vedder, "The Provisionality of Thinking in Heidegger," and Vedder, *De voorlopigheid van het denken.*

98. Derrida, *Psyché,* 67.

Notes to Chapter 4

1. Ricoeur, *The Rule of Metaphor,* 43.

2. See Sallis, "Heidegger's Poetics"; IJsseling, *Mimesis;* Lacoue-Labarthe, *L'imitation des modernes; La fiction du politique;* and *Heidegger.*

3. Heidegger, *Introduction to Metaphysics,* 185.

4. See "*Platons Staat: Der Abstand der Kunst (Mimesis) von der Wahrheit (Idee),*" in Heidegger, *Nietzsche I,* 173–90.

5. IJsseling, *Mimesis,* 47, 59.

6. Heidegger, *Nietzsche I,* 182.

7. Ibid., 185.

8. Ibid., 180.

9. Ibid., 182.

10. Ibid., 189.

11. On displacement, see Heidegger, *Holzwege,* 40; on mimesis, see *Nietzsche I,* 175, 187.

12. Heidegger, *Off the Beaten Track,* 44. See also Sallis, "Heidegger's Poetics," 187.

13. Lacoue-Labarthe, *Heidegger,* 100.

14. See Lacoue-Labarthe, *La fiction du politique,* 114–33.

15. Heidegger's use of the word "holy" should not be understood as a further mystification on Heidegger's part. By using this word, he suggests that it is this world that is disclosed, and with it the presence of the gods. This world open to the Greeks is in important ways concealed to us.

16. Heidegger, *Holzwege,* 30.

17. See Sallis, "Heidegger's Poetics"; IJsseling, *Mimesis;* Lacoue-Labarthe, *L'imitation des modernes; La fiction du politique;* and *Heidegger.*

18. Heidegger, *Vorträge und Aufsätze,* 230.

19. Heidegger, *What Is Philosophy?,* 47. Partly quoted in Derrida, *Politiques de l'amitié,* 371–72.

20. Heidegger, *Vorträge und Aufsätze,* 230.

21. Cf. IJsseling, "Mimesis and Translation."

22. Heidegger indicates this with emphasizing the first and the second part of the German term *Übersetzen*, respectively; *Parmenides*, 16–18. For Heidegger's account of language, see Gondek, *"Das Übersetzen denken"*; Escoubas, *"De la traduction"*; Dastur, *Heidegger*.

23. "Das sogenannte Übersetzen und Umschreiben folgt immer nur dem Übersetzen unseres ganzen Wesens in den Bereich einer gewandelten Wahrheit" (Heidegger, *Parmenides*, 18).

24. Ibid., 16.

25. Heidegger, *Hölderlins Hymnen "Germanien" und "Der Rhein*," 63; *Hölderlins Hymne "der Ister,"* 75.

26. Heidegger, *Parmenides*, 61.

27. Heidegger, *Holzwege*, 7–8.

28. Ibid., 57.

29. Heidegger, *Hölderlin's Hymn "The Ister,"* 48.

30. "Das Fremde freilich, durch das hindurch die Heimkehr wandert, ist kein beliebiges Fremdes im Sinne des bloßen unbestimmten Nicht-Eigenen. Das auf die Heimkehr bezogene, d. h. mit ihr einige Fremde, ist die Herkunft der Heimkehr und ist das gewesene Anfängliche des Eigenen und Heimischen" (Heidegger, *Hölderlins Hymne "Der Ister,"* 67).

31. Dastur only seems to take this first affecting seriously when she claims that contamination is typical for every translation in Heidegger's work; see Dastur, *Heidegger*, 173. However, despite the fact that the foreign language is the provenance of one's own language, Heidegger carefully distinguishes this affecting from *wirre Vermischung*.

32. Cf. Heidegger, *Hölderlins Hymne "der Ister,"* 67–68, 176.

33. Heidegger, *Hölderlin's Hymn "The Ister,"* 66.

34. Derrida, *Heidegger et la question*, 88–89.

35. Heidegger, *Parmenides*, 18.

36. Heidegger, *Parmenides* (translation), 12.

37. Heidegger, *On the Way to Language*, 163.

38. See *"Die Herd als das Sein,"* in Heidegger, *Hölderlins Hymne "der Ister,"* 134–36.

39. Aristotle, *Poetics*, 1450a3; all reference to Aristotle from Barnes, *Complete Works of Aristotle*.

40. Ricoeur, *Time and Narrative*, 1:66.

41. Ricoeur, *Temps et récit*, 1:111–12.

42. Ibid., 135.

43. For a more extensive account of the difference between redescription and refiguration, see Tengelyi, "Redescription and Refiguration."

44. See in particular the chapter entitled *"Renonce à Hegel,"* in which Ricoeur shows how a total mediation, leading to the primacy of the concept needs to be avoided; Ricoeur, *Temps et récit*, 3:349–73.

45. Ibid., 1:129–31.

46. Ibid., 3:262–63.

47. Ibid., 3:271.
48. Ricoeur, *Time and Narrative,* 3:154; my italics.
49. Ricoeur, *Le conflit des interprétations,* 27–28.
50. Ricoeur, *Temps et récit,* 3:280.
51. Ibid., 1:137–44.
52. Ibid., 1:146.
53. Ibid., 1:140.
54. Ricoeur, *Time and Narrative,* 1:77.
55. Derrida, "Two Words for Joyce," 149.
56. Lacoue-Labarthe, *Heidegger,* 103, 106.
57. Derrida, *Writing and Difference,* 120.
58. The difference between good (or true) and bad (or false) infinity in Hegel runs parallel to the distinction between potential and actual infinity in Aristotle. The typical example of bad infinity is the sequence of numbers 1, 2, 3, . . . This sequence is infinite in the sense of endless: it never attains its end since the sequence is never completed. Therefore, Hegel also calls it continued finitude. In contrast, good infinity is a form of complete infinity in the sense that it sublates (*aufheben*) finitude.
59. Kant, *Kritik der reinen Vernunft,* B536–43.
60. Ibid., B536.
61. Ibid., B540.
62. Ricoeur, *Le conflit des interprétations,* 23.
63. Ricoeur, *Freud and Philosophy,* 526.
64. Ricoeur, *Du texte à l'action,* 105, 109, 377.
65. Kearney, *On Paul Ricoeur,* 136.
66. See especially the final chapter of Ricoeur, *Soi-même comme un autre.*
67. Ibid., 387.
68. "La relation qui va du visage à l'Absent, est en dehors de toute révélation et de toute dissimulation" (Levinas, "*La trace de l'autre,*" 618).
69. Ibid., 620.
70. Ricoeur, *Soi-même comme un autre,* 369–409.
71. Ricoeur, *Oneself as Another,* 339.
72. "Für die Verständigung im Gespräch ist solche Beherrschung der Sprache geradezu eine Vorbedingung. Jedes Gespräch macht die selbstverständliche Voraussetzung, daß die Redner die gleiche Sprache sprechen" (Gadamer, *Wahrheit und Methode,* 388).
73. Derrida, *Memoires* (translation), 38.
74. These discussions are collected in Ricoeur, *Sur la traduction.*
75. Ricoeur, *On Translation,* 29.
76. Ricoeur, *Sur la traduction,* 9, 41–42.
77. Ibid., 10.
78. Rosenzweig, "*Die Schrift und Luther,*" 194.
79. Ricoeur, *Sur la traduction,* 16–19, 42.
80. In each of the three essays, Ricoeur discusses this problem; see *Sur la tra-*

duction, 12–14, 39, 60. For the argument of the third man, see Plato, *Parmenides* 132a–b; and *Republic* 597c.

81. Ricoeur, *On Translation,* 22.

82. Ibid., 37; Ricoeur, *Sur la traduction,* 66.

83. Ricoeur, *On Translation,* 19.

84. Ibid., 37.

85. Ibid., 23. In his account of translation, Ricoeur is clearly inspired by the magnificent study Berman, *L'épreuve de l'étranger.*

86. Ricoeur, *On Translation,* 10.

87. Even Nancy's notion of *partage*—sharing in/sharing out—to characterize dialogue does not solve this problem; see Nancy, *Le partage des voix.* If we listen to a language that we do not know, the moment of sharing in presupposes translation. Hence, the activity of translation precedes also this dimension of dialogue. Differently put, the experience of *partage* is only possible if we are not completely foreign to the other's language. This, of course, is completely in line with Plato's *Ion* and Nancy's reading of it: the language of rhapsody is not completely foreign to Socrates since he is capable of playing the role of the rhapsode.

88. Derrida, *La dissémination,* 203, 208.

89. Ibid., 208–09.

90. Ibid., 219.

91. Derrida, *Dissemination,* 193.

92. Derrida, *La dissémination,* 218.

93. Ibid., 216.

94. Ibid., 218.

95. Derrida, *Dissemination,* 193.

96. Ibid., 193.

97. See IJsseling, *Mimesis,* 56.

98. Lacoue-Labarthe, *La fiction du politique,* 24.

99. Despite Lacoue-Labarthe's critique of Hegel, it is important to note that Hegel's attention to the necessity of mimesis and of finite media in the self-realization of spirit is also a source of inspiration for both Derrida's and Lacoue-Labarthe's thought on mimesis. This necessity is ultimately used to criticize the Hegelian understanding of this mimetic movement as a movement of spirit.

100. Heidegger, *Sein und Zeit,* 322.

101. Ibid., 324; Derrida, *Apories,* 55–56.

102. Ibid., 60–61, 97.

103. Heidegger, *Being and Time,* 312.

104. Ricoeur, *Soi-même comme un autre,* 393–409.

105. "Das Dasein ruft im Gewissen sich selbst" (Heidegger, *Sein und Zeit,* 365); Ricoeur, *Soi-même comme un autre,* 409.

106. Heidegger, *Sein und Zeit,* 367.

107. "Ce rapport à soi…suppose l'autre au-dedans de son être-soi-même comme différent de soi" (Derrida, *Apories,* 111).

108. Derrida, *Sovereignties in Question*, 140.

109. Derrida, "Heidegger's Ears," 187.

110. Heidegger, *Sein und Zeit*, 494–97.

111. Shakespeare, *Hamlet*, 1.5.188, in Graig, *Complete Works Shakespeare*, 950.

112. See for this analysis Derrida, *Spectres de Marx*, 47–57; Heidegger, "*Der Spruch des Anaximander*," in *Holzwege*, 321–73.

113. Derrida, *Spectres de Marx*, 55.

114. Heidegger, *Holzwege*, 329; Derrida, *Spectres de Marx*, 54.

115. Ibid., 56–57.

116. See Vedder, *De voorlopigheid van het denken;* "The Provisionality of Thinking."

117. Derrida, *Mémoires*, 56.

118. Derrida, *Memoires* (translation), 37.

119. Ibid., 38.

120. Derrida, *Specters of Marx*, 28.

121. For a beautiful overview, see Crépon, "Deconstruction and Translation."

122. Berman, "*L'essence platonicienne de la traduction.*"

123. Derrida, *Marges de la philosophie*, 272. In his reading of Descartes, Derrida tries to show how the former considers the Latin languages to have "an essential relationship with the possible-impossible of language," which is the impossible possibility of a universal language still to be built; see Derrida, *Du droit à la philosophie*, 327. Only such a *mathesis universalis* would be able to "vindicate the obscurities, ambiguities, equivocities of the mother tongue," ibid., 329.

124. The former is noted in Thomas, *Reception of Derrida*, 10–15; the structure of supplementarity in translation is noted in Derrida, *Du droit à la philosophie*, 373.

125. See Crépon, "Deconstruction and Translation," 311. Derrida explicitly considers this theme in his reading of Benjamin in Derrida, *Psyché*, 214.

126. Derrida, "What Is a 'Relevant' Translation?," 175.

127. Derrida, *Sovereignties in Question*, 168, 162.

128. Derrida, *Psyché*, 203–35.

129. Benjamin, "*Die Aufgabe des Übersetzers*," 169.

130. Derrida, *Psyché*, 214–15, 220. On the latter page, Derrida quotes a translation of Benjamin's claim, "So ist die Übersetzung zuletzt zweckmäßig für den Ausdruck des innersten Verhältnisses der Sprachen zueinander" (Benjamin, "*Die Aufgabe des Übersetzers*," 159).

131. Ricoeur, *Sur la traduction*, 18.

132. Derrida, *Psyché*, 220.

133. Derrida, *Psyche* (translation), 224. The signature refers to the idiomatic mark a translation leaves on its promise of showing the affinities between languages; see Derrida, "What Is a 'Relevant' Translation?," 178.

134. Derrida, *Psyche* (translation), 214. To some extent this seems to have escaped Crépon in his thorough essay on translation in the work of Derrida since he does not qualify this untouchable affinity between language; see Crépon, "Deconstruction and Translation."

135. Benjamin, "*Die Aufgabe des Übersetzers*," 168.

136. Derrida, *Sovereignties in Question*, 103.

137. Heidegger, *Hölderlins Hymne "der Ister,"* 177–78.

138. Derrida, "What Is a 'Relevant' Translation?," 176, 199.

Notes to Conclusion

1. This idea is developed in Nancy, *Le partage des voix*. For Heidegger's determination of hermeneutics, see also "*Die Faktizität der Hermeneutik*," in Vedder, *Was ist Hermeneutik?*, 93–113.

2. Heidegger, *On the Way to Language*, 29.

3. A similar explication of *hermēneuein* can be found in §7 of *Sein und Zeit*, where Heidegger writes, "The *logos* of the phenomenology of Dasein has the character of a *hermēneuein*, through which the authentic meaning of Being, and also those basic structures of Being which Dasein itself possesses, are *made known* [*kundgegeben*] to Dasein's understanding of Being" (*Being and Time*, 62).

4. Heidegger, *Hölderlins Hymnen "Germanien" und "Der Rhein,"* 31–32.

5. Nancy, *Le partage des voix*.

6. Ricoeur, *De l'interprétation*, 477–78.

7. Ricoeur, *Interpretation Theory*, 78.

8. Derrida has paid a lot of attention to the notion of the preface in his "*Hors livre*," in Derrida, *La dissémination*, 7–67.

9. Kierkegaard, *Prefaces*, 4.

10. Ibid., 5.

11. Ibid., 3.

12. "*La structure, le signe et le jeu dans le discours des sciences humaines*," in Derrida, *L'écriture et la différence*, 409–28.

13. Derrida, *Writing and Difference*, 292–93.

14. The theme of the transcendental signified plays an important role at the beginning of the essay from which the above quote stems; cf. Derrida, *L'écriture et la différence*, 411.

15. Cf. Derrida, *Heidegger et la question*, 182–83.

BIBLIOGRAPHY

WORKS BY JACQUES DERRIDA

Works in French

Apories: Mourir — s'attendre aux "limites de la vérité." Paris: Galilée, 1996.

Béliers. Le dialogue ininterrompu. Entre deux infinis, le poème. Paris: Galilée, 2003.

La carte postale: De Socrate à Freud et au-delà. Paris: Flammarion, 1980.

Le "concept" du 11 septembre: Dialogues a New York avec Jürgen Habermas et Giovanna Borradori. Paris: Galilée, 2004.

De la grammatologie. Paris: Minuit, 1967.

La dissémination. Paris: Seuil, 1972.

Donner la mort. Paris: Galilée, 1999.

Donner le temps 1: La fausse monnaie. Paris: Galilée, 1991.

Du droit à la philosophie. Paris: Galilée, 1990.

L'écriture et la différence. Paris: Seuil, 1967.

Force de loi. Paris: Galilée, 1994.

Glas. Paris: Galilée, 1974.

Heidegger et la question: De l'esprit et autres essais. Paris: Flammarion, 1990.

Khôra. Paris: Galilée, 1993.

"*Les langages et les institutions de la philosophie.*" *Texte* 4 (1985): 9–39.

Marges de la philosophie. Paris: Minuit, 1972.

Mémoires pour Paul de Man. Paris: Galilée, 1988.

L'origine de la géométrie. Paris: PUF, 1962.

Parages. Paris: Galilée, 1986.

Politiques de l'amitié. Paris: Galilée, 1994.

Positions. Paris: Minuit, 1972.

Psyché: inventions de l'autre. Paris: Galilée, 1987.

Psyché: inventions de l'autre, II. Paris: Galilée, 2003.

"*Qu'est-ce qu'une traduction 'relevante'?*" *L'Herne: Derrida* 83 (2004): 561–76.

Sauf le nom. Paris: Galilée, 1993.

Schibboleth: pour Paul Celan. Paris: Galilée, 1986.

Spectres de Marx. Paris: Galilée, 1993.

Le toucher, Jean-Luc Nancy. Paris: Galilée, 2000.

Ulysse gramophone: Deux mots pour Joyce. Paris: Galilée, 1987.

La voix et le phénomène. Paris: PUF, 1967.

Voyous: Deux essais sur la raison. Paris: Seuil, 2003.

Derrida, Jacques, and Évelyne Grossman. "*La Langue n'appartient pas. Entretien avec Jacques Derrida.*" *Europe* 79 (2001): 81–91.

Works in Translation

The Derrida Reader: Writing Performances. Edited by Julian Wolfreys. Chicago: University of Nebraska Press, 1998.

Dissemination. Translated by Barbara Johnson. Chicago: University of Chicago Press, 1981.

Edmund Husserl's Origin of Geometry: An Introduction. Translated by John P. Leavey Jr. Lincoln: University of Nebraska Press, 1989.

"Heidegger's Ears: *Geschlecht IV*: Philopolemology." In *Reading Heidegger,* edited by John Sallis, 163–218. Bloomington: Indiana University Press, 1993.

Limited Inc. Edited and translated by Elisabeth Weber. Paris: Galilée, 1990.

Margins of Philosophy. Translated by Alan Bass. Chicago: University of Chicago, 1982.

Memoires for Paul de Man. Rev. ed. Translated by Cecile Lindsay, Jonathan Culler, Eduardo Cadava, and Peggy Kamuf. New York: Columbia University Press, 1989.

Of Grammatology. Translated by Gayatri Chakravorty Spivak. Baltimore: Johns Hopkins University Press, 1976.

Of Spirit: Heidegger and the Question. Translated by Geoffrey Bennington and Rachel Bowlby. Chicago: University of Chicago Press, 1989.

"On Reading Heidegger: An Outline of Remarks to the Essex Colloquium." *Research in Phenomenology* 17 (1987): 171–88.

Positions. Translated by Alan Bass. Chicago: University of Chicago Press, 1982.

Psyche: Inventions of the Other. Vol. 1. Edited by Peggy Kamuf and Elizabeth Rottenberg. Stanford: Stanford University Press, 2007.

Psyche: Inventions of the Other. Vol. 2. Edited by Peggy Kamuf and Elizabeth Rottenberg. Stanford: Stanford University Press, 2008.

"The Retrait of Metaphor." Translated by Alan Bass. *Enclitic* 2, no. 2 (1978): 5–33.

Rogues: Two Essays on Reason. Translated by Pascale-Anne Brault and Michael Naas. Stanford: Stanford University Press, 2005.

Sovereignties in Question: The Poetics of Paul Celan. Edited by Thomas Dutoit and Outi Pasanen. New York: Fordham University Press, 2005.

Specters of Marx: The State of the Debt, the Work of Mourning, and the New International. Translated by Peggy Kamuf. With an introduction by Bernd Magnus and Stephen Cullenberg. New York: Routledge, 1994.

Speech and Phenomena, and Other Essays on Husserl's Theory of Signs. Translated by David B. Allison. With a preface by Newton Garver. Evanston: Northwestern University Press, 1973.

"Two Words for Joyce." In *Post-Structuralist Joyce: Essays from the French.* Edited by Derek Attridge and Daniel Ferrer, 148–58. Cambridge: Cambridge University Press, 1984.

"What Is a 'Relevant' Translation?" Translated by Lawrence Venuti. *Critical Inquiry* 27, no. 2 (2001): 174–200.

"The 'World' of the Enlightenment to Come (Exception, Calculation, Sovereignty)." Translated by Pascale-Anne Brault and Michael Naas. *Research in Phenomenology* 33 (2003): 9–52.

Writing and Difference. Translated by Alan Bass. Chicago: University of Chicago Press, 1978.

WORKS BY MARTIN HEIDEGGER

Works in German

Der Begriff der Zeit. Gesamtausgabe, vol. 64. Frankfurt am Main: Vittorio Klostermann, 2004.

Der Satz vom Grund. Gesamtausgabe, vol. 10. Frankfurt am Main: Vittorio Klostermann, 1997.

Die Grundbegriffe der Metaphysik: Welt—Endlichkeit—Einsamkeit. Gesamtausgabe, vol. 29/30. Frankfurt am Main: Vittorio Klostermann, 1983.

Einführung in die Metaphysik. Gesamtausgabe, vol. 40. Frankfurt am Main: Vittorio Klostermann, 1983.

Einführung in die phänomenologische Forschung. Gesamtausgabe, vol. 17. Frankfurt am Main: Vittorio Klostermann, 1994.

Erläuterungen zu Hölderlins Dichtung. Gesamtausgabe, vol. 4. Frankfurt am Main: Vittorio Klostermann, 1982.

Feldweg-Gespräche. Gesamtausgabe, vol. 77. Frankfurt am Main: Vittorio Klostermann, 1995.

Hölderlins Hymne "der Ister." Gesamtausgabe, vol. 53. Frankfurt am Main: Vittorio Klostermann, 1982.

Hölderlins Hymnen "Germanien" und "Der Rhein." Gesamtausgabe, vol. 39. Frankfurt am Main: Vittorio Klostermann, 1980.

Holzwege. Gesamtausgabe, vol. 5. Frankfurt am Main: Vittorio Klostermann, 1977.

Identität und Differenz. Gesamtausgabe, vol. 11. Frankfurt am Main: Vittorio Klostermann, 2006.

Kant und das Problem der Metaphysik. Gesamtausgabe, vol. 3. Frankfurt am Main: Vittorio Klostermann, 1991.

Logik, die Frage nach der Wahrheit. Gesamtausgabe, vol. 21. Frankfurt am Main: Vittorio Klostermann, 1976.

Nietzsche I. Gesamtausgabe, vol. 6.1. Frankfurt am Main: Vittorio Klostermann, 1996.

Nietzsche II. Gesamtausgabe, vol. 6.2. Frankfurt am Main: Vittorio Klostermann, 1996.

Parmenides. Gesamtausgabe, vol. 54. Frankfurt am Main: Vittorio Klostermann, 1982.

Phänomenologie des religiösen Lebens. Gesamtausgabe, vol. 60. Frankfurt am Main: Vittorio Klostermann, 1995.

Platon: Sophistes. Gesamtausgabe, vol. 19. Frankfurt am Main: Vittorio Klostermann, 1992.

Reden und andere Zeugnisse eines Lebensweges. Gesamtausgabe, vol. 16. Frankfurt am Main: Vittorio Klostermann, 2000.

Sein und Wahrheit. Gesamtausgabe, vol. 36/37. Frankfurt am Main: Vittorio Klostermann, 2001.

Sein und Zeit. Gesamtausgabe, vol. 2. Frankfurt am Main: Vittorio Klostermann, 1977.

Unterwegs zur Sprache. Gesamtausgabe, vol. 12. Frankfurt am Main: Vittorio Klostermann, 1985.

Vom Wesen der Wahrheit: Zu Platons Höhlengleichnis und Theätet. Gesamtausgabe, vol. 34. Frankfurt am Main: Vittorio Klostermann, 1988.

Vorträge und Aufsätze. Gesamtausgabe, vol. 7. Frankfurt am Main: Vittorio Klostermann, 2000.

Was heißt Denken? Gesamtausgabe, vol. 8. Frankfurt am Main: Vittorio Klostermann, 2002.

"*Was ist das—die Philosophie?*" In *Identität und Differenz,* Gesamtausgabe, vol. 11, 3–26. Frankfurt am Main: Vittorio Klostermann, 2006.

Wegmarken. Gesamtausgabe, vol. 9. Frankfurt am Main: Vittorio Klostermann, 1976.

Zur Sache des Denkens. Gesamtausgabe, vol. 14. Frankfurt am Main: Vittorio Klostermann, 2007.

Works in Translation

Basic Writings from Being and Time (1927) to The Task of Thinking (1964). Edited, with general introduction and introductions to each selection, by David Farrell Krell. New York: Harper and Row, 1977.

Being and Time. Translated by John Macquarrie and Edward Robinson. New York: Harper-Collins, 1962.

Being and Time. Translated by Joan Stambaugh. Albany: SUNY Press, 1996.

Early Greek Thinking: The Dawn of Western Philosophy. Translated by David Farrell Krell and Frank A. Capuzzi. New York: Harper and Row, 1975.

The Essence of Truth: On Plato's Parable of the Cave and the Theaetetus. Translated by Ted Sadler. London: Continuum Books, 2002.

Hölderlin's Hymn "The Ister." Translated by Will McNeill and Julia Davis. Bloomington: Indiana University Press, 1996.

Identity and Difference. Translated by Joan Stambaugh. New York: Harper and Row, 1969.

An Introduction to Metaphysics. Translated by Ralph Manheim. New Haven: Yale University Press, 1959.

Off the Beaten Track. Edited and translated by Julian Young and Kenneth Haynes. Cambridge: Cambridge University Press, 2002.

On the Way to Language. Translated by Peter D. Hertz. New York: Harper and Row, 1971.

On Time and Being. Translated by Joan Stambaugh. New York: Harper and Row, 1972.

Parmenides. Translated by André Schuwer and Richard Rojcewicz. Bloomington: Indiana University Press, 1993.

Pathmarks. Edited by William McNeill. Cambridge: Cambridge University Press, 1998.

Plato's Sophist. Translated by Richard Rojcewicz and André Schuwer. Bloomington: Indiana University Press, 1997.

Poetry, Language, Thought. Translated by Alfred Hofstadter. New York: Harper and Row, 1971.

The Principle of Reason. Translated by Richard Lilly. Bloomington: Indiana University Press, 1977.

What Is Called Thinking? Translated by Fred. D. Wieck and John Glenn Gray. New York: Harper and Row, 1968.

What Is Philosophy? Translated, with an introduction, by William Kluback and Jean T. Wilde. New Haven: College and University Press, 1958.

WORKS BY PAUL RICOEUR

Works in French

A l'école de la phénoménologie. Paris: Vrin, 1986.

Autrement. Paris: PUF, 1997.

Le conflit des interprétations. Paris: Seuil, 1969.

De l'interprétation, essai sur Freud. Paris: Seuil, 1965.

Du texte à l'action: Essais d'herméneutique II. Paris: Seuil, 1986.

Histoire et vérité. Paris: Seuil, 1967.

La mémoire, l'histoire, l'oubli. Paris: Seuil, 2000.

La métaphore vive. Paris: Seuil, 1975.

Parcours de la reconnaissance. Paris: Stock, 2004.

Philosophie de volonté: Finitude et culpabilité. I. L'homme faillible. Paris: Aubier, 1960.

Philosophie de volonté: Finitude et culpabilité. II. La symbolique du mal. Paris: Aubier, 1960.

Réflexion faite: autobiographie intellectuelle. Paris: Esprit, 1995.

Soi-même comme un autre. Paris: Seuil, 1990.

Sur la traduction. Paris: Bayard, 2004.

Temps et récit. 3 Volumes. Paris: Seuil, 1983–1985.

Vivant jusqu'à la mort: Suivi de Fragments. Paris: Seuil, 2007.

Works in Translation

"Between Rhetoric and Poetics." In *Essays on Aristotle's Rhetoric*, edited by Amélie Oksenberg Rorty, 324–84. Berkeley and Los Angeles: University of California Press, 1996.

The Conflict of Interpretations: Essays in Hermeneutics. Edited by Don Ihde. Evanston: Northwestern University Press, 1974.

Freud and Philosophy: An Essay on Interpretation. Translated by Denis Savage. New York: Yale University Press, 1970.

From Text to Action: Essays in Hermeneutics II. Translated by Kathleen Blamey and John B. Thompson. Evanston: Northwestern University Press, 1991.

Hermeneutics and the Human Sciences: Essays on Language, Action and Interpretation. Edited and translated by John B. Thompson. Cambridge: Cambridge University Press, 1981.

Interpretation Theory: Discourse and the Surplus of Meaning. Fort Worth: Texas Christian University Press, 1976.

Memory, History, Forgetting. Translated by Kathleen Blamey and David Pellauer. Chicago: University of Chicago Press, 2004.

Oneself as Another. Translated by Kathleen Blamey. Chicago: University of Chicago Press, 1992.

On Translation. Translated by Eileen Brennan. London: Routledge, 2006.

The Rule of Metaphor: Multi-Disciplinary Studies in the Creation of Meaning in Language. Translated by Robert Czerny with Kathleen McLaughlin and John Costello. London: Routledge, 1978.

Time and Narrative. 3 Volumes. Translated by Kathleen McLaughlin and David Pellauer. Chicago: University of Chicago Press, 1984–88.

SECONDARY SOURCES

Agamben, Giorgio. *Homo Sacer: Sovereign Power and Bare Life.* Translated by Daniel Heller-Roazen. Stanford: Stanford University Press, 1998.

———. *Language and Death: The Place of Negativity.* Translated by Karen E. Pinkus with Michael Hardt. Minneapolis: University of Minnesota Press, 1991.

Amalric, Jean-Luc. *Ricoeur, Derrida: L'enjeu de la métaphore.* Paris: PUF, 2006.

Badiou, Alain. *L'être et l'événement.* Paris: Seuil, 1988.

———. *Manifeste pour la philosophie.* Paris: Seuil, 1989.

———. *Saint Paul: La fondation de l'universalisme.* Paris: PUF, 1997.

Barnes, Jonathan, ed. *The Complete Works of Aristotle.* 2 vols. The revised Oxford edition. Princeton: Princeton University Press, 1984.

Benjamin, Walter. "*Die Aufgabe des Übersetzers.*" In *Das Problem des Übersetzens,* Hans Joachim Störig, 156–69. Darmstadt: Wissenschaftliche Buchgesellschaft, 1973.

Bennington, Geoffrey, and Jacques Derrida. *Jacques Derrida.* Translated by Geoffrey Bennington. London: University of Chicago Press, 1993.

Benveniste, Émile. *Problèmes de linguistique générale.* Paris: Gallimard, 1966.

Berman, Antoine. *L'épreuve de l'étranger. Culture et traduction dans l'Allemagne romantique.* Paris: Gallimard, 1984.

———. "*L'essence platonicienne de la traduction.*" *Revue d'esthétique* 12 (1986): 63–73.

Bernasconi, Robert. *The Question of Language in Heidegger's History of Being*. Atlantic Highlands: Humanities Press, 1985.

———. "The Transformation of Language at Another Beginning," *Research in Phenomenology* 13 (1983): 1–23.

Bernet, Rudolf, et al. *Derrida et la phénoménologie. Revue de phénoménologie*. Paris: Alter, 2000.

Biemel, Walter, and Friedrich-Wilhelm von Herrmann, eds. *Kunst und Technik: Gedächtnisschrift zum 100. Geburtstag von Martin Heidegger*. Frankfurt am Main: Vittorio Klostermann, 1989.

Bourgeois, Patrick L. *Extension of Ricoeur's Hermeneutics*. The Hague: Nijhoff, 1975.

Bourgeois, Patrick L., and Frank Schalow. *Traces of Understanding: A Profile of Heidegger's and Ricoeur's Hermeneutics*. Amsterdam: Rodopi, 1990.

Buckley, R. Philip. *Husserl, Heidegger, and the Crisis of Philosophical Responsibility*. Phaenomenologica 125. Dordrecht: Kluwer, 1992.

Cohen, T., ed. *Jacques Derrida and the Humanities: A Critical Reader*. Cambridge: Cambridge University Press, 2001.

Cooper, John M., ed. *Plato: Complete Works*. Indianapolis: Hackett, 1997.

Crépon, Marc. "Deconstruction and Translation: The Passage into Philosophy." *Research in Phenomenology* 36 (2006): 299–313.

Dastur, Françoise. *Heidegger: La question du Logos*. Paris: Vrin, 2007.

Derrida, Jacques, V. Descombes, J.-F. Lyotard, Jean-Luc Nancy & Philippe Lacoue-Labarthe. *La faculté de juger*. Paris: Minuit, 1985.

DiCenso, James. *Hermeneutics and the Disclosure of Truth: A Study in the Work of Heidegger, Gadamer, and Ricoeur*. Virginia: University Press of Virginia, 1990.

Ellison, Ralph. *The Invisible Man*. New York: Vintage Books, 1972.

Escoubas, Elaine. "*De la traduction comme 'origine' des langues: Heidegger et Benjamin.*" *Les Temps Modernes* 44 (1989): 97–142.

———. "Ontology of Language and Ontology of Translation in Heidegger." In *Reading Heidegger*, edited by John Sallis, 341–47. Bloomington: Indiana University Press, 1993.

Figal, Günter. *Der Sinn des Verstehens: Beiträge zur hermeneutischen Philosophie*. Stuttgart: Philipp Reclam, 1996.

————. *Gegenständlichkeit: Das Hermeneutische und die Philosophie.* Tübingen: Mohr Siebeck, 2006.

Figal, Günter, and Hans-Helmuth Gander, eds. *"Dimensionen des Hermeneutischen": Heidegger und Gadamer.* Martin-Heidegger-Gesellschaft Schriftenreihe, vol. 7. Frankfurt am Main: Vittorio Klostermann, 2005.

France, Anatole. *Le jardin d'Epicure.* Paris: Calmann Lévy, 1921.

Frank, Manfred. *Was ist Neostrukturalismus?* Frankfurt am Main: Suhrkamp, 1984.

Gadamer, Hans-Georg. *Griechische Philosophie III.* Gesammelte Werke, vol. 7. Tübingen: Mohr Siebeck, 1999.

————. *Neuere Philosophie I.* Gesammelte Werke, vol. 3. Tübingen: Mohr Siebeck, 1999.

————. *Wahrheit und Methode: Ergänzungen.* Gesammelte Werke, vol. 2. Tübingen: Mohr Siebeck, 1999. Translated by Joel Weinsheimer and Donald G. Marshall as *Truth and Method* (London: Continuum, 2004).

————. *Wahrheit und Methode: Grundzüge einer philosophischen Hermeneutik.* Gesammelte Werke, vol. 1. Tübingen: Mohr Siebeck, 1999.

Gasché, Rodolphe. *Inventions of Difference.* Cambridge, Mass.: Harvard University Press, 1994.

————. *The Tain of the Mirror.* Cambridge, Mass.: Harvard University Press, 1986.

Gondek, H. *"Das Übersetzen denken: Übersetzen und Über*setzen.*" Heidegger Studies* 12 (1996): 37–55.

Graig, W. J., ed. *The Complete Works of William Shakespeare.* London: Pordes, 1984.

Greisch, Jean. *Herméneutique et grammatologie.* Paris: CNRS, 1977.

————. *"Identité et différence dans la pensée de Martin Heidegger."* Revue des Sciences Philosophiques et Théologiques* 57 (1973): 71–111.

————. *"Les mots et les roses: la métaphore chez Martin Heidegger."* Revue des Sciences Philosophiques et Théologiques* 57 (1973): 433–55.

————. *"Vers une herméneutique du soi: la voie courte et la voie longue."* Revue de Métaphysique et de Morale* 98, no. 3 (1993): 413–27.

Hantaï, Simon. *La connaissance des textes: Lecture d'un manuscrit illisible (Correspondances).* With Jacques Derrida and Jean-Luc Nancy. Paris: Galilée, 2001.

Hatab, Lawrence J. "Heidegger and Myth: A Loop in the History of Being." *Journal of the British Society for Phenomenology* 22 (1991): 45–64.

Hegel, G. W. F. *Vorlesungen über die Ästhetik* I. Werke 13. Frankfurt am Main: Suhrkamp, 1970.

Hofer, Michael, and Mirko Wischke, eds. *Gadamer verstehen/Understanding Gadamer*. Darmstadt: Wissenschaftliche Buchgesellschaft, 2003.

Howells, Christina. *Derrida: Deconstruction from Phenomenology to Ethics*. Cambridge: Polity Press, 1998.

Husserl, Edmund. *Die Krisis der europäischen Wissenschaften und die transzendentale Phänomenologie*. Husserliana VI. The Hague: Martinus Nijhoff, 1954.

Hyland, Drew A. *Questioning Platonism: Continental Interpretations of Plato*. New York: State University of New York Press, 2004.

Ihde, Don. *Hermeneutic Phenomenology: The Philosophy of Paul Ricoeur*. Foreword by Paul Ricoeur. Evanston: Northwestern University Press, 1971.

IJsseling, Samuel. *"Heidegger en het geschreven woord."* *Tijdschrift voor filosofie* 54, no. 2 (1992): 195–213.

———. *Mimesis: Over schijn en zijn*. Baarn: Ambo, 1990.

———. *Mimesis: On Appearing and Being*. Translated by Hester IJsseling and Jeffrey Bloechl. Kampen: Kok Pharos, 1997.

———. "Mimesis and Translation." In *Reading Heidegger*, edited by John Sallis, 348–52. Bloomington: Indiana University Press, 1993.

———. *Retoriek en filosofie*. Bilthoven: Ambo, 1975. Translated by Paul Dunphy as *Rhetoric and Philosophy in Conflict* (The Hague: Nijhoff, 1976).

———. *"Sprache und Schrift."* In *Philosophie und Poesie: Otto Pöggeler zum 60. Geburtstag*, edited by Annemarie Gethmann-Siefert, 105–24. Stuttgart: Frommann-Holzboog, 1988.

IJsseling, Samuel, ed. *Jacques Derrida: Een inleiding in zijn denken*. Baarn: Ambo, 1986.

Inwood, Michael. "Truth and Untruth in Plato and Heidegger." In *Heidegger and Plato*, edited by Emad Partenie, 72–95. Evanston: Northwestern University Press, 2005.

Kant, Immanuel. *Kritik der reinen Vernunft*. Werkausgabe vols. 3 and 4. Frankfurt am Main: Suhrkamp, 1974.

———. *Kritik der Urteilskraft.* Werkausgabe vol. 10. Frankfurt am Main: Suhrkamp, 1974.

Kates, Joshua. "Derrida, Husserl and the Commentators: Introducing a Developmental Approach." *Husserl Studies* 19 (2003): 101–29.

———. *Essential History: Jacques Derrida and the Development of Deconstruction.* Evanston: Northwestern University Press, 2005.

Kearney, Richard. *On Paul Ricoeur: The Owl of Minerva.* Hampshire: Ashgate, 2004.

———. *Poetics of Imagining: Modern to Postmodern.* London: Harper Collins Academic, 1998.

Kierkegaard, Søren. *Either/Or, Part I.* Kierkegaard Writings III. Edited and translated with introduction and notes by Howard V. Hong and Edna H. Hong. Princeton: Princeton University Press, 1987.

———. *Prefaces: Writing Sampler.* Kierkegaard Writings IX. Edited and translated with introduction and notes by Todd W. Nichol. Princeton: Princeton University Press, 1997.

Kisiel, Theodore, and John van Buren, eds. *Reading Heidegger from the Start: Essays in His Earliest Thought.* New York: State University of New York Press, 1994.

Kockelmans, Joseph J., ed. *A Companion to Martin Heidegger's "Being and Time."* Washington: University Press of America, 1986.

———. *On Heidegger and Language.* Translation by Joseph J. Kockelmans. Evanston: Northwestern University Press, 1972.

Lacoue-Labarthe, Philippe. *Heidegger, Art, and Politics.* Translated by Chris Turner. Oxford: Basil Blackwell, 1990.

———. *Heidegger: La politique du poème.* Paris: Galilée, 2002.

———. *L'imitation des modernes: Typographies II.* Paris: Galilée, 1986.

———. *La fiction du politique: Heidegger, l'art et la politique.* Paris: Christian Bourgois, 1987.

———. *Typography: Mimesis, Philosophy, Politics.* Edited by Christopher Fynsk. With an introduction by Jacques Derrida. Cambridge, Mass.: Harvard University Press, 1989.

Lacoue-Labarthe, Philippe, and Jean-Luc Nancy. *L'absolu littéraire: Théorie de la littérature du romantisme allemand.* Paris: Seuil, 1978.

Lacoue-Labarthe, Philippe, and Jean-Luc Nancy, eds. *Les fins de l'homme: A partir du travail de Jacques Derrida.* Paris: Galilée, 1981.

Lafont, Christina. *Heidegger, Language, and World-Disclosure.* Cambridge: Cambridge University Press, 2000.

———. *The Linguistic Turn in Hermeneutic Philosophy.* Cambridge, Mass.: MIT Press, 1999.

Lawlor, Leonard. *Derrida and Husserl: The Basic Problem of Phenomenology.* Bloomington: Indiana University Press, 2002.

———. "Dialectic and Iterability." *Philosophy Today* 32, no. 3 (1988): 181–94.

———. *Imagination and Chance.* New York: State University of New York Press, 1992.

Levinas, Emmanuel. *Humanisme de l'autre homme.* Montpellier: Fata Morgana, 1972.

———. *"La trace de l'autre."* *Tijdschrift voor Filosofie* 25, no. 3 (1963): 605–23.

———. *Totalité et infini: essai sur l'extériorité.* Phaenomenologica 8. The Hague: Martinus Nijhoff, 1961.

———. *"Tout autrement."* *L'Arc* 54 (1973): 33–37.

Marrati-Guénoun, Paola. *La genèse et la trace: Derrida lecteur de Husserl et Heidegger.* Phaenomenologica 146. Dordrecht: Kluwer, 1998.

McNeill, Will. "The first principle of hermeneutics." In *Reading Heidegger from the Start*, edited by Theodore Kisiel and John van Buren, 393–408. New York: State University of New York Press, 1994.

Merleau-Ponty, Maurice. *Notes de cours sur* L'origine de la géométrie *de Husserl.* Paris: Epiméthée, 1998.

Michelfelder, Diane P., and Richard E. Palmer, eds. *Dialogue and Deconstruction: The Gadamer-Derrida Encounter.* Albany: State University of New York Press, 1989.

Montaigne, Michel de. *The Complete Essays of Michel de Montaigne.* Translated by Donald M. Frame. Stanford: Stanford University Press, 1958.

Montefiore, A., ed. *Philosophy in France Today.* Cambridge: Cambridge University Press, 1983.

Naas, Michael. *Taking on the Tradition: Jacques Derrida and the Legacies of Deconstruction.* Stanford: Stanford University Press, 2003.

Nancy, Jean-Luc. *La communauté désoeuvré.* Paris: Bourgois, 1986.

———. *Le partage des voix.* Paris: Galilée, 1982.

————. *Le sens du monde.* Paris: Galilée, 1993.

Nietzsche, Friedrich. "*Ueber Wahrheit und Lüge im aussermoralischen Sinne.*" In *Nachgelassene Schriften 1870–1873.* Critical edition of the *Complete Works,* div. 3, vol. 2, 367–84. Edited by Giorgio Colli and Mazzino Montinari. Berlin: Walter de Gruyter, 1973.

Oksenberg Rorty, Amélie, ed. *Essays on Aristotle's Rhetoric.* Berkeley and Los Angeles: University of California Press, 1996.

————. *The Identities of Persons.* Berkeley and Los Angeles: University of California Press, 1976.

Orth, Ernst Wolfgang, ed. *Studien zur neueren französischen Phänomenologie: Ricoeur, Foucault, Derrida. Phänomenologische Forschungen* 18. Freiburg: Alber, 1986.

Partenie, Catalin, ed. *Heidegger and Plato: Toward Dialogue.* Evanston: Northwestern University Press, 2005.

Parvis, Emad. "Thinking More Deeply into the Question of Translation." In *Reading Heidegger,* edited by John Sallis, 323–40. Bloomington: Indiana University Press, 1993.

Peperzak, Adriaan T. "Heidegger and Plato's Idea of the Good." In *Reading Heidegger,* edited by John Sallis, 258–85. Bloomington: Indiana University Press, 1993.

Pöggeler, Otto. *Der Denkweg Martin Heideggers.* Pfullingen: Verlag Günther Neske, 1963.

Robbins, Tom. *Skinny Legs and All.* New York: Bantam, 1991.

Rosen, Stanley. "Remarks on Heidegger's Plato." In *Heidegger and Plato,* edited by Emad Partenie, 178–91. Evanston: Northwestern University Press, 2005.

Rosenzweig, Franz. "*Die Schrift und Luther.*" In Störig, *Das Problem des Übersetzens,* 194–222.

Rushdie, Salman. *The Ground Beneath Her Feet.* New York: Henry Holt and Company, 2000.

Sallis, John. "Deformatives: Essentially Other Than Truth." In *Reading Heidegger,* edited by John Sallis, 26–46. Bloomington: Indiana University Press, 1993.

————. "Heidegger's Poetics: The Question of Mimesis." In *Kunst und Technik: Gedächtnisschrift zum 100. Geburtstag von Martin Heidegger,* edited by Walter Biemel and Friedrich-Wilhelm von Herrmann, 175–88. Frankfurt am Main: Vittorio Klostermann, 1989.

Sallis, John, ed. *Deconstruction and Philosophy*. Chicago: University of Chicago Press, 1987.

———. *Heidegger and the Path of Thinking*. With an introduction by John Sallis. Pittsburgh: Duquesne University Press, 1970.

———. *Reading Heidegger: Commemorations*. Bloomington: Indiana University Press, 1993.

Saussure, Ferdinand de. *Cours de linguistique générale*. Lausanne: Payot, 1916.

Schürmann, Reiner, ed. *Heidegger on Being and Acting: From Principles to Anarchy*. Translated by Christine-Marie Gras. Bloomington: Indiana University Press, 1987.

Scully, Stephen. *Plato's Phaedrus*. Newburyport: Focus Publishing, 2003.

Silverman, Hugh J. *Textualities: Between Hermeneutics and Deconstruction*. New York: Routledge, 1994.

Silverman, Hugh J., ed. *Hermeneutics and Deconstruction*. Albany: State University of New York Press, 1985.

Steiner, George. *After Babel*. 3rd edition. Oxford: Oxford University Press, 1998.

Stellardi, Giuseppe. *Heidegger and Derrida on Philosophy and Metaphor: Imperfect Thought*. Amherst: Humanity Books, 2000.

Stiegler, Bernard. *La technique et le temps: 1. La Faute d'Épiméthée*. Paris: Galilée, 1994.

Störig, Hans Joachim. *Das Problem des Übersetzens*. Darmstadt: Wissenschaftliche Buchgesellschaft, 1973.

Taylor, Charles. *Human Agency and Language: Philosophical Papers I*. Cambridge: Cambridge University Press, 1985.

———. *Sources of the Self: The Making of Modern Identity*. Cambridge: Cambridge University Press, 1989.

Tengelyi, László. "Redescription and Refiguration of Reality in Ricoeur." *Research in Phenomenology* 37, no. 2 (2007): 160–74.

Thomas, Michael. *The Reception of Derrida: Translation and Transformation*. New York: Palgrave Macmillan, 2006.

Vedder, Ben. *De voorlopigheid van het denken*. Leuven: Peeters, 2004.

———. "Heidegger on Desire." *Continental Philosophy Review* 31 (1998): 353–68.

————. "On the Meaning of Metaphor in Gadamer's Hermeneutics." *Research in Phenomenology* 32 (2002): 196–209.

————. "The Provisionality of Thinking in Heidegger." *The Southern Journal of Philosophy* 43, no. 4 (2005): 643–60.

————. *Was ist Hermeneutik? Ein Weg von der Textdeutung zur Interpretation der Wirklichkeit.* Stuttgart: Kohlhammer, 2000.

Visser, Gerard. *De druk van de beleving: Filosofie en kunst in een domein van overgang en ondergang.* Nijmegen: SUN, 1998. Translated as *Erlebnisdruck: Philosophie und Kunst im Bereich eines Übergangs und Untergangs* (Würzburg: Königshausen und Neumann, 2005).

Wilde, Jean T., ed. *The Search for Being; Essays from Kierkegaard to Sartre on the Problem of Existence.* New York: Twayne Publishers, 1962.

Wood, David. *On Paul Ricoeur.* London: Routledge, 1991.

————. *Philosophy at the Limit.* London: Unwin Hyman, 1990.

Index

alētheia (unconcealment): and being, 13;
   Derrida on, 123; and forgetting, 34, 38,
   39–40, 106, 123; Heidegger on, 6, 11,
   29, 32–33, 180, 236; and *lēthē*, 37–38,
   177; in memory, 123; and metaphysics,
   180; and mimesis, 183–84; Mnemosyne
   as, 106; truth as, 29, 32, 219, 220, 236;
   and unthought, 248n52. *See also lēthē*
alienation: of nature, 219; and science, 72,
   83; of writing from speech, 64–65, 68,
   71–72, 80, 94
alterity: and configuration and gathering,
   227; and foreign languages, 195; and
   mimesis, 202; and self, 211, 212. *See
   also* otherness
analogy, 140, 142; and metaphor, 150–51
Angst (anxiety), 43, 258n18
announcement: Heidegger on, 52,
   238–39; Plato on, 239; Ricoeur on,
   240
anticipation, 54, 180, 209; and projection,
   19–21; and provisionality, 229, 262n97;
   and thrownness, 22. *See also* promise
appropriation: and concealment, 49–50;
   Derrida on, 261n87; and disclosure,
   79, 135; distanciation in, 80, 86; and
   expropriation, 112; Heidegger on,
   48–49, 56, 112, 114, 119, 130, 131,
   176, 193–94, 230; of language, 48–49,
   51; and poetics, 131; Ricoeur on, 78,

80, 85, 86; and translation, 193–94,
   195, 216, 230; and writing, 80–81, 85.
   See also Ereignis
Aquinas, Thomas, 13, 150
Aristotle: Derrida on, 178; on God, 16;
   Heidegger on, 13, 108, 135–39; on
   language as sign, 135–36; on *legein,*
   53; on *logos,* 26, 53; on metaphor, 4,
   124, 126, 129, 132–33, 135–39, 140,
   142, 144, 146–47; on mimesis, 5, 84,
   182, 197, 218–20, 221; on *muthos,* 6,
   187, 197; on nature and art, 240–41;
   on plot, 55; on poetics, 4–5, 6, 187;
   Ricoeur on, 138, 144–48, 197, 254n62;
   on writing and speech, 65
—works: *Metaphysics,* 6, 150; *On
   Interpretation,* 26, 135–36, 247n30,
   252n21; *Poetics,* 124, 126, 129, 132,
   140, 197; *Rhetoric,* 4, 5, 132, 137, 138,
   144; *Topics,* 146–47, 166
art: and disclosure, 185, 187; gathering of,
   187; and mimesis, 185–88, 220, 237
articulation: and disclosure, 26; and
   interpretation, 8, 26, 72; and language,
   5, 47, 50, 52, 65–67, 68, 71; and
   metaphor, 172; and metaphysics, 52;
   poetic, 4
assertion: Heidegger on, 26–28, 36, 62,
   76, 247n31; and interpretation, 24–28,
   76; and metaphor, 144

33–35, 35–36, 115, 237; and writing,
60, 62, 100–01

unconcealment. *See alētheia*
undecidable, 95–96
understanding: and fore-understanding,
198; Heidegger on, 76, 85; Kant on,
209; language as medium of, 65–68,
94; and metaphor, 165; and mimesis,
203; Ricoeur and Gadamer on, 86;
self-understanding, 66, 86, 197, 212,
223–24; and translation, 217
univocity, 166, 231

Vedder, Ben, 229
Versagen (refuse, withhold), 42, 44, 177
Verstellen (disguise, distort, displace), 177;
Heidegger on, 22–23, 24, 34, 35,
42–44, 242; meanings of, 22, 237,
248n56; and mimesis, 184–85, 187–88;
and the trace, 24. *See also pseudos*
Vorstellung, 90

withdrawal: Derrida on, 167–70, 171,
174, 176, 177–78; Heidegger on,
16–17, 39, 135, 168, 170. *See also*
metaphor

writing: as alienation, 64–65, 68, 71–72,
80, 94; appropriation of, 80–81, 85;
Aristotle on, 65; as concealment, 63–64,
69, 89–90, 96, 97–101; as danger, 59,
63; Derrida on, 42, 58, 59, 63, 77,
81, 89–90, 91, 93, 94, 96, 99,
100, 105, 110; and dialogue, 60, 62,
71; and disclosure and displacement,
59, 96–97; dissemination of, 81, 89,
96–97, 109; as distanciation, 72,
78–81; feebleness of, 63; as fleeing
from thinking, 59, 108; Gadamer on,
64–65, 68–72, 80, 94; and handwriting,
110; Heidegger on, 59, 68, 108, 109,
110; and ideality, 68–71, 80, 92–93;
and language, 58, 59, 63, 80, 100;
and *logos,* 99, 100, 106; materiality
of, 80, 239; and myth, 42; Plato on,
59–64, 97–101; and *pseudos,* 59, 61,
87; Ricoeur on, 42, 58, 59, 77, 80, 89,
93; seduction of, 97, 98; and speech,
60, 62, 65, 71–72, 77, 81–82, 99, 110;
as supplement, 91–94; transference of,
59, 64, 71–72, 73, 78, 80–81, 92, 103,
119–21; and truth, 60, 62, 100–01;
typewriter and, 110. *See also* language